Creating a Data-Driven Organization
Practical Advice from the Trenches

Carl Anderson

Beijing · Boston · Farnham · Sebastopol · Tokyo

Creating a Data-Driven Organization

by Carl Anderson

Copyright © 2015 Carl Anderson. All rights reserved.

Printed in the United States of America.

Published by O'Reilly Media, Inc., 1005 Gravenstein Highway North, Sebastopol, CA 95472.

O'Reilly books may be purchased for educational, business, or sales promotional use. Online editions are also available for most titles (*http://safaribooksonline.com*). For more information, contact our corporate/institutional sales department: 800-998-9938 or *corporate@oreilly.com*.

Editor: Tim McGovern	**Indexer:** Lucie Haskins
Production Editor: Colleen Lobner	**Interior Designer:** David Futato
Copyeditor: Kim Cofer	**Cover Designer:** Ellie Volckhausen
Proofreader: Amanda Kersey	**Illustrator:** Rebecca Demarest

August 2015:   First Edition

Revision History for the First Edition

2015-07-20:   First Release

See *http://oreilly.com/catalog/errata.csp?isbn=9781491916919* for release details.

978-1-491-91691-9

LSI

Table of Contents

Preface

Summary

In this book, I address two core questions:

- What does it mean for an organization to be data-driven?
- How does an organization get there?

Many organizations think that simply because they generate a lot of reports or have many dashboards, they are data-driven. Although those activities are part of what an organization does, they are typically backward-looking. That is, they are often a declaration of past or present facts without a great deal of context, without causal explanation of *why* something has or has not happened, and without recommendations of what to do next. In short, they state what happened but they are not prescriptive. As such, they have limited upside.

In contrast, consider more forward-looking analyses, such as predictive models that optimize ad spend, supply chain replenishment, or minimize customer churn. They involve answering the "why" questions—or more generally, "w-questions": who, what, when, why, and where—making recommendations and predictions, and telling a story around the findings. They are frequently a key driver in a data-driven organization. Those insights and recommendations, *if* acted upon, have a huge potential impact upon the organization.

However, such insights require collecting the right data, that the data is trustworthy, the analysis is good, that the insights are considered in the decision, and that they drive concrete actions so the potential can be realized. Phew! I call this sequence—the flow from collection to final impact—the *analytics value chain*.

This last step in the chain is critical. Analytics is not data-driven if its findings are never seriously considered or acted upon. If they are unread, ignored, and the boss is going to do whatever he or she wants to do, regardless of what the data says, then they are ineffectual. To be data-driven, an organization must have the right processes and the right culture in place to augment or drive critical business decisions with these analyses and therefore have a direct impact on the business.

Culture, then, is the key. This is a multifaceted problem that involves data quality and sharing, analyst hiring and training, communication, analytical organizational structure, metric design, A/B testing, decision-making processes, and more. This book will elucidate these ideas by providing insights and illustrative examples from a variety of industries. I also bring in the voices of experience in interviews that provide advice and insights of what worked and what didn't from a variety of data science and analytics leaders. I hope to inspire all our readers to become more data-driven.

Moreover, throughout the book I emphasize the role that data engineers, analysts, and managers of analysts can play. I suggest that a data-driven organization and requisite culture can and should be built not only from top-down leadership but also from the bottom up. As Todd Holloway, head of data science at Trulia, remarked at the 2014 Chief Data Officer Executive Forum, "The best ideas come from the guys closest to the data." Not only are they the ones who work directly with the data sources and who recognize and can remedy the data-quality issues and understand how best to augment the data, but "they often come up with the good product ideas." In addition, they can help educate the rest of the organization to be more data literate. Part of that comes from developing their skill set and using it to do good work. Another part, however, comes from being more business savvy—learning the right questions to ask and business problems to tackle—and then "selling" their insights and recommendations to the decision-makers and making a compelling case of what the finding or recommendation means to business and why it makes an impact.

And there are great impacts and gains to be had. One report,[1] controlling for other factors, found that data-driven organizations have a 5%–6% greater output and productivity that their less data-driven counterparts. They also had higher asset utilization, return on equity, and market value. Another report[2] claims that analytics pays back $13.01 for every dollar spent. Being data-driven pays!

Data-drivenness is not a binary but rather a continuum: you can always be more data-driven, collect more high-quality relevant data, have a more skilled analytics organization, and do more testing. Moreover, you can always have a better decision-making process. In this book, I'll discuss the hallmarks of great data-driven organizations. I'll cover the infrastructure, skills, and culture needed to create organizations that take data, treat it as a core asset, and use it to drive and inform critical business decisions and ultimately make an impact. I will also cover some common anti-patterns, behavior that inhibits a business from making the most from its data.

The goals of the book, then, are to inspire the analyst organization to play its part, to provide pause for thought—to ask "are we making the most of our data?" and "can we be more data-driven?"—and to stimulate discussion about what more can be done to make use of this key resource. It is never too early to be thinking about this. Senior management and founders should be working to bake this into the very fabric of their company at an early stage. So, let's find out more about what is entailed.

Who Should Read This Book?

The information here will help you build and run an internal analytics program, deciding what data to gather and store, how to access it and make sense of it, and, most crucially, how to act on it.

Whether you're the only data scientist at a startup (and wearing a half-dozen other hats, to boot!), or the manager at an established organization with a room—or a department—full of people report-

---

1 Brynjolfsson, E., L. M. Hitt, and H. H. Kim. "Strength in Numbers: How Does Data-Driven Decisionmaking Affect Firm Performance?" (*http://bit.ly/brynjolfsson-strength/*) Social Science Research Network (2011).

2 Nucleus Research, "Analytics pays back $13.01 for every dollar spent," (*http://bit.ly/nucleus-analytics*) O204 (Boston, MA: Nucleus Research, 2014), 5.

ing to you, if you have data and the desire to act more quickly, effi-
ciently, and wisely, this book will help you develop not just a data
program but a data-driven culture.

Chapter Organization

Roughly speaking, this book is organized by thinking about that
flow along that value chain. The first chapters cover data itself, in
particular choosing the right data sources and ensuring that they are
high quality and trustworthy. The next step in that chain is analysis.
You need the right people with the right skills and tools to do good
work, to generate impactful insights. I call this group the "analysts,"
deliberately using the term in its broadest sense to cover data analysts, data scientists, and other members of the analytics organization. I do that to be inclusive because I believe that everyone, from a
junior data analyst fresh out of school to a rockstar data scientist,
has a role to play.I cover what makes a good analyst, how they can
sharpen their skills, and also cover organizational aspects: how those
analysts should be formed into teams and business units. The next
few chapters cover the actual analytical work itself, such as performing analyses, designing metrics, A/B testing, and storytelling. I then
proceed to the next step in the chain: making decisions with those
analyses and insights. Here I address what makes decision-making
hard and how it can be improved.

Throughout all these chapters, there is a very strong message and
theme: being data-driven is not just about data or the latest big data
toolset, but it is *culture*. Culture is the dominant aspect that sets
expectations of how far data is democratized, how it is used and
viewed across the organization, and the resources and training
invested in using data as a strategic asset. Thus, I draw all the lessons
from the various steps in the value chain into a single culture chapter. One of the later chapters then discusses top-down data leadership and in particular, the roles of two relatively new C-suite
positions: the chief data officer and the chief analytics officer. However, culture can be shaped and influenced from the bottom up, too.
Thus, throughout the book I directly address analysts and managers
of analysts, highlighting what they can do to influence that culture
and maximize their impact upon the organization. A true data-
driven organization is a data democracy and has a large number of
stakeholders who are vested in data, data quality, and the best use of

data to make fact-based decisions and to leverage data for competitive advantage.

Conventions Used in This Book

The following typographical conventions are used in this book:

Italic
> Indicates new terms, URLs, email addresses, filenames, and file extensions.

`Constant width`
> Used for program listings, as well as within paragraphs to refer to program elements such as variable or function names, databases, data types, environment variables, statements, and keywords.

`Constant width bold`
> Shows commands or other text that should be typed literally by the user.

`Constant width italic`
> Shows text that should be replaced with user-supplied values or by values determined by context.

 This element signifies a tip or suggestion.

 This element signifies a general note.

Safari® Books Online

 *Safari Books Online* is an on-demand digital library that delivers expert content in both book and video form from the world's leading authors in technology and business.

Technology professionals, software developers, web designers, and business and creative professionals use Safari Books Online as their primary resource for research, problem solving, learning, and certification training.

Safari Books Online offers a range of plans and pricing for enterprise, government, education, and individuals.

Members have access to thousands of books, training videos, and prepublication manuscripts in one fully searchable database from publishers like O'Reilly Media, Prentice Hall Professional, Addison-Wesley Professional, Microsoft Press, Sams, Que, Peachpit Press, Focal Press, Cisco Press, John Wiley & Sons, Syngress, Morgan Kaufmann, IBM Redbooks, Packt, Adobe Press, FT Press, Apress, Manning, New Riders, McGraw-Hill, Jones & Bartlett, Course Technology, and hundreds more. For more information about Safari Books Online, please visit us online.

How to Contact Us

Please address comments and questions concerning this book to the publisher:

O'Reilly Media, Inc.
1005 Gravenstein Highway North
Sebastopol, CA 95472
800-998-9938 (in the United States or Canada)
707-829-0515 (international or local)
707-829-0104 (fax)

We have a web page for this book, where we list errata, examples, and any additional information. You can access this page at *http://bit.ly/data-driven-org*.

To comment or ask technical questions about this book, send email to *bookquestions@oreilly.com*.

For more information about our books, courses, conferences, and news, see our website at *http://www.oreilly.com*.

Find us on Facebook: *http://facebook.com/oreilly*

Follow us on Twitter: *http://twitter.com/oreillymedia*

Watch us on YouTube: *http://www.youtube.com/oreillymedia*

Acknowledgments

Despite having a single authorship, this book is really the sum of contributions, ideas, and help from a lot of great experts and colleagues in the field. I would like to thank the following people for their extremely helpful advice, suggestions, insights, and support: Andrew Abela, Peter Aiken, Tracy Allison Altman, Samarth Baskar, Lon Binder, Neil Blumenthal, Yosef Borenstein, Lewis Broome, Trey Causey, Brian Dalessandro, Greg Elin, Samantha Everitt, Mario Faria, Stephen Few, Tom Fishburne, Andrew Francis Freeman, Dave Gilboa, Christina Kim, Nick Kim, Anjali Kumar, Greg Linden, Stephen Few, Jason Gowans, Sebastian Gutierrez, Doug Laney, Shaun Lysen, Doug Mack, Patrick Mahoney, Chris Maliwat, Mikayla Markrich, Lynn Massimo, Sanjay Mathur, Miriah Meyer, Julie-Jennifer Nguyen, Scott Pauly, Jeff Potter, Matt Rizzo, Max Schron, Anna Smith, Nellwyn Thomas, Daniel Tunkelang, James Vallandingham, Satish Vedantam, Daniel White, and Dan Woods. Thanks too, in general, to my colleagues at Warby Parker, who were all very supportive. Sincerest apologies to anyone whom I may have inadvertently missed from this list.

I would especially like to thank Daniel Mintz, Julie Steele, Dan Woods, Lon Binder, and June Andrews, who acted as a technical reviewers and who all provided very thorough, sage, and concrete suggestions that greatly helped improve the book.

Thanks also to the organizers from Data Driven Business (*http://www.datadrivenbiz.com/*), especially Antanina Kapchonava, and the participants of the Chief Data Officer Executive Forum held in New York City on November 12, 2014.

James Vallandingham generously re-created and modified Figure 4-1 especially for this book. Thanks, Jim!

I would like to thank Sebastian Gutierrez for some interesting conversation and for letting me steal some examples from his excellent data-visualization course.

I would also like to recognize the support of my friends and family, especially my long-suffering wife, Alexia, who described herself as a "book widow" at month two; and my mother, who has been incredibly supportive throughout my life.

Finally, I would like to extend my gratitude to all the great staff of O'Reilly, especially Tim McGovern, who edited the work and who pushed and shaped it in all the right places. Thanks, too, to Mike Loukides, Ben Lorica, Marie Beaugureau, and especially the production team: Colleen Lobner, Lucie Haskins, David Futato, Kim Cofer, Ellie Volckhausen, Amanda Kersey, and Rebecca Demarest.

CHAPTER 1

What Do We Mean by Data-Driven?

Without data you're just another person with an opinion.
—William Edwards Deming

Data-drivenness is about building tools, abilities, and, most crucially, a *culture* that acts on data. This chapter will outline what sets data-driven organizations apart. I start with some initial prerequisites about data collection and access. I then contrast reporting and alerting versus analyses in some detail because it is such an important distinction. There are many different types of forward-looking analysis, varying in degrees of sophistication. Thus, I spend some time going over those types, describing them in terms of "levels of analytics" and "analytics maturity," in particular, discussing the hallmarks of an analytically mature organization. What does that look like?

Let us start us on the way to answering our first question: what does it mean for an organization to be data-driven?

Data Collection

Let's get a couple of obvious prerequisites out of the way.

Prerequisite #1: An organization must be collecting data.

Data undoubtedly is a key ingredient. Of course, it can't just be any data; it has to be the *right* data. The dataset has to be relevant to the question at hand. It also has to be timely, accurate, clean, unbiased; and perhaps most importantly, it has to be trustworthy.

This is a tall order. Data is always dirtier than you imagine. There can be subtle hidden biases that can sway your conclusions, and cleaning and massaging data can be a tough, time-consuming, and expensive operation. I often hear that data scientists spend 80% of their time obtaining, cleaning, and preparing data, and only 20% of their time building models, analyzing, visualizing, and drawing conclusions from that data (for example, http://bit.ly/nyt-janitor and http://bit.ly/im-data-sci). In my experience, this is entirely plausible. In the next chapter, I'll cover aspects of data quality in much more detail.

Even if you do have quality data, and even if you have *a lot* of quality data, you will only get so far and; despite the hype that you might hear, it does not make you data-driven. Some people, especially certain big data vendors and service providers, pimp big data as a panacea: if you collect everything, somewhere in there are diamonds (or golden nuggets or needles or one of many other metaphors) that will make any company successful. The hard truth is that data alone is not enough. A small amount of clean, trustworthy data can be far more valuable than petabytes of junk.

Data Access

Prerequisite #2: Data must be accessible and queryable.

Having accurate, timely, and relevant data, though, is not sufficient to count as data-driven. It must also be:

Joinable
    The data must be in a form that can be joined to other enterprise data when necessary. There are many options, such as relational databases, NoSQL stores, or Hadoop. Use the right tool for the job. For instance, for a long while, the financial analysts at Warby Parker were using Excel to compute the key metrics reported to senior management. They sucked down huge amounts of raw data from different sources and ran VLOOK-UPS (an Excel function to find cross-references in the data) to join all that data to get a top-level look at the numbers. This worked well initially, but as the company's sales and customer base were scaling rapidly, the data got larger and larger, the Excel file approached 300 MB, their computers maxed out their RAM, and the VLOOKUPS would take 10 hours or more, frequently crash, and had to be restarted. They had stretched the

tool and approach as far as they could go. Excel had been an appropriate tool, but company hypergrowth changed that. The mechanics of getting those numbers became a huge time-sink for the analysts and a source of stress as to whether they would get their numbers or have to wait another 10 hours to rerun those VLOOKUPS. It turned them from analysts into Microsoft data engineers. My team helped to bring that whole dataset into a MySQL relational database. We wrote queries to crunch the numbers for them, allowing them to focus on analysis, trends, and presentation of that data—a far better use of their time. Now that they have better tools and more time, they are producing deeper, richer analyses.

Shareable

There must be a data-sharing culture within the organization so that data can be joined, such as combining customers' clickstream with their transactional history. Imagine a patient admitted to a hospital ER, receiving treatment and then being released with a requirement to attend an outpatient clinic for additional treatment and checkups. The patient is going to receive worse customer service and more importantly worse care if the hospital and clinic don't share data—when, where, and why was he admitted, what issues did he present, what treatment did he receive, etc. From the healthcare providers' perspective, their analysts are going to find it hard or impossible to analyze and improve the process and care if they don't have a coherent, accurate picture of patient flow, diagnostic processes, and complete longitudinal data of those patients. So, siloed data is always going to inhibit the scope of what can be achieved. When more data is available to more parts of a system, the whole is greater than the sum of the parts.

Queryable

There must be appropriate tools to query and slice and dice the data. All reporting and analysis requires filtering, grouping, and aggregating data to reduce the large amounts of raw data into a smaller set of higher-level numbers that help our brains comprehend what is happening in a business. I need to be able to see trends or understand differences among customer segments. Analysts have to have tools that allow them to compute those metrics relatively easily.

(All of these topics will be covered in greater detail in later chapters.)

OK, so now we have data and it is accessible. Is this sufficient? No, not yet. You need people with the right skills to use that data. That can mean the mechanics of filtering and aggregating data, such as through a query language or Excel macros, but it also means people who design and choose the appropriate metrics to extract and track (this topic is covered in Chapter 6). Those metrics might be resubscription rates (for subscription services such as Netflix or the *Wall Street Journal*), lifetime values, or growth metrics, but someone needs to decide upon them and someone (else) needs to create some process to provide those values.

So, for an organization to be data-driven, there have to be humans in the loop, humans who *ask the right questions* of the data, humans who have the skills to extract the right data and metrics, and humans who use that data to inform next steps. In short, data alone is not going to save your organization.

Reporting

Let's suppose you have an analytical group with access to accurate data. The group extracts sales data and generates a report proudly claiming that the company's bookings grew 5.2% from April to May (Figure 1-1).

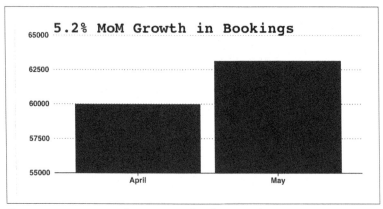

Figure 1-1. 5.2% month-over-month sales growth!

This is certainly now sounding more like a data-driven company. However, this is still deeply insufficient. Certainly it is good that they are tracking these metrics. The CFO and CEO will definitely be interested in those numbers. What, however, does this value of 5.2%

really tell you? Very little, in fact. There are many possible reasons why the company sales grew by this amount:

- Suppose that you sell a highly seasonal product, such as beachwear. Maybe 5.2% is much lower than normal. Maybe most years, May's growth is more than 7% over the prior month and this year's growth is well below average.
- Maybe your chief marketing officer spent a lot of money on a national campaign to drive brand awareness. How much of that 5.2% growth was generated from that campaign, and was that campaign a good value for the money?
- Maybe your CEO appeared on *Good Morning America*, or your product was featured in *Techcrunch*, or a video went viral, and that was the driver. That is, growth can be traced back to a specific unusual driving event (which might drive transient or sustained growth).
- Maybe monthly sales are low in volume and highly variable. Maybe that growth was just luck and maybe the overall trend is *downward*. (If you have ever traded stocks, you will surely understand.)
- Maybe the data is just wrong. If your sales are relatively stable, and you see a spike, and you are not aware of any unusual events, perhaps there is a data quality problem.

All of these are possibilities. The reported number is just that, a numerical value with little to no context.

> "As orgs grow larger and complex, people at the top depend less on firsthand experience, and more on heavily processed data." — John Gardner
>
> —John Maeda (@johnmaeda)
> August 16, 2014 (*http://bit.ly/maeda-gardner*)

Alerting

Ding, ding, ding! Web-app server #14 has just averaged more than 98% CPU utilization for the last five minutes.

Alerts are essentially reports about what is happening right now. They typically provide very specific data with well-designed metrics. But like reports, they don't tell you why you are seeing a spike in CPU utilization, and they don't tell you what to do, right now, to rectify the problem. As such, like reports, they lack this crucial context. There is no causal explanation. This is the point at which performance engineers or system administrators dive into the production logs to ascertain what is going on, why it is happening, and what the options are to fixing it: rollback some code, spin up some more servers, reconfigure the load balancer, etc.

Figure 1-2 shows an example of server load over time. There is some variability, but most of the day is spent with a run queue of about 0.5 or fewer. At 1 a.m., load starts to spike, shooting up to more than 5, a tenfold increase over "normal," in the space of 30 minutes. It seems highly unusual. What's going on? Maybe someone should fix that, but how?

In this case, it is just the weekly backups running. This happens every Thursday at 1 a.m.—perfectly normal, nothing to see here. This makes the point that there is great data here and a good metric that's presented clearly. But the context—that it is caused by backups, that it happens on a particular schedule and this 1 a.m. time slot is expected, and that the server can handle this load without problems—is all lacking.

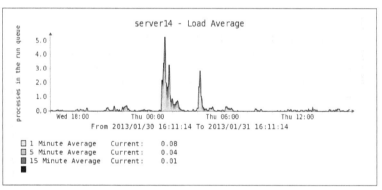

Figure 1-2. Example of server load over time (from http://bit.ly/bwf-back).

From Reporting and Alerting to Analysis

Reporting and alerting are necessary but not sufficient characteristics of being data-driven. We should, however, not understate the importance of both these activities. Reporting especially is a highly valuable component of a data-driven organization. You can't have an effective one without it. However, the reverse is not true: there are many organizations that focus on reporting and may have little to no real (objective) analysis. For one thing, reporting may be driven by legal requirement and responsibilities, such as Sarbanes-Oxley compliance and generating earnings reports to shareholders, and not from an internal cultural drive to improve the business.

Reporting tells you what happened in the past. It also provides a baseline from which to observe changes and trends. It can be interesting and can keep some investors and shareholders happy, but it is a fundamentally backward view of the world. To be data-driven, you have to go beyond that. To be *forward-looking* and engage in analysis, dig in, and find out why the numbers are changing and, where appropriate, make testable predictions or run experiments to gather more data that will shed light on why.

Let's be more explicit and compare and contrast the two. Here is one set of definitions:

Reporting
> "The process of organizing data into informational summaries in order to monitor how different areas of a business are performing"[1]

Analysis
> "Transforming data assets into competitive insights that will drive business decisions and actions using people, processes and technologies"[2]

Reporting says what happened—we hit a peak of 63,000 simultaneous visitors on the website on Thursday at 10:03 a.m. It tends to provide a very specific scope.

Analysis says why it happened—the company was mentioned in a piece on the TV newsmagazine show *60 Minutes* at 10:01 a.m.—and *should* recommend what the organization can or should do to generate more or less of the same.

Reporting is matter of fact, descriptive. Analysis, on the other hand, is prescriptive.

---

1 Dykes, B., "Reporting vs. Analysis: What's the Difference?" (*http://bit.ly/dykes-reporting*) Digital Marketing Blog, October 19, 2010.

2 Faria, M., "Acting on Analytics: How to Build a Data-Driven Enterprise." (*http://bit.ly/faria-acting*) BrightTALK, September 11, 2013.

In Table 1-1, we summarize the differences between the two. Hopefully it is now clear why analysis and being data-driven is such a powerful facet or cultural component of a business. This is what can drive a business in new directions or to greater levels of efficiency.

Table 1-1. Key attributes of reporting versus analysis (mostly gleaned from Dykes, 2010).

Reporting	Analysis
Descriptive	Prescriptive
What?	Why?
Backward-looking	Forward-looking
Raise questions	Answer questions
Data → information	Data + information → insights
Reports, dashboards, alerts	Findings, recommendations, predictions
No context	Context + storytelling

A useful framework for understanding analytics is Davenport et al.[3] (see Table 1-2).

Table 1-2. Davenport's hypothesized key questions addressed by analytics (modified from Davenport et al., 2010). D) is valuable analytics but only E) and F) are data-driven and then if and only if information is acted upon (more explanation in text).

	Past	Present	Future
Information	**A) What happened?** Reporting	**B) What is happening now?** Alerts	**C) What will happen?** Extrapolation
Insight	**D) How and why did it happen?** Modeling, experimental design	**E) What's the next best action?** Recommendation	**F) What's the best/worst that can happen?** Prediction, optimization, simulation

---

3 Davenport, T.H., J. G. Harris, and R. Morison. *Competing on Analytics*. Boston: Harvard Business Press, 2010.

Here we can see insight-driving activities in the bottom row. As I noted earlier, reporting (A) and alerting (B) are simply not data-driven: they state what happened in the past or that something unusual or undesirable is happening now; there is no explanation of why it is happening or why it did happen, and no recommendations as how to resolve or reproduce the situation. Digging down to understand causal factors through models or experiments (D) is a precursor to data-drivenness. Only by understanding why something happened can you formulate a plan or set of recommendations (E). E) and F) are truly data-driven but if and only if the information is acted upon—explained in detail below.

(C is a danger zone: it can be easy enough to extend a perceived trend out to the future—in Excel, click "Chart" and then "Add trendline"—that is, extrapolate outside the current's data range and make a naïve prediction. Even making a sensible choice about a functional form for the model, there are many reasons why that prediction may be misleading or plain wrong. To have confidence in those predictions, you should strive to have a causal model. Types of analysis is covered in Chapter 5.)

In summary, the bottom row highlights forward-looking activities that include elements of causal explanation. Now we are starting to touch upon what it means to be data-driven.

Hallmarks of Data-Drivenness

There are several types of activities that truly data-driven organizations engage in:

- A data-driven organization may be continuously testing. It might be A/B testing checkout flow on a website or testing email subject lines in a marketing campaign. LinkedIn, for instance, runs 200 experiments per day, whereas Etsy runs dozens of experiments simultaneously. Tests may also include user testing—working directly with actual customers or users to obtain direct feedback on possible new features or products.
- A data-driven organization may have a continuous improvement mindset. It may be involved in repeated optimization of core processes, such as shaving minutes off manufacturing times or decreasing cost per acquisition. This comes about

through careful analysis, crafting mathematical or statistical models, and simulation.

- A data-driven organization may be involved in predictive modeling, forecasting sales, stock prices, or company revenue, but importantly feeding the prediction errors and other learning back into the models to help improve them (we cover this further in Chapter 10).

- A data-driven organization will almost certainly be choosing among future options or actions using a suite of weighted variables. Resources are always finite, and there are always pros and cons for different reasonable courses of action. One should gather data for each of the set of variables that are of concern or interest and determine weights among those to generate a final leading decision. For instance, when Warby Parker selected its first office location outside New York, it considered a large set of variables—Gallup's Well-being index, talent pool, cost of living, number and cost of flights to New York, etc.—and ranked and weighted them as part of the final decision. Marissa Mayer (CEO of Yahoo!) tells a similar story when choosing among competing job offers and making her decision to work for Google.[4]

A true data-driven organization will be doing at least one of these things, something forward-looking where data is a first-class citizen.

OK, now we have an organization that has high-quality data and skilled analysts who are engaged in these forward-looking activities. Surely, that makes it data-driven!

Unfortunately, not necessarily. Like a tree falling in a forest with no one to hear it, if analysts are putting out analyses but no one takes notice, if they don't influence decision makers' decisions, which are still based on gut and opinion, it is not data-driven. Analytics has to inform and influence the influencers.

Dykes talks about this in terms of an "analytics value chain" (see Figure 1-3). Data has to drive reports, which should lead to deeper dives and analysis. Those analyses have to get to the decision maker who incorporates those into her decision-making process. This step is key to being data-driven. An organization needs that data and that

---

4 Bosker, B., "Google Exec Marissa Mayer Explains Why There Aren't More Girl Geeks." (*http://bit.ly/hpo-girl-geeks*) The Huffington Post, July 6, 2011.

analysis to drive a decision that changes strategy or tactics and makes an ultimate impact to the organization in some manner. Technology and training can do the first part: enable analysts to run analyses and write up their findings. However, it is the *culture* that sets up the mindset and process to take notice of those findings, trust them, and act upon them.

Finally, we get to the crux of what being data-driven means. A data-driven organization will use the data as critical evidence to help inform and influence strategy. There will be an evidence-based culture in which data can be trusted and the analysis is highly relevant, informative, and used to determine next steps.

Therein lies the challenge. If your organization is making gut decisions, how do you make a case for more data-driven decision making? It is not easy and it is not quick, so don't expect radical changes overnight, but everyone in an organization can contribute significantly to such an improvement. In this book, we will examine a number of ways an organization's culture should be driving to be more data-driven.

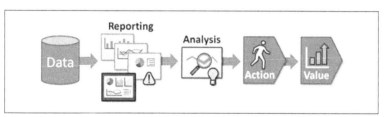

Figure 1-3. The analytics value chain (from Dykes, 2010). In a data-driven organization, the data feed reports, which stimulate deeper analysis. These are fed up to the decision makers who incorporate them into their decision-making process, influencing the direction that the company takes and providing value and impact. Figure from http://bit.ly/dykes-reporting.

Analytics Maturity

In 2009, Jim Davis, the senior vice president and chief marketing officer of SAS Institute, declared that there are eight levels of analytics:[5]

---

5 SAS, "Eight Levels of Analytics," (*http://bit.ly/sas-8-levels/*) (Cary, NC: SAS Institute, Inc., 2008), 4.

Standard reports

What happened? When did it happen? *Example*: monthly financial reports.

Ad hoc reports

How many? How often? Where? *Example*: custom reports.

Query drill down (or online analytical processing, OLAP)

Where exactly is the problem? How do I find the answers? *Example*: data discovery about types of cell phone users and their calling behavior.

Alerts

When should I react? What actions are needed now? *Example*: CPU utilization mentioned earlier.

Statistical analysis

Why is this happening? What opportunities am I missing? *Example*: why are more bank customers refinancing their homes?

Forecasting

What if these trends continue? How much is needed? When will it be needed? *Example*: retailers can predict demand for products from store to store.

Predictive modeling

What will happen next? How will it affect my business? *Example*: casinos predict which VIP customers will be more interested in particular vacation packages.

Optimization

How do we do things better? What is the best decision for a complex problem? *Example*: what is best way to optimize IT infrastructure given multiple, conflicting business and resource constraints?

The ideas appear to form the basis of a figure in Davenport and Harris's 2007 influential book *Competing on Analytics*,[6] shown here as Figure 1-4.

---

6 Despite appearing two years earlier, Davenport and Harris' source is cited as "adapted from a graphic produced by SAS."

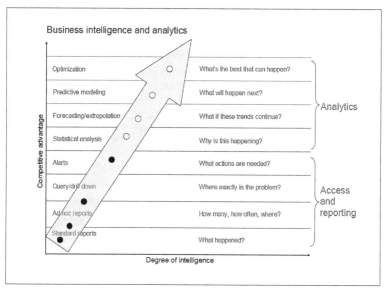

Business intelligence and analytics

Optimization	What's the best that can happen?
Predictive modeling	What will happen next?
Forecasting/extrapolation	What if these trends continue?
Statistical analysis	Why is this happening?

Analytics

Alerts	What actions are needed?
Query/drill down	Where exactly is the problem?
Ad hoc reports	How many, how often, where?
Standard reports	What happened?

Access and reporting

Competitive advantage

Degree of intelligence

Figure 1-4. "Business Intelligence and Analytics" of Davenport and Harris' Competing on Analytics. HBR Press, previously derived from Jim Davis' levels of analytics.

(You can see that this is also where Davenport's framework and Table 1-2 is based. You can easily map the first four levels to the upper information row and the second set of four to the lower insight row of Table 1-2.)

I like the general concept and the labels. However, in the way that both Davis (2009) and Davenport and Harris (2007) present their ideas, especially with the big sweeping upward arrow, it is too easy to interpret this as a progression or some sort of hierarchy, kind of like a video game where you progress to each next level only after having conquered the previous level.

This pseudo-progression is often labeled as analytics maturity. If you do a Google image search for "analytics maturity," you will see what I mean; that many BI vendors and practitioners present this as set of stepping stones with unidirectional arrows pointing from one level to the next. Analytics is not like that: it cuts across levels within an analysis, and different parts of the organization can be engaged in analyses of differing degrees of sophistication at any one time. Ron Shevlin[7] makes some great points:

> From a capabilities perspective, there's no reason why a firm couldn't forecast something likes sales ("level" 6) without knowing where exactly the "problem" with sales is ("level" 3)...How could I, as a manager, address the question of "what actions are needed now?" without some understanding of "what if these trends continue?" and "what will happen next?" ("levels" 6 and 7)?

The correct way, I think, to interpret this is to think of the *maximum* level that the organization is engaged in is positively correlated with the level of commitment, investment, and utility of analytics and, as Davenport and Harris argue, the analytical competitiveness. For instance, if you have an operations research team of Ph.D.s dedicated to optimizing your global supply chain, you are clearly heavily invested in data and analytics. If your organization only gets to alerts and query drilldowns, you have a lower investment and are less data-driven.

The underlying implication is that more sophisticated analytics are better; they make and organization more competitive. Is that true? In a fascinating study,[8] MIT Sloan Management Review collaborated with IBM Institute for Business Value to survey 3,000 managers and analysts across 30 industries about their use of and beliefs about the value of analytics.

One survey question asked about the organization's competitive position where the possible responses were:

1. Substantially outperform industry peers
2. Somewhat outperforming industry peers
3. On par with industry peers
4. Somewhat or substantially underperforming industry peers

Those organizations that chose answers 1 or 4 were deemed top and lower performers, respectively. Interestingly, compared to lower performers, top performers were:

---

7 Shevlin, R., "The Eight Levels Of Analytics?" (*http://bit.ly/fb-8-levels*) The Financial Brand, October 27, 2009.

8 LaValle, S., M. S. Hopkins, E. Lesser, R. Shockley, N. Kruschwitz, "Analytics: The New Path to Value." (*http://bit.ly/sloan-big-data*) MIT Sloan Management Review, October 24, 2010.

- Five times more likely to use analytics
- Three times more likely to be *sophisticated* analytics users
- Two times more likely to use analytics to guide day-to-day operations
- Two times more likely to use analytics to guide future strategies

There are certainly complicating factors in the methodology. There may be significant survivor bias, and there will likely be correlation of top performers with organization size (we know that revenue of these organizations ranged from less than $500 million to more than $10 billion). For instance, perhaps only larger, more successful organizations have the bandwidth and resources to develop sophisticated operations research departments that can develop and run supply chain simulation models. However, there was broad agreement that better and more sophisticated analytics drove business value.

The authors identified three levels of analytics capability: aspirational, experienced, and transformed. These are summarized in Table 1-3.

Table 1-3. Levels of analytics capability: aspirational, experienced, and transformed. Modified from http://bit.ly/sloan-big-data.

	Aspirational	Experienced	Transformed
Use analytics to...	Justify actions	Guide actions	Prescribe actions
Use rigorous approaches to make decisions	Rarely	Sometimes	Mostly
Ability to capture, aggregate, and analyze or share information and insights	Limited	Moderate	High
Functional proficiency	• Finance and budgeting • Operations and production • Sales and marketing	• All aspirational functions • Strategy / biz-dev • Customer service • Product R&D	• All aspirational and experienced functions • Risk management • Customer experience • Workforce planning • General management • Brand and marketing management

Compared to aspirational organizations, transformed organizations were:

- Four times more likely to capture information very well
- Nine times more likely to aggregate information very well
- Eight times more likely to analyze information very well
- Ten times more likely to disseminate information and insights very well
- 63% more likely to use a centralized analytics unit as the primary source of analytics (analytics organizational structures are covered in Chapter 4)

Again, there is a complicated tangle of cause and effect and biases here, but there is an association between competitive advantage, relative to industry peers, and analytics sophistication.

So, what is stopping organizations from adopting analytics widely? Two of the top three answers were lack of understanding of how to use analytics and lack of skills internally in the line of business (see Figure 1-5).

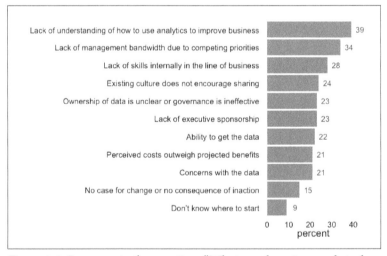

Figure 1-5. Response to the question, "What are the primary obstacles to widespread adoption and use of information and analytics in your organization?"

Those are something that everyone, including every analyst, can help drive. For instance, analysts can help "level up" their skill set and can be more proactive about doing good work and communicating its value to their managers and to the business. They can do more research to dig up case studies of how other organizations tackled similar business problems through analytics. Managers of the data engineers can assign resource to data integration and quality so that data is trusted. Senior managers can promote or demand greater sharing of data and designate clearer ownership and stewardship of data, such as appointing a chief analytics officer or chief data officer (covered in Chapter 11). Everyone has a role.

Overview

We'll dive into these issues in more detail in the following chapters. More concretely, I'll examine the needs in terms the foundation: the raw and aggregated data itself and its quality (Chapters 2 and 3). Next, I'll examine the analyst organization itself: the types of analysts, the skills they should possess, and how they should be structured (Chapter 4). I'll cover aspects of data analysis (Chapter 5), metric design (Chapter 6), and storytelling with data (Chapter 7). Chapter 8 covers A/B testing. Crucially, we'll cover the culture and decision-making process that are the hallmarks of a great data-driven organization (Chapters 9 and 10). I'll discuss what's needed to manage the culture and change management, especially in larger organizations: a data-driven C-suite. In particular, I'll cover three new executive positions: chief data officer, chief digital officer, and chief analytics officer (Chapter 11). Chapter 12 covers ethics and privacy issues of data and how an organization that respects its users' data may in fact limit what its analysts may do with the data. I'll end with some general conclusions (Chapter 13).

CHAPTER 2

Data Quality

80% of my time was spent cleaning the data.
Better data will always beat better models.
—Thomson Nguyen

Data is the foundation of a data-driven organization.

If you don't have timely, relevant, and trustworthy data, decision-makers have no alternative other than to make decisions by gut. Data quality is key.

 In this chapter, I'm using "quality" in a very broad sense, considering it primarily from an analyst's perspective.

Analysts need the right data, collected in the right manner, in the right form, in the right place, and at the right time. (They are not asking for much.) If any of those aspects are missing or lacking, analysts are limited in the questions that they can answer and the type or quality of insights that they can derive from the data.

In this chapter and the next, I will cover this broad topic of data quality. First, I'll discuss how to ensure that the data collection process is right. This is quality in the sense that it is accurate, timely, coherent, etc. Then, in the next chapter, I'll cover how to make sure that we are collecting the right data. This is quality in the sense of choosing and supplying the best data sources to augment existing data and so enable better insights. In short, I'll cover collecting the data right followed by collecting the right data.

This chapter focuses on the ways that we know that data is reliable, and all the ways that it can be unreliable. I'll first cover the facets of data quality—all the attributes that clean data has. After, I will delve into the myriad ways that data can go bad. That latter section is relatively detailed for a couple of reasons. First, because there are numerous ways data quality can be impaired. These different ways are not theoretical. If you've worked with data for a while, you will have encountered many, if not most, of them. They are a reality and happen more often than we would like. There is a reason that most data scientists spend the vast majority of their time cleaning data. Moreover, the likelihood of encountering these issues increases with scale. A former colleague, Samer Masry, says, "When working at scale, always remember issues that are one in a million can happen every second!" Second, and perhaps more importantly, as I suggest, proactively checking and maintaining data quality is a shared responsibility. Everyone in the analytics value chain should be an active participant in data quality. Thus, having a deeper understanding of data quality issues and sources, some of which are subtle and can introduce profound biases into data sources, is to everyone's benefit.

With that, let us examine what data quality means.

Facets of Data Quality

Data quality is not something that can be reduced down to a single number. Quality isn't a 5 or a 32. The reason is that the term covers a suite of facets or dimensions. Consequently, there are degrees of quality, with some issues more serious than others. The severity of those issues, however, can depend on the *context* of the analysis to be performed with the data. Thus, if you have a customer address table where the state code is present but the ZIP code is mostly absent, then missing ZIP codes would be a major blocker or impediment if you intended to analyze by ZIP but not if you intended to analyze at the state level.

More concretely, data quality has a number of facets. The data should be:

Accessible

An analyst has access to the data. This not only covers permissions but also the appropriate tooling that makes the data usable and analyzable. For instance, while a SQL (Structured Query Language: how people query databases) dump file may contain the data that the analyst may need, it is not in a useful form. It has to be exposed in a running database or in a business intelligence tool (on top of the database) for analysts to be able to analyze the data.

Accurate

Values represent the true value or state of the entity. For instance, a miscalibrated thermometer, a mistyped date of birth, and an out-of-date customer address all represent inaccurate data.

Coherent

Data can be combined with other relevant data in an accurate manner. For instance, a sales order should be able to be tied to a customer, one or more products in the order, a billing and/or shipping address, and possibly payment information. That suite of information provides a coherent picture of the sales order. Coherence is driven by the set of IDs or keys that bind the data in different parts of the database together.

Complete

There is no missing data. This can mean a single piece of data within a single record, such as a missing first name in a customer record, or complete records that are missing, such as a whole customer record that failed to get saved to a database.

Consistent

Data is in agreement. For example, an email address for a particular customer in one data source matches the email address for the same customer in another data source. When there are conflicts, one source should be considered the master source or they are both unused until the source of disagreement is understood and fixed.

Defined

Individuals data fields each have a well-defined, unambiguous meaning. Well-named fields accompanied by a data dictionary (discussed later) aid quality.

Relevant

Data has bearing on the data analysis being conducted. For instance, the historical stock trading prices of AAPL, while interesting, may have little bearing on an analysis of pork belly futures.

Reliable

Data is both complete (you have all the data that you should expect) and it is accurate (the data provides the correct information).

Timely

There is a short or reasonable duration between the collection of the data and the availability or release to analysts. In practice, this means that the data arrives in time for analysts to complete analysis before it is due. I recently heard of a major corporation whose data warehouse had a latency of one month. With those delays, the data is next to useless (yet still represents a maintenance and storage cost) and can only reasonably be used for long-term strategic planning and forecasting.

A slip in just *one* of these facets can render the data useless, partially usable, or the worst of all: seemingly usable but misleading.

In the rest of this chapter, I cover some of the processes and problems that drive down data quality, some approaches to detect and mitigate the issues, and who is responsible for data quality.

Dirty Data

Data can go bad in lots of ways and at every step of the data collection process. I'll trace the data all the way through its life cycle, from its generation to its analysis, covering the ways that bad data can be introduced at each point.

Data is always dirtier than we imagine. According to one study,[1] dirty or poor data quality costs US businesses $600 billion annually (that's 3.5% of GDP!).

---

1 Eckerson, W., "Data Warehousing Special Report: Data Quality and the Bottom Line." (*http://bit.ly/eckerson-quality*) (Chatsworth, CA: 101communications LLC, 2002), 34.

In many situations, analysts have little control in the collection and primary processing of data. Typically, they receive a dataset far downstream in a long chain of steps covering data generation, recording, transfer, processing, and blending. However, it is important to be aware of and appreciate the types of data quality issues that can arise and their potential remedies.

The goal of this section is to highlight the common data quality problems and pitfalls, to show how some of these issues can be avoided in the first place, and to briefly cover how they can be identified in datasets. Moreover, as will become clearer later, it is a call to action for members of the analytics teams to be full stakeholders in data quality wherever possible.

So, starting off at the source, what makes data dirty, and what can be done about it?

Data Generation

Data generation is the most upstream source of issues and can arise from errors in hardware (sensors), software (bugs), and wetware (humans).

In hardware, sensors may be miscalibrated or uncalibrated, which can result in inaccurate readings. For instance, a temperature sensor might be reading high: it says 95°F when in reality it is only 93°F. That may be easy to fix: where possible, calibrate it against some source of truth, such as another trusted sensor or meter, during setup.

Sensors may also be plain unreliable. I once worked on a DARPA (Defense Advanced Research Projects Agency) grant involving swarm robotics. We had a collection of simple robots whose task was to map the environment collaboratively. The problem was that the infrared sensors on these robots were shockingly bad. Instead of focusing on developing a decentralized algorithm to map a building, I spent most of my time working on algorithmic filters to deal with the quality of the sensors that measured distance to the nearest wall or other robots. Values would be dropped or the distance estimates to the nearest wall would suddenly jump around one meter or more (>50% error) from a stationary robot—you just couldn't trust the information coming out of those sensors.

When humans are involved, there are countless way to introduce errors into the collection process. They may not know how to use equipment properly, they may rush, or otherwise be sloppy. They may misinterpret instructions. They may not follow protocols set out: imagine nurses in two different clinics measuring patients' weights. In one, they weigh the patients with their shoes on, in the other with shoes off. Clear protocols and training are needed to fix these types of issues. Just like any experiment, you need to try to control and standardize as much of the process as possible so that the data stands the best chance of being usable, reliable, and comparable.

Data Entry

When data is generated manually—such as the nurses measuring patients' weights—it has to be recorded, ultimately in some sort of computer. Despite the promise of paperless offices, data is still far too often recorded on paper forms as an intermediate step before it is entered into a computer. These hardcopy stages can introduce a lot of errors.

When handwritten forms are transcribed, mistakes will happen. (If you see my handwriting, you will understand.) Healthcare providers have done the most research in this area, in part because the consequences of inaccurate information can be so serious in terms of patients' health but also because the cost, such as giving a patient an unnecessary test, is so high. In one study, 46% of medication errors (which had a base rate of 11% of all orders) were attributed to transcription mistakes.[2] Disturbingly, some fields in clinical research databases were found to have error rates of 27%.[3] Such errors can arise from people misreading or misinterpreting writing, not hearing or not understanding bad audio quality or unusual words when transcribing aurally, or miskeying the information into a computer.

---

2 Seely, C. E., D. Nicewander, R. Page, and P.A. Dysert, "A baseline study of medication error rates at Baylor University Medical Center in preparation for implementation of a computerized physician order entry system." (*http://bit.ly/seeley-med-errors*) *Proc (Bayl Univ Med Cent). 2004 Jul* 17(3): 357–361.

3 Goldberg, S. I., A. Niemerko, and A. Turchin, "Analysis of Data Errors in Clinical Research Databases." (*http://bit.ly/goldberg-errors*) *AMIA Annu Symp Proc. 2008:* 242–246.

For instance, I used to work in a healthcare modeling company. A key government dataset we frequently used was called NHANES (National Health and Nutrition Examination Survey). This is essentially a US census for health. Mobile clinics tour the country and sample people: they take blood pressure readings, measure weight, ask about family history of diabetes and cancer, and so on. When we looked at the distribution of heights of people in one of their datasets we found a whole bunch of adults listed at five inches tall! These are trained staff that survey people day in and day out. Because measuring height is a relatively simple procedure, the most likely explanation is a data entry problem. Maybe they were five feet tall, but it's just as possible that they were five feet, five inches, or six feet five, but because we couldn't tell for sure, we had to set those values as unknown.

Fortunately, five-inch-tall people is such an obvious error that we could detect it with a simple histogram and be confident that there was a problem. That, however, is not always the case. There are degrees of detectability. Imagine transcribing a paragraph and instead of copying "allergies: cats and dogs," the data entry clerk transposed two characters and typed "allergies: ctas and dogs." Ctas is just nonsense. It is not a dictionary word. This is easy to catch and you can use the context to work out what it should be. A more subtle error is cases where transposition of characters can lead to other valid words: think "form" transposed to "from." That is harder to detect. In this case, the context will hopefully allow you to work out what it should be, but it is not guaranteed. Finally, now imagine a value of 56.789 has two digits transposed to 56.798. That is going to be very difficult, if not impossible, to detect.

More generally, data entry issues manifest themselves as four types of issues:

Transcription
   Words or values entered are not those that were in original data.

Insertion
   Additional characters were introduced. 56.789 → 564.789.

Deletion
   One or more characters were omitted. 56.789 → 56.89.

Transposition
   Two or more characters were swapped. 56.789 → 56.798.

Special subcategories of insertion and deletion are *dittography*, where a string or value is copied twice (56.789 → 56.7789) and *haplography*, where a double string or value is only copied once (56.779 → 56.79). The terms come from text criticism, where scholars reconstruct damaged and hand-copied ancient texts, a special kind of bad-data problem.

Dates are especially subject to transposition errors involving days and months. I am British and my native format for dates is day/month/year. However, I live in the US, where the format is typically month/day/year. This was certainly confusing to me for the first few years that I lived here, and it can be confusing for others, too. Imagine a website with users across the globe enter a free-form text field for a date. Users may have different expectations of date format, and without sufficient messaging or validation, data can be incorrectly entered. Some dates might easily be caught: 25 March (3/25 in the US) cannot be month=25/day=3. What about something like 4/5 though? Can you be sure that all users mean that to be April 5?

So, what can be done about these types of errors?

Data entry error mitigation

The first thing to do, if possible, is reduce the number of steps from data generation to input. To state the obvious, if you can avoid an intermediate paper form, you should do so and enter data directly into the computer.

Where possible, add field validation to your electronic forms (Figure 2-1). That is, if the data is well-structured and has an expected format—a US ZIP code must be five or nine digits digits or a Social Security number must be nine digits—check that the data meets that format, and if it doesn't, reject the data and guide the user to correcting any mistakes. Validation is not limited to single values. For instance, you should check that a return flight time is after the outbound flight. In short, validate as much as possible and prevent "garbage in, garbage out" at source.

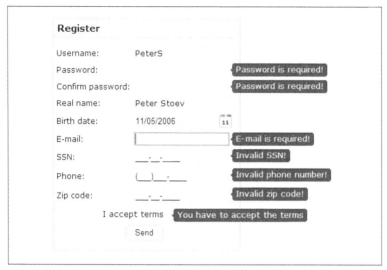

Figure 2-1. Example of field validation in an online registration form, from http://www.jqwidgets.com/.

Where there is a set of valid values, such as state abbreviations, you can use a dropdown menu for the user to choose from. Autocomplete is another alternative. In general, you want users to type as little input as possible: get them to choose from a set of options that you provide—unless, of course, it is an open-ended question with a free-form text field.

Ideally, try to remove the human element as much as possible from the data collection process and have as much as possible collected and stored automatically.

If you have the time and resources, you can have two people independently transcribe the data, or the same person transcribe the data twice, and then compare results and then recheck where the data doesn't match. This is known as double entry. I once had an intern transcribe measurements from a set of technical drawings and then he, on his own volition, redid the task and checked for differences. As the consumer of the data, that gave me a lot of confidence that the data was as accurate as we could reasonably expect.

An interesting approach used when transmitting important numbers such as bank account numbers, Social Security numbers, and even the ISBN number of this book is to use a *check digit*. This is an extra digit tacked onto the end of a number that is some function of the other digits and is used to check that the rest of the number was transmitted correctly from one system to another. Let's imagine that you need to transmit a ZIP code: 94121. Let's detail a very simple scheme. You sum the digits to get 17. Now you sum those digits to get 8. You transmit 941218. The receiving system at the other end would do the same operation: chop off the last digit, 94121 → 17 → 8. This matches that check digit of 8 and so 94121 is correct. If there was a transcription error and you transmitted 841218 instead, you could detect 84121 → 16 → 7 ≠ 8.

This scheme isn't very robust: 93221 (double transcription error) or 94211 (transposition error) would provide the same check digit value. Real check digit functions are more mathematically complex and robust than this and they are designed to deal with a number of transcription and transposition errors. Routing numbers of US banks (*http://bit.ly/wiki-routing*) (the nine-digit number in the bottom left of your checks) are one such example and have a trailing check digit. Those routing numbers must satisfy

$$3 \times (d_1 + d_4 + d_7) + 7 \times (d_2 + d_5 + d_8) + d_3 + d_6 + d_9 \mod 10 = 0$$

(mod means the remainder if we take out multiples of 10, so 32 mod 10 = 2 as 32 = 3 × 10 + 2) and can be checked with simple Python code, such as:

```
routing_number = "122187238"
d = [int(c) for c in routing_number]
checksum = ( # do the math!
            7 * (d[0] + d[3] + d[6]) +
            3 * (d[1] + d[4] + d[7]) +
            9 * (d[2] + d[5])
          ) % 10
print(d[8] == checksum)
```

As can be seen, there are a number of things that you can do to try to maintain high-quality code at the data entry stage, but they are not infallible. So, you have some data in the system and it flows down to an analyst. Now what?

Exploratory data analysis

When analysts receive some data, they should generally do some exploratory data analysis (Chapter 5) to assess data quality. One simple way to check for glaring errors, such as the five-inch-tall people, is to summarize the data. For each variable, one can compute a five-number summary: minimum, the lower quartile (25th percentile), the mean and/or median, the upper quartile (75th percentile), and the maximum. Take a look at the minimum and maximum. Do they make sense? Are they higher or lower than you would expect? Five inches is clearly way too low.

Here is an example of R's summary() function on the Iris dataset—R (*http://www.r-project.org/*) is a free open source software environment for statistical computing and graphics popular with statisticians and data scientists. Iris (*http://bit.ly/wiki-iris-data*), a type of flower, is the source of a well-known dataset collected by Edgar Anderson but made famous by the statistician R. A. Fisher, consisting of measurements of 50 samples of three iris species:

```
> summary(iris)
 Sepal.Length    Sepal.Width    Petal.Length    Petal.Width        Species
 Min.   :4.300   Min.   :2.000   Min.   :1.000   Min.   :0.100   setosa    :50
 1st Qu.:5.100   1st Qu.:2.800   1st Qu.:1.600   1st Qu.:0.300   versicolor:50
 Median :5.800   Median :3.000   Median :4.350   Median :1.300   virginica :5
 Mean   :5.843   Mean   :3.057   Mean   :3.758   Mean   :1.199
 3rd Qu.:6.400   3rd Qu.:3.300   3rd Qu.:5.100   3rd Qu.:1.800
 Max.   :7.900   Max.   :4.400   Max.   :6.900   Max.   :2.500
```

You can easily scan the rows and columns to get a sense of the data (1st Qu. = 1st quartile or 25th percentile; 3rd = 75th percentile). You can also obtain the same information (plus outliers) visually by generating boxplots (Figure 2-2).

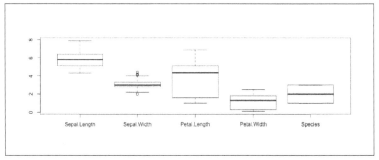

Figure 2-2. Boxplots of the iris dataset by calling R's boxplot() function.

Figure 2-3 illustrates some of the issues that you might be able to detect with a simple histogram of your data. In the NHANES dataset, I also looked at the blood pressure measurements. Running sum mary(), I saw maximum blood pressure values that seemed extremely high, far higher than seems normal. I thought that those were erroneous, too. However, when viewed as a distribution, they were at the tail of the distribution but at a reasonable frequency. Checking the medical literature, I was able to confirm that blood pressures could be as high as those observed. However, these were people who likely had an *untreated* medical condition. Remember that this was a general sample of the US population and not patients from a medical facility where presumably they would be treated— context is everything.

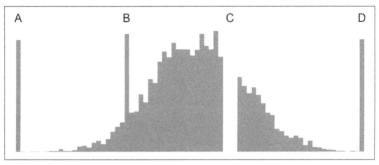

Figure 2-3. Example of the sorts of errors and features that can be detected with a simple histogram: A) default values, such as –1, 0, or 1/1/1900; B) incorrectly entered or duplicate data; C) missing data; and D) default values, such as 999.

Developing expectations of the data and the related ability to esti-mate[4] are two skills that analysts should develop. I was wrong about the blood pressure values because I was used to thinking about nor-mal healthy individuals. However, I found out more, increased my domain knowledge, adjusted my expectations of the range of values that I should expect to see, and was comforted that the data was likely correct.

It goes to show that initially you can't necessarily trust any data source. I always assume that there is something wrong with the data, and it is my job to find out where the problems lie. I don't get obses-sive, but I will do some work (such as R's summary(), pairs(), and boxplot()) to assure myself that there are not any obvious issues. In

---

4 Guesstimation is an underrated analyst skill. I would recommend Chapter 7 of P.K. Janert's (2011) *Data Analysis with Open Source Tools* (O'Reilly).

the case of the NHANES data, my colleagues and I plotted histograms of all the variables to look for odd patterns, bimodal distributions, and other outliers. Counting number of records by date is another simple test. Exploratory data analysis such as this can be simple, quick, and highly valuable.

Missing Data

One of the most significant issues with data is incomplete or missing data (Figure 2-3C). That can manifest itself in two ways: missing data within a record, or wholly missing records.

Filling in the Blanks: Imputation

There are statistical approaches than can be used to "impute" or fill in the missing data with the most likely values (I happen to like R's Amelia package (*http://bit.ly/amelia-package*) and Google's imputation service (*http://bit.ly/google-imputation*) for its spreadsheets). Their success depends upon a number of factors, including sample sizes, the number and pattern of missing data, the types of variables (whether they are categorical, continuous, discrete, etc.), and the noisiness of the data. One of the simplest approaches is to fill in the missing values with the mean of that variable. More sophisticated approaches, however, often use iteration of a technique called expectation-maximization with maximum-likelihood. See *Missing Data* by P.D Allison (Sage) and *Statistical Analysis with Missing Data, Second Edition* by R.J. A. Little and D.B. Rubin (Wiley). It is a powerful technique but, depending upon the characteristics of the data, is going to produce at least some incorrect predictions.

Why then, might you use such an approach? Why risk it? In many cases, especially in medical and social sciences, data is very expensive to collect, and you might only have one chance to collect it. Imagine collecting blood pressure from a patient on the third day of a clinical trial; you can't go back and repeat that. A core problem, a catch-22 situation in fact, is that the smaller the sample size, the more precious each record is. However, the less data an imputation algorithm has to work with, the worse its predictions will be.

A single missing value within a record can render the whole record useless. This would typically be true if it represented the primary key—i.e., the value that uniquely identified the subject of the record

—such as a customer ID or order ID (and which would be needed to join to other data). It would also be true of other fields if those were the focus of the analysis. For instance, if you intended to analyze sales by ZIP code, and ZIP code was missing from a particular record, then clearly you could not use that record. If you are lucky, you may not need the field with the missing value and so you do not suffer reduced sample size.

As mentioned earlier, data can be missing for a variety of reasons. In surveys, for instance, people may not understand or skip a question, their handwriting might be illegible to the transcribers, or they might give up on the survey halfway through. In hardware, a server might die or a sensor might fail. Because biases can kill the quality of your data, what is really important to figure out is *how* the data is missing.

Imagine that a web server disk dies, taking with it the locally stored data you need. This would be an example of wholly missing records. If you have a load balancer that distributes the load randomly to each of 20 web servers, one of which failed, it is inconvenient for sure—you've lost 5% of your data—but so long as the missing data is a random sample of all data, all is not lost. However, if there is some pattern or bias, you can be in trouble. If that web server typically serves a particular geographic region, you may be missing a disproportionate amount of data from a given set of ZIP codes, and that could significantly impact the analysis.

A more biased scenario is the following: imagine that you send out a customer survey and give recipients two weeks to respond. Any responses that arrive after the cutoff are excluded from the analysis. Now imagine a set of customers who are suffering from shipping issues and receive their orders late. They might be more likely to be both unhappy and to send off their responses later. As such, you might exclude a higher proportion of unhappy customers. You have a biased sample. In his statistics teaching material, Daniel Mintz (*http://bit.ly/mintz-bias*) provides an especially clear example of bias: "Question. Do you like to answer surveys: yes or no?" Who will and will not complete that?

The type of missingness is critical. (I blame statisticians for the following terminology, which I think is terrible.) You need to investigate whether the data is:

MCAR

> Missing completely at random, such as the randomly allocated web server traffic.

MAR

> Missing at random, meaning that the data is missing as a function of the *observed* or nonmissing data, such as the geo-serving web server that resulted in a lower sample size for a subset of ZIP codes.

MNAR

> Missing not at random, where data is missing as a function of the *missing* data, such as the unhappy customers and their survey responses. This is the most pernicious case where there is a significant bias.

The lower down this list, the more trouble you are in and the fewer options you have to resolve the situation.

They key is that you recognize and understand any biases that you are facing. Sometimes you can at least say directionally the impact in the metrics or place some bounds. Counterintuitively, there are even some unusual situations where biased missing data can have no impact on your metric.

When I used to teach statistics, I would use the following example to teach the properties of the median: there is an unusual sport of pigeon racing where "pigeon fanciers" drive their pigeons, say, a hundred miles from home, release them, then frantically drive back home and wait for the birds to arrive. It's a race, and as each bird arrived, they note the time—pigeon number six arrived after 2 hours and 3 minutes, pigeon number 11 arrived at 2 hours and 13 minutes, etc. Inevitably, some pigeons don't make it. They might get blown off course or fall prey to a raptor. We can't know the *average* flying time of all the birds because some birds have missing data. However, so long as fewer than half the birds are missing, we can compute the *median* flying duration. We know the original sample size, we know the durations of more than half the sample, and significantly we know that all missing data is slower than the last bird to arrive, so we can compute the true median value: it is robust to this set of missingness criteria. Thus, sometimes the right metric choice can salvage a situation. (The choice of metrics is covered further in Chapter 6.)

Duplicates

Duplicate data is another common problem. Duplicates can mean the same exact record appearing multiple times. This can happen for different reasons; for instance, suppose that you have 10 datafiles and you accidentally load the 6th file twice, or you are loading a file, and halfway through, you encounter a corrupted record that breaks the load. If you edit the file to fix or delete that record and reload the file, then the first half of the file is duplicated in your database. Duplicates can arise from multiple sign-ups. For instance, a customer might sign up for an account multiple times with the same or different email, resulting in different customer IDs but with the same other personal information. (While it sounds simple, entity disambiguation such as this can be very tricky.) Duplicates could also arise from overlapping sensors in which two sensors record the same event. In that medication error study mentioned earlier, 35% of errors were due to data not being transferred correctly from one system to another; sometimes the data didn't make it, and sometimes the orders were duplicated. According to Johns Hopkins Hospital, 92% of the duplicates in its data occur during inpatient registration.

In terms of databases, there are several ways to prevent this type of duplication. The safest is to add a constraint to your database table. Let it be the gatekeeper. A combination key defines the set of one or more fields that makes a record unique. By adding this key constraint to your database table, it will complain about and reject any records where that same combination of data already exists in the table. In addition, you can wrap the load in a transaction, which provides all-or-nothing load behavior. That is, the database notes the current status (think of it taking a snapshot), starts to load a new set of data, and if there are any problems, it rolls back to the beginning, to that snapshot point, with no new data saved. This gives you a chance to work out why the file is corrupted and means that you don't have to clean up any mess in the database. A third, less efficient, approach is to run two queries per record: first a SELECT query that asks if this record is already present. If not, then an INSERT query adds the new record.

Duplicates like these are more common than you think. If you are not aware that there are duplicates, this may influence your metrics, but probably more serious is that at some point one of the analysts

---

will notice. Once the quality of the data is brought into question, the data team has lost credibility, and there is a reduced chance that the data will be used or trusted and be incorporated in a decision-making process.

Truncated Data

When data is loaded into a database, it can get truncated (anderson → anders or 5456757865 → 54567578). In the best case, you may lose a few characters of a free-form response field; and in the worst case, two different IDs may be truncated so that they look like the same shorter, incorrect ID value; i.e., you inadvertently combine data from different orders or customers.

Why can this happen? In typical relational databases when creating a table, you have to specify each field's name and type: for example, there will be a column called last_name, and it will be a string with at most 32 characters; or there will be a customer_id column, and it will be an integer ranging from 0 to 65535. The problem is that you don't always know in advance the maximum string or integer length of the values that you will encounter. You might obtain a data sample, estimate the field lengths, and add a buffer such as doubling those estimates, but you don't really know for sure until you process the data in production. Moreover, databases typically default to truncation errors as *warnings*; they output a message, but they keep chugging away consuming the data. As such, these problems can be easy to miss. One way to fix this is to set your database to strict mode so that warnings become full-blown errors that you can more easily catch.

Units

Another source of data quality is inconsistent units, especially in international teams and datasets. CNN (*http://bit.ly/cnn-nasa-orbiter*) reports:

> NASA lost a $125 million Mars orbiter because a Lockheed Martin engineering team used English units of measurement [pounds-seconds] while the agency's team used the more conventional metric system [Newton-seconds] for a key spacecraft operation.

Yeah, it's really that important. The only way to avoid this is to have very clear, explicit communication. Have a requirements document that sets out unambiguously how items are measured and recorded and their units. The resulting dataset should also be accompanied by a detailed data dictionary.

Currencies are another area where units are critical. Imagine an international e-commerce website where an order of value 23.12 was placed. In the US, we would expect that to be $23.12; but in France, we would expect that to be 23.12€. If orders from different countries are combined without a currency metadata field into one dataset, the resulting analysis will be biased toward the weaker currency (because they have larger numerical values for the same item) and will be useless.

Datasets have to provide as much metadata and context as necessary to avoid ambiguities such as these.

You can also just adopt and stick to the metric system (wake up, America!).

Default Values

Another issue with data, sometimes something that can be hard to track down and disambiguate, is default values (Figure 2-3A and D). Missing data might appear as a NULL in a database, but it could also appear as some default value that you specify. For instance, Jan 1, 1900 is a common date default. There are a couple of issues. First, if you forget that there is such a default, you may be left puzzling about the results. Suppose that you made a date of birth field have a default of 1/1/1900. Analysts may wonder why so many people in your database appear to be more than 100 years old. Second, and more serious, if you make a bad choice, you may not be able to distinguish missing data from actual data. For instance, if a default value is set as 0, but nonmissing data for that field may also take a value 0, then you can't determine which really had a measured value of 0 and which were unknown. Choose default values wisely.

Data Provenance

When data quality issues are found, it is crucial to trace them back to their origin. That way, the whole subset of data can be removed from analysis or better processes or protocols can be devised and put in place to remedy the problem. Metadata that stores the origin and change history of data is known as lineage, pedigree, or as I use here, data provenance.

There are two primary classes of provenance: *source provenance*, which tracks where data comes from, and *transformation provenance*, which tracks changes made to data.

In my team, for instance, we collect datafiles daily from a variety of vendors and load them into our database for reporting and analysis. Typically, those raw data receiving tables, which are called landing or staging tables, have two extra fields: loadtime (the time at which we start the load for that file or batch) and filename. That way, if we discover quality issues, it makes it very easy to identify which file the data came from, for us to inspect the exact line in the raw datafile, and for us to ask the vendor to investigate. This is an example of source provenance.

In transactional databases (databases used to support live applications and uses such as processing orders as opposed to reporting), it's fairly common to see a pair of fields in a table: `created_at` and `last_modified`. As the names suggest, these fields specify when the record was first created (you write that metadata once on creation and never update) and when the most recent change was made (update with current time any time any part of the record is changed). Sometimes you may also encounter an additional field, such as `modified_by`, which lists the user who made the most recent change. This can be helpful to identify whether a change to, say, an order or email preference was made by users themselves or by a customer service representative working on their behalf. Here, `created_at` is an element of source provenance while `last_modified` and `modified_by` are elements of transformation provenance. The most fine-grained provenance is a separate logging table or logging statements that lists precisely what was changed, by whom, and when.

Provenance metadata should be an element of a proactive strategy of checking, maintaining, and improving data quality.

There is a good chance that data provenance is going to grow in importance. It is increasingly easy to instrument systems to collect and store more of one's own data and to purchase relevant supplemental data from third parties (such as demographics from ZIP code or shopping history from email). These organizations should be creating richer contexts around their customers and both their explicit and implicit event and transaction data. That requires creating objects from multiple sources of data, modifying existing data, such as imputing missing values, or annotating data with other attributes, such as inferred gender, intent, and so on. All of these should be traceable back to the original data value, its source, and any reason or metadata for any modification or transformation.

Data Quality Is a Shared Responsibility

The ways in which data can be inaccurate or of poor quality are end-less. In addition to those mentioned previously, there are line-ending issues, encoding issues where unicode values are squished into ASCII (this happens all the time), corrupted data, truncated files, late data, and names and addresses that don't match up (sum-marized in Table 2-1). Data quality shouldn't be left just to the data engineers; it should be an enterprise-wide responsibility.

Table 2-1. Summary of just some of the types of data quality issues and potential remedies. For a more detailed list, see Singh and Singh, "A descriptive classification of causes of data quality problems in data warehousing," IJCSI Intl. J. Comp. Sci 7, no. 3 (2010): 41–50.

Facet	Issue	Solutions
Accuracy	*Data entry*: character insertion	*Web*: drop-down menu, autocomplete. *Analog*: double entry.
Accuracy	*Data entry*: character deletion	*Web*: drop-down menu, autocomplete. *Analog*: double entry.
Accuracy	*Data entry*: character mutation	*Web*: drop-down menu, autocomplete. *Analog*: double entry.
Accuracy	*Data entry*: transposition	*Web*: drop-down menu, autocomplete. *Analog*: double entry.
Accuracy	*Data entry*: out-of-range values	*Web*: form validation. *Database*: field constraints.
Accuracy	*Data entry*: ambiguous date formats	*Web*: datepicker or explicit form. *Database*: create data dictionary, standardize (e.g., to YYYY-MM-DD).
Accuracy	Duplicates records	*Database*: combination key constraints, dedupe data.
Accuracy	Data corruption	Check digits or check sums.
Accuracy	Differing encoding (e.g., one table is UTF-8 while another is ASCII) or encoding conversion loss (e.g., José stored as ASCII might end up as Jos?)	*Database*: try to standardize on a single, broad character set, such as Latin1 or UTF-16.

Facet	Issue	Solutions
Accuracy / coherence	Value truncation	*Database*: larger field type; elevate database warnings to errors.
Coherence	Combined fields (e.g., "Doe, Joe" makes it very hard to join to other tables where same person might be "Joe Doe")	*Application or database*: use separate fields.
Coherence	Differing primary keys for same entity in different system making it hard to associate data correctly	*Application or database*: unified ID system.
Consistence	Conflicting data (e.g., differing address for same person in different systems)	*Database*: central user system or rule-based resolution to decide which is more reliable.
Confusion	Confusing or ambiguous time zones	*Web*: datepicker. *Database*: create data dictionary, standardize (e.g., to UTC).
Confusion	Field abuse: stuff a field with other data (e.g., use an unused `mid dle_name` field to store order status)	*Application or Database*: best practices, strict clearly documented schema.
Confusion	Confusing codes (e.g., HiLowRangeTZ3)	*Database*: create data dictionary.
Confusion	Ambiguous missing data: does value of 0 mean missing or actual value of 0?	*Application or database*: choose sensible default values outside value range.
Completeness	Partial loading errors	Database: alerts, transactions, (e.g., rollback to prior snapshot on error)
Completeness	Data missing completely at random (MCAR)	*Analysis*: oversample, use category weights.
Completeness	Data missing at random (MAR): data is missing as function of the observed or nonmissing values.	*Analysis*: restrict analysis to where data can be used safely.
Completeness	Data missing not at random (MNAR): data is missing as function of the missing data	*Analysis*: redesign or restart collection process.
Completeness	Incorrect number of delimiters in flat causing fewer or extra columns	Quote fields, source quality checks.
Timeliness	Stale data from slow updates (e.g., backlog of change of address forms)	Better, faster automation.
Provenance	Unclear when or why a data field was changed	*Application or database*: better logging, add provenance database fields.

A frontend developer can add ZIP code validation into a website form, a data engineer can add in a check digit during transmission to another data repository, and a database administrator can check for and prevent duplicates or monitor for loading errors. However, you can't expect them to know what are out-of-range systolic blood pressure values. When input data forms are part of your organization's operations, business owners (meaning managers in the business units), domain experts, and analysts should be working with the frontend developers to provide range check bounds. They should also be part of the requirements and project management process to make sure that data quality elements are incorporated into the data flow process where appropriate. As mentioned earlier, the analytics organization should be a stakeholder in the data collection machinery.

Downstream, business owners and domain experts should proactively check data quality. Analysts should be doing exploratory data analysis or developing their own repeatable processes to check that data is within ranges, that certain expected relationships hold true (such as the ratio of systolic to diastolic blood pressures), to ascertain the level of missingness, and so on. At the farmer's market, a chef will pick up produce, squeeze the avocados, sniff the basil. Those, after all, are literally his raw ingredients. Likewise, analysts should have the same attitude to data. It is their raw ingredients and must pass their sniff test, too.

Business owners are likely responsible for the decision to purchase datasets from a third-party vendor or for designing the experiments to sample people in customer surveys or in online A/B tests. They, too, should be thinking about and seeking out biases in the data. They should be running or delegating exploratory data analysis, plotting distributions, and finding those five-inch-tall people.

CHAPTER 3

Data Collection

> *Errors using inadequate data are much*
> *less than those using no data at all.*
> —Charles Babbage

> *It's difficult to imagine the power that you're going to have*
> *when so many different sorts of data are available.*
> —Tim Berners-Lee

In the previous chapter, I covered data quality and collecting data right. In this chapter, we switch focus to choosing the right data sources to consume and provision to the analysts. That is, collecting the right data. I'll cover such topics as prioritizing which data sources to consume, how to collect the data, and how to assess the value that the data provides to the organization.

Collect All the Things

Imagine that you are rolling out a new checkout process on your website. You will want to know exactly *how it is performing* against your metrics—you will want to track conversion, basket size, and so on—but it will also be instructive and insightful to understand *how it is being used*. For instance, on some sites, "add to cart" is a painless single click, so a pattern of customer behavior might be to add a bunch of items to the cart as a holding area and then prune that down to their final choices before clicking the checkout submit button. On other sites, however, "add to cart" might involve multiple clicks, and removing items might be harder or ambiguous—in short, there is more friction—so that customers essentially need to make their final decision before adding items to the cart. You can see why instrumenting the checkout process as much as possible can lead to deeper insights about the feature and can drive ideas for feature additions or refinements and further tests.

In his book, *Building Data Science Teams* (*http://bit.ly/data-sci-teams*) (O'Reilly), DJ Patil remarks:

> It's easy to pretend that you're data driven. But if you get into the mindset to collect and measure everything you can, and think about what the data you've collected means, you'll be ahead of most of the organizations that claim to be data driven.

Collect and measure everything that you can. You never know what you might need, you often only have one chance to collect the data, and you'll kick yourself later when you need it and it is no longer accessible. The more data that you collect, the greater the chance that you have to model and understand the users' behavior (as in the checkout example) and, importantly, their *context*—context is king. That is, the more that an organization understands about the individual users, their tastes, intentions, and desires, the more it can improve the user experience through personalization, recommendation, or more fine-grained services that reach down the "long tail."[1]

When developing online products, collecting everything is a no-brainer. It is a data source that you control, and a click on one feature can use the same or similar collection mechanism as a click on another feature. That is, you can make use of common patterns, data flows, and storage mechanisms. A strongly data-driven organization, however, will likely be thinking much broader than this: data-driven marketing, data-driven sales, data-driven customer service, data-driven supply chain, data-driven HR. If each of those has a suite of internal and external *data sources* with different formats, latency, data quality issues, security and compliance requirements, etc., then this starts to become daunting for the data team. That's when "collect everything" sounds great in practice but is a major headache when the rubber meets the road.

---

1 Anderson, C. *The Long Tail: Why the Future of Business Is Selling Less of More*. New York: Hachette Books, 2005.

Moreover, it is not free. While more data is better[2] (see Appendix A for some examples and reasoning why), it can come at a hefty price. It costs money to build pipelines to suck down, cleanse, transform, and store those data. There is a cost to maintain those systems, to back up the data, and to integrate those data sources to provide a holistic view of the business. There can also be a significant down-stream cost to provide quality tools for analysts to make good use of disparate data sources. You need all of that to get the right data into the hands of the analysts.

The Three Vs of Big Data

Big data practitioners and vendors tend to think about data collection and processing at scale in terms of three Vs: volume, variety, and velocity.[3]

Volume
> Refers to the amount of data. This incurs direct costs in terms of storage and data transfer. Although it is true that storage costs are decreasing exponentially (*http://bit.ly/storage-cost*)—they are now about $0.03 per GB compared to about $10 per GB in the year 2000—the number of sources of data available, and the rate at which those sources can be sampled, have increased so significantly that they counter those storage cost decreases.

Variety
> Another important dimension of data. On the one hand, a varied set of sources provide a richer context and more holistic view. Thus, pulling down weather information, inflation data, as well as chatter on social media, may provide fruitful insights into sales of your products. However, the more varied your data sources and data types (CSV from one source, JSON objects from another source, hourly weather here but rapid stock ticks here), the greater will be your integration costs. It is hard to bring these data together to paint a coherent picture.

---

2 Fortuny, E. J. de, D. Martens, and F. Provost, Predictive Modeling with Big Data: Is Bigger Really Better?" (*http://bit.ly/defortuny-predictive*) *Big Data* 1, no. 4 (2013): 215–226.

3 First coined by Laney, D., "3D Data Management: Controlling Data Volume, Velocity, and Variety," (*http://bit.ly/laney-3d-data*) Application Delivery Strategies by META Group Inc., February 6, 2001.

Velocity

How much data you need to process per unit time. Imagine sampling Twitter data during a presidential debate to provide current sentiment. You have to not only process a huge amount of information, but do so at a rapid clip to be able to provide some real-time sense of how the nation is feeling about the remarks during the debate. Large-scale, real-time processing is complex and costly.

(Occasionally, you will see some vendors slip in another *V*, *veracity*, that reflects data quality.)

Even organizations that collect a huge amount—Facebook, Google, and yes, the NSA, too—didn't make it happen overnight. You build the data sources, connections among them, and processing capabilities over time. You have to have a rational, well-thought-out data acquisition or provisioning *strategy*. Further, data teams in most organizations are resource-constrained; they can't do everything at once, and so they have to prioritize which data sources to tackle very carefully. The reality is that when collecting data, things happen sequentially and slowly—there are always unforeseen delays and problems, and so you have to focus on value, return on investment, and the impact that a new data source will make upon the organization. That's a primary focus of this chapter.

Prioritizing Data Sources

How does a typical, smaller, resource-constrained organization, where data engineers have competing calls on their time, choose which data source to consume next? In prioritizing those data sources for consumption and provisioning, a data-driven organization should focus on a fourth and more important *V*: *value* to the business.

The primary motivation of the data team should be to meet the business units' and their analysts' needs and help provide an impact to the organization. Each team or unit is likely to have a set of "core" data. For a customer service team, that might mean the various forms of interaction data, such as emails, phone calls, social media, perhaps instant message data, case data, and the sales order data. With that, they can perform their primary function—to deliver amazing customer service—but they can combine these sources to produce a holistic view of the set of interactions per case; they can view the high-level metrics about team productivity, such as average time to resolve a case; and they can analyze the type of interactions per source. Teams have to have their core data. However, in addition, they might have another set of data that would augment their core data. For instance, this might be defect rate data from manufacturing or A/B test data that might highlight where customers are getting confused by a new feature. Those might help the team predict the rate and topics of cases that are expected to come in. Those other data sources are likely valuable and impactful but not crucial.

The problem in a resource-constrained organization is that the customer service team is only one of many teams. Other teams have their set of core and nice-to-have data needs, too. Imagine a data engineer or data team project manager trying to balance all these requests from different teams. Table 3-1 sets out a number of dimensions that may help them determine priority. The key facet is return on investment (ROI), but ease, complexity, data quality, and other issues are a consideration.

Table 3-1. Points to consider when prioritizing which new data sources to bring into the organization in a resource-constrained data engineering team

Priority	Reason	Explanation
High	Data is truly and urgently needed.	If there is a genuine need from the business unit and a hard deadline, you need to serve those internal customers ASAP.
High	Data will deliver high value.	If there is a high return on investment (ROI), for instance, they can help generate significantly higher revenue or reduce costs, this source should be a high priority.
High	Multiple teams need the same data.	There is a higher ROI if you can satisfy multiple business owners simultaneously.
High	Data is ephemeral or streaming.	Some streaming social media APIs or hardware devices only allow you to query a certain short time window after which the data is lost forever. It is a case of use it or lose it.
Medium	Augment existing data in value-driving way.	New data will augment existing data and provide a significantly richer context. (This is discussed in detail in the next section.)
Medium	Data engineers can reuse existing data processing code.	If the team has some familiarity with the data source or its API and can make use of existing code, there are likely to be fewer unknowns or surprises.

Priority	Reason	Explanation
Medium	Easy to pull down.	Sometimes a request might jump the queue because there exists a nice Python client or API that makes it very easy to pull data down or the data has a clean and simple schema. If this is a data source you can knock out in an afternoon or a day or two, and it will provide some demonstrable value, it might be worth just getting it done quickly.
Medium	Good API that allows you to bring down historical data.	If you don't urgently need the data right now, and you know that you can always go back and retrieve historical data, then there are probably other higher-priority data sources to go after. For instance, if you wanted to pull down raw Google Analytics data for archiving purposes, you can always get it when you really need it.
Low	Analysts have some data access and a workaround.	If the analyst has some access to the data source, even if not ideal, such as through a vendor dashboard, but there is a workaround (such as exporting data to CSV that meets their immediate needs), then this is low priority. There are likely other data sources that organization does not currently have access to that might deliver more immediate value.
Low	Low-quality data.	If there is little confidence in the quality of the data, then it may, at best, provide little value and, at worst, be counterproductive.
Low	Data has to be screen-scraped.	Screen-scraping is where one extracts data from web pages. Because website owners frequently change the underlying HTML and CSS of pages, and they are not always well structured, such data processes tend to be complex, very brittle, and require a lot of maintenance.
Low	Low likelihood of the data being used.	If it is only a "nice to have" and is without a clear use case, this is a low ROI choice.

As you can see, there are a lot of competing considerations that determine what new data source it makes sense to bring into the organization next. There is a delicate balance of the cost and complexity to deliver that new data versus the value that data provides to the analysts and the organization as a whole.

Connecting the Dots

While there is clear value to consuming data across your organization—you obtain some data from digital marketing, some from sales, some from supply chain, etc.—for deeper analytics, there is even greater value when you start to link up "adjacent" data items. What do I mean by that?

Imagine that you are given a thousand-piece jigsaw puzzle, but there is no picture on the box. As you sort the pieces, you identify a group of blue pieces. Those are probably the sky. A group of individual green pieces look like grass. Here is an eye. Is that human or animal? You can get a vague sense of the overall image, but it lacks any detail. The detail comes when you start to click adjacent pieces together. You click that piece with the eye to the piece with an ear. Now you have greater clarity. Let's translate this more explicitly to analytics.

Suppose that you use Google Analytics to analyze how people come to your website. This gives you a breakdown of referring pages and search terms, locations in the world, and so on, which gives you a sense or picture at the sample or *population* level (those are the pieces of the sky). You analyze the suite of customer survey responses over the last three months: 75% love the price, 20% were amazed by the customer service, and so on (those are like the pieces of grass). You get a sense of the state of the business, but only a 50,000-foot view because these are independent data points.

Now, in contrast, imagine a single sales order (Figure 3-1). Belinda Smith orders an outdoor patio set. If you can join the sales order to the transacting session from her clickstream, you can gain greater insight: she spent 30 minutes clicking around 15 different patio sets before she decided on one. Clearly, she did not arrive with a particular patio set in mind. How did she get to the page? If you join in referrer data, she did a Google search for "patio tables" and that led her to your site. That confirms your intuition about her browsing behavior. Now, if you add in her complete sales history, you realize that Belinda is a frequent shopper, often for home goods, and interestingly has a spike in the last month. Together, the information that she used a Google search and is a frequent shopper implies that she may not be brand loyal and that you need to work hard to reacquire her. Each time you add in another dataset at this *individual*-level, you get a much deeper, richer sense of this person. Let's keep going. Let's pull in US census data that maps gender probability given a first name: Belinda is almost certainly female. OK. When she paid, she added in a shipping address. Let's pull in demographic data from that ZIP code. This is an affluent suburban neighborhood with large lot sizes. What else can we do with that address? Let's look up that address on the multiple listing service (MLS), which is a central repository of house sales. Interestingly, the listing shows that the house has a pool. That could be useful for recommendations. What else? The house was sold just six weeks ago. Aha, she likely recently moved to that address. From other analysis we have done, we know that new homeowners tend to buy occasional rugs, beds, and lamps (yes, it is true, I did this analysis). Finally, she clicked on a refer-a-friend widget to get a coupon during checkout. Because she accepted Facebook's terms of service in the process, this opens up her social network. (We'll cover privacy and ethics in detail in Chapter 12.)

For a data analyst or data scientist, this deep profile and context offers a huge amount of raw material to work with. You can get a clear sense of her history, demographic, and even, in this case, current motivation. Do this for some of your other customers, and automate even just some of this analysis, and you have a powerful strategic advantage.

Connecting the dots at this individual level, in contrast to the segment level, has huge value and should drive the decisions about which datasets to bring into the organization next (without violating ethical or privacy concerns) and how to connect them at the individual level.

Data Collection

Now that we have considered the question of what data to collect, let us briefly consider the question of how it should be collected.

For many data sources, you simply take a *systematic* approach and suck down all the available data for that source (or subset of the fields). There are many ways to consume data feeds. You can use an API, or collect files from an FTP site, or you can even screen-scrape and collect what you can. If this is a one-time dump, you are done. If the data, however, is updated or added to frequently, and this is an ongoing data stream, you have to decide how to consume that data. For small files or tables, it can be easier simply to blow away existing tables and replace them with the current, larger dataset. In my team, we consider "small" to be tables with 100,000 rows or fewer. For larger data sources, you have to set up some more complex delta process. The simplest case is where new data is always entirely new rows (an example is transaction logs where updates or deletes to existing rows should not happen). In that case, you can just append (INSERT) the new data to the existing data table. In more complex cases, you have to work out several cases: a new data row is an INSERT, or it is a DELETE, or it is an UPDATE.

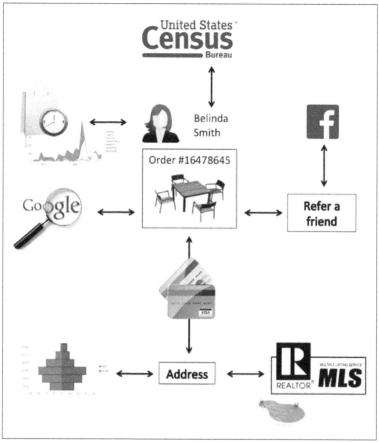

Figure 3-1. Adding a rich context to Belinda's order using a suite of data sources. From http://bit.ly/anderson-ddo-sea.

For other data sources, you may have to *sample* data. It may be very expensive to send out and process surveys, run clinical tests, or even dip into Twitter's firehose. How you sample has very important implications to data quality. We will cover experimental design in Chapter 8, but a poor design can introduce severe bias and reduce data quality and utility dramatically. The simplest approach is a "simple random sample" (*http://bit.ly/wiki-simple-random-sample*) where one essentially flips a coin to choose randomly those that are in the sample and those that are not. The goal is that the sample is truly representative from the larger population or sample from which it is drawn.

One thing to consider is sampling for longitudinal datasets. Imagine that you wish to sample website sessions per day. You sample 10% of sessions and load those into a database for further analysis. If you do this each day, you will have a set of independently and randomly chosen sessions, but you may miss out on data from visitors that visit the website on consecutive days. That is, your dataset may not contain any individuals with multisession data—they might be in sample on Monday but out of sample on their return on Wednesday. So, if you are more interested in following multiple sessions, and your site tends to have visitors that return frequently, you may fare better, and have higher-quality data to work with, by randomly sampling individuals and following their sessions over time, than by sample sessions. (You will, however, likely suffer attrition as individuals drop out and fail to return.) How you sample should be driven by the business question that you are trying to answer.

One final point: should you consume raw or aggregated data? Some vendors provide dashboards where data has been aggregated up to the key metrics that the analysts need. Those can provide significant value to the analysts. However, if the data is valuable, what I tend to see is that analysts want more; they want to drill down further and slice and dice the data in ways that the vendor dashboard does not support. While those reports and dashboards can be consumed as-is for archiving purposes, my take is that it is usually better to suck down the raw data where possible because you can always aggregate up to those metrics but not vice versa. With the raw data, you can, in principle, support slicing and dicing the data in all the ways that the analyst can imagine. There are cases where consuming raw data is not feasible, such as where the raw data is huge and costly to store, or the vendor provides a valuable service to compute those metrics (a process that you could not perform yourself), but raw is typically the better option.

Purchasing Data

While there is typically a wealth of information from an organization's internal data systems alone, and it can be supplemented with publicly available data, sometimes you just need to shell out for additional data from third parties.

There are many reasons why you might purchase external datasets. Earlier, we used the example of Belinda Smith's patio set purchase to make the case about the value of context. First, other partners, vendors, or even government agencies may simply have the data that can provide that context and add the "adjacent pieces" in your puzzle. Second, you may have internal data but a third party can provide higher-volume or higher-quality data.

Sometimes, you may have little choice as to where to purchase data. For instance, MLS has a practical monopoly on housing sales data. In other cases, however, there is direct competition. For instance, you can purchase customer profile data, based on credit card purchases, from a suite of providers, such as Datalogix, Axciom, Epsilon, or Experian. There is a market.

When there is a choice of sources—for instance, a dataset that maps ZIP code to metropolitan area—one has to weigh a number of dimensions, including:

Price
> Analysts and their bosses love free, but sometimes it is better to pay for higher-quality data. You have to consider whether it is a fair price and consider the value that it will provide to your organization. This is considered in detail in the next subsection.

Quality
> How clean and reliable is the data?

Exclusivity
> Is this a proprietary, exclusive dataset that will provide an advantage over your competitors if used well?

Sample
> Can you obtain a sample that will allow you to judge the content and quality and review the format sufficiently without having to make a firm commitment?

Updates
> How frequently does the data change, become stale, or irrelevant? How frequently is the data updated?

Reliability
> If calling a web service API, what's its up time? What are the limits on API calls or other service-level agreements?

Security

If the data is sensitive, is it encrypted and transmitted securely?

Terms of use

Are there any licensing terms or restrictions that will limit the value that you can derive from the data?

Format

We all have our favored formats, but generally human-readable formats, such as CSV, JSON, or XML (and which would exclude binary formats, excepting standard compression) are preferred because they are more easily parsed and provide more options to do so. At the end of the day, is this a format that you can easily support, or do you need to chalk up additional development costs and time to consume and support it?

Documentation

Well-documented sources should be favored. Typically, you want to know how data is collected (to know whether it can be trusted and if it provides value) and have a data dictionary (that lists the fields, their data types, example values, and any important business logic incorporated into that field's value; see Table 3-2). Randall Grossman, the chief data officer of Fulton Financial, has said that "A trusted data dictionary is the most important thing that a CDO can provide to business users."

Volume

Can you support the volume and storage needs? Valuable datasets need not be large, however. For instance, a ZIP code to DMA (designated market area, i.e., TV viewing region defined by the Nielsen Company) may only have 41,000 rows but can be immensely valuable to a marketing team evaluating TV ad spend.

Granularity

Does it go down to the level of resolution you need?

Table 3-2. Example of a data dictionary, this one from a public health project in California

SAS variable name (eHARS)	Label	Description	Values	SAS format	HARS variable name
aids_age_mos	Age at AIDS diagnosis (months)	The calculated age at AIDS (HIV, stage 3) diagnosis, in months.			age_mos
aids_age_yrs	Age at AIDS diagnosis (years)	The calculated age at AIDS (HIV, stage 3) diagnosis, in years.			age_yrs
aids_categ	AIDS case definition category	The CDC case definition for AIDS (HIV, stage 3) met by the patient; calculated based on lab information and opportunistic diseases entered for a person. For a description of the algorithm used to calculate aids_categ, refer to section 8 of the eHARS Technical Reference Guide.	**7** - AIDS (HIV, stage 3) case defined by immunologic (CD4 count or percent) criteria **A** - AIDS (HIV, stage 3) case defined by clinical disease (OI) criteria **9** - Not an AIDS (HIV, stage 3) case	$A_CAT	categ
aids_cdc	CDC case definition for AIDS	Has this person met the CDC AIDS (HIV, stage 3) case definition? To meet the CDC AIDS (HIV, stage 3) case definition, the case must be defined by immunologic criteria or clinical disease criteria (aids_categ = A or 7).	**Y** - Yes **N** – No	$YN	N/A

It is clear from a good data dictionary how the data is defined, what the formats and allowable values are, and, in this case, how the data is used by a software package. These are a few rows from eHARS (*http://bit.ly/ehars-hiv*) (Enhanced HIV/AIDS Reporting System) in California. (SAS is statistical application suite popular in medicine.)

How Much Is a Dataset Worth?

It is relatively easy to work out how much your data costs you. You can examine the direct storage cost bill (such as from Amazon Web Services), the cost of backup services, the paycheck and overheads to the data team staff who manage and maintain the data, and of course the purchase price of the data (if any). However, a data-driven organization needs to identify the value to the business. What is the ROI? That is more tricky to ascertain.

d'Alessandro et al.[4] provide a principled framework that can estimate direct ROI values, in dollars, at least in certain situations. They work in the world of advertising, developing predictive models to compute the best ads to show to each user. They get paid if a user clicks an ad. Thus, in this scenario, the outcome and return is clear: they get paid, say $1, if the user clicks, and $0 if the user does not. They also have their own data that drives their models. Some of that is derived from historical bidding activity, and some that was purchased in the past (which they regard as sunk cost). The question they ask is, "what is my ROI for models built on our own data versus models built with additional third-party data?" This requires determining three components:

1. What is the value of an action? In this example, the action is a click, and it is worth $1.
2. What is the expected value of a model with our own data?
3. What is the expected value of a model with our own data plus additional third-party data?

Combining those:

Value of data = expected value(model with third-party data) − expected value(model without third-party data)

---

[4] d'Alessandro, B., C. Perlich, and T. Raeder, "Bigger is Better, But At What Cost?" (*http://bit.ly/dalessandro-bigger*) *Big Data* 2, no. 2 (2014): 87–96.

and

incremental return = value(click) × value of data.

Thus, suppose that a model with their own data only has a 1% chance of being clicked upon but a model with additional third-party data has a 5% chance of being clicked upon. The value of the data is a 4% lift, and the incremental value of that data is $1 × (5% − 1%) = $0.04.

Armed with a concrete value such as this, you can then objectively determine the value of purchasing that data. If it would cost $0.04 to purchase those incremental data points, then it is not worth it. If the cost is only $0.01, then it is a no-brainer.

You are not restricted to evaluating the incremental value of third-party data in addition to your own data. As is so often the case in data, context is everything. Interestingly, d'Alessandro et al. ran an experiment where they compared incremental value of third-party data against randomly targeting users, that is, no data versus third-party data only. They showed positive incremental value across a range of segments with segment value / 1000 users as high as $1.80. They then ran an experiment with their own data plus third-party data. What would you expect to happen? The incremental value tanked! Segment value per 1,000 users was now around $0.02 or less. In the context of data they already possessed, the extra data provided positive but negligible value (Figure 3-2), most likely because of redundancies in the data.

This general approach works well because it is possible, at least from their data providers, to obtain a sample of data that they can test. If the economics works out, they can purchase a full dataset. That is, they are not committed to making the data purchase until they have run some experiments to estimate the value. That is not always the case with vendors. However, you may be in a situation where you pay a monthly fee for a data feed. If so, you can run experiments such as these to determine the value of the data and make a decision as to whether it provides a positive ROI or not. If not, cancel the service.

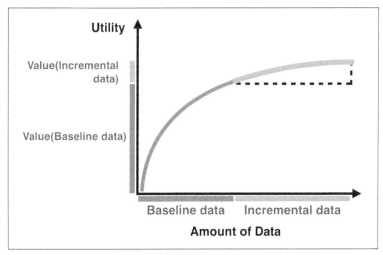

Figure 3-2. Adding additional data likely adds value, but there are diminishing returns. From http://bit.ly/dalessandro-predictive).

As the authors conclude:

> As "big data" becomes the panacea for many business optimization decisions, it is increasingly important for managers to be able to evaluate their data-driven decisions and justify the investments made in acquiring and using data. Without the tools to make such evaluations, big data is more of a faith-based initiative than a scientific practice.

Amen!

Data Retention

In this chapter, we have focused on obtaining and integrating additional data, increasing the data that analysts have to work with. However, data can become stale or irrelevant. We touched on some of the costs in the previous section: storage costs, maintenance costs, and acquisition costs. There are also costs and risks that are less easy to estimate: if there is a data breach, what will be the damage and cost to your business? So, one thing to consider is when to delete data (reduce risk and cost) and when to move data to an appropriate storage medium.

Data has a habit of replicating. You may load a dataset into a relational database, but that isn't the end of it. A given data point might flow down to one or more slave databases, just in case the master database server dies. Now you have two copies. Then you may do backups onto a server. Typically, you have several days or maybe a week's worth of backups available in case things go wrong. Now we are up to nine copies of that data point. All those copies cost money. One thing that you can do is match the datasets to the relevant latency required in order to use or restore them.

An example is the following: Amazon S3 (*http://aws.amazon.com/ s3/*) (Simple Storage Service) is a cheap and easy-to-use location with which to store data. For instance, it is almost certainly cheaper to store those backups on a service such as this than maintain an additional server to house those backups. When you need the data, you can pull them down instantly. Amazon, however, also provides a similar service called glacier (*http://aws.amazon.com/glacier/*). This is essentially the same as S3 but is meant as an archiving service; however, it can take four to five hours to restore the data. At current prices, this is about *one third* the cost of S3. If something went wrong, would you need that data instantly, or could you live for half a day or a day without it?

A data-driven organization should think carefully about the value of its data. Primary focus should be on its core data, where any downtime may have a real impact. It should consider deleting old, irrelevant data (this is easier said than done); but if nothing else, it should consider moving it to the cheapest suitable medium, such as offsite tape archives.

A more data-driven organization, for instance, one that has reached the "level" of predictive modeling, can create "rich" data models that capture the key features of the data and discard the rest. For instance, according to Michael Howard (*http://bit.ly/howard-real-data*), CEO of C9, "Salesforce, for example, doesn't keep a history of a deal for more than 90 days." If that is the case, then it is imperative that you select details carefully.

As we have shown, a data-driven organization has to think very strategically about its data sources and the organization's resources to garner and maintain them. Analysts have an important role here by researching possible sources and vendors, obtaining samples and, where possible, determining quality and putting the samples to work to ascertain their value.

In the next chapter, we consider who those analysts are, what their role is, and how they should be organized.

The Analyst Organization

*A really great data analyst should get people excited...
I knew I was the first to get the data, so I was the
first to know the story. It's fun discovering stuff.*
—Dan Murray

The human component of a great data-driven organization is a great analytics organization. Who are those people, and how should they be organized?

In this chapter, I will cover the analytics organization itself: the types of staff that comprise it and the skills that they should possess. I'll examine the breadth of analytics positions, and we'll meet some of the people in those varied roles. In addition, there are a number of ways in which analysts can be organized, each with a different set of pros and cons, and so I'll step through various organizational structures.

Types of Analysts

A data-driven organization is likely to have a variety of analyst roles, typically organized into multiple teams. Different people describe different analyst roles differently, and many of the skills are overlapping among them, but I'll outline a general description of my version of data analysts, data and analytics engineers, business analysts, data scientists, statisticians, quants, accountants and financial analysts, and data-visualization specialists. For each, I'll describe the types of skills they tend to possess, the tools they use, and provide an example of someone in that role. Your organization may have a different set of titles, but the skills described here are generally necessary in order to make the most of your data.

Data Analyst

This is the broadest, most common term, at least compared to the more specialized roles discussed next. In many cases, they are T-shaped: they have shallower experience across a broad spectrum of skills but deep skills and domain knowledge in a dominant area. Data analysts range from entry-level positions, which are often more focused on data gathering and preparation, to highly skilled and very specialized analysts. Such analysts are often domain experts, focusing on a wealth of different areas, such as voice of the customer, loyalty programs, email marketing, geo-specialized military intelligence, or certain segments of the stock market. The particular roles in an organization depend on the organization's size, maturity, domain, and market. In all these roles, their output is likely to be a mix of both reporting and analysis. As well as breadth of domain, analysts vary widely in their level of technical skills.

At one end are analysts who work solely in the world of Excel and vendor dashboards. At the other end are people, such as Samarth, who write Scala code against raw, large-scale data stores at Etsy. Samarth's background is in political science, but he got his analytics training while working on Barack Obama's 2012 re-election campaign. There he picked up R, SQL, and Python—the typical data scientist's trifecta—to run web and email experiments. He is now data analyst at Etsy in New York, where he still works on web and email experiments but also clickstream analysis, analyzing trends, and writing reports and white papers. He works with a variety of product managers, engineers, and designers across the company to help design experiments, analyze them with Scala/Scalding, R, and SQL, and interpret those results. He also writes general company-wide white papers as well as more specific memos for executives to understand trends, user behavior, or specific features.

An analyst with a very different profile is Samantha. She has a bachelor's degree in accountancy and works as a data analyst for Progressive Insurance in Cleveland, Ohio at in their claims control finance team. She manages an escheatment (the transfer of unclaimed or abandoned property to the state) process for claims through audit, analysis, and compliance with state escheatment laws. That involves creating reports to track abandoned property, analyzing outstanding drafts, and summarizing the financial risk associated with those. She uses a mix of SAS, Excel, and Oracle, as well as domain-specific tools, such as ClaimStation. She has a broad set of internal "customers" who rely on her work including Corporate Tax, Financial Operations, IT, Claims Business Leaders, as well as individual claims representatives in the field and is driven, she says, by "seeing my analysis pay off to the financial benefit of both Progressive and our insured customers." Being in a more heavily regulated industry and with particular responsibilities for ensuring that Progressive comply with state laws, attention to detail is an especially important trait in her role.

Data Engineers and Analytics Engineers

Primarily responsible for obtaining, cleaning, and munging data and getting it into a form that analysts can access and analyze. They are responsible for operational concerns, such as throughput, scaling, peak loads, and logging, and may also be responsible for building business intelligence tools that analysts use.

Meet Anna. While working toward a Ph.D. in physics, she realized her true passion lay in data science and joined Bitly as a data scientist, leaving her graduate program with a master's degree. At Bitly she created visualizations from large datasets, crunched data with Hadoop, and implemented machine learning algorithms. She then joined Rent The Runway and is now a data engineer. Using tools such as SQL, Python, Vertica, and bash, she now maintains the data infrastructure that supports the analysts, develops new tools to make data more reliable, timely, and scalable, and she acts as the touchpoint with the rest of the organization's engineers to understand any changes that they are making that will impact data.

Business Analysts

Analysts who typically serve as the interface between business stakeholders (such as department heads) and the technology department (such as software developers). Their role is to improve business processes or help design and develop new or enhanced features in backend systems or frontend systems, such as an enhanced checkout flow on a customer-facing website.

Lynn is senior business analyst for Macys.com. With a bachelor's degree in fine arts, experience as an application developer, and Project Management Professional certification, Lynn has a decade of experience of project management and business analysis, mostly in bookselling ecommerce. Her role involves analysis of project requirements, understanding clients' needs, process improvement, and project management, often using an agile approach. "There isn't a typical day," she said. "Some days I talk with the users" (i.e., merchants who use Macy's product information management system) "about their needs, some days I review user stories with the developers, or answer questions from QA or developers about the user stories."

Data Scientists

A broad term that tends to include more mathematically or statistically inclined staff, typically with both advanced degrees (often in quantitative subjects, such as math, sciences, and computer science) and developed coding skills. I like Josh Wills' (*http://bit.ly/wills-data-sci*) pithy definition: "Data Scientist (n.): Person who is better at statistics than any software engineer and better at software engineering than any statistician." However, it doesn't fully capture their role, which might be to build "data products," such as recommendation engines using machine learning, or to do predictive modeling and natural language processing.[1]

Trey, a senior data scientist at Zulily, a daily-deals site based in Seattle, is one such data scientist. With a master's degree in sociology, Trey splits his time working on a variety of projects ranging from building statistical models and recommendation algorithms that improve customer experience to helping product managers interpret the results of an A/B test. He mostly uses Python (using libraries such as pandas, scikit-learn, and statsmodels) and will pull down data to analyze using SQL and Hive. While he has the technical skills to build statistical models, he considers the the ability to explain those models to nonexperts a crucial data science skill. This love of teaching is reflected in his hobby, the spread (*http://*

---

1 Conway, D., "The Data Science Venn Diagram," (*http://bit.ly/conway-data-venn*) September 30, 2010.
Anderson, C., "What is a data scientist?" (*http://bit.ly/anderson-data-sci*) December 3, 2012.

thespread.us/), a blog that teaches data science concepts using American football data as well as how to become more informed consumers of sports statistics.

Statisticians

Skilled personnel who focus on statistical modeling across the organization. They typically have at least a master's degree in statistics and are especially prevalent in insurance, healthcare, research and development, and government. One quarter of statisticians in the US (*http://bit.ly/bls-stats*) work for federal, state, and local government. They are often involved in not just analysis but the design of surveys, experiments, and collection protocols to obtain the raw data.

Meet Shaun, a statistician supporting quantitative marketing at Google's Boulder office. With a bachelor's degree in mathematics and computational science and a Ph.D. in statistics, Shaun now has a varied role supporting employees on other teams, often moving from project to project as needs arise. One on hand, his work can involve pulling, cleaning, visualizing, and verifying the quality of a new data source. One the other, he taps into his statistical skills to develop clustering algorithms to improve online search geo-experiments, develop Bayesian structural time series models, or to estimate individual-level viewership from household-level data using Random Forests. He spends most of his time in R, especially to analyze and visualize data (notably packages like ggplot2, plyr/dplyr, and data.table). However, he also extracts data with SQL-like languages and uses some Python and Go.

Quants

Mathematically skilled quantitative analysts who typically work in the financial services sector modeling securities, risk management, and stock movements on both the buy and sell side of the market. For example, a pension fund may employ a quant to put together an optimal portfolio of bonds to meet the fund's future liabilities. They often come from mathematics, physics, or engineering backgrounds, and some—especially algorithmic trading analysts (the highest paid of all analyst positions)—are especially strong programmers in languages, such as C++, that can process data and generate actions with very low latency.

Satish is a quant at Bloomberg in New York, coming to the role with a strong background in both applied math and electrical engineering, including a Ph.D. He uses R (ggplot2, dplyr, reshape2), Python (scikit-learn, pandas), and Excel (for pivot tables) to build a range of statistical models and then C/C++ to roll some of those into production. Those models often cover relative value for various fixed-income asset classes. However, he also serves as an internal consultant and thus gets to work on a diverse set of problems ranging from credit models for mortgage-backed securities to predicting wind power supply in the UK. "The vast amounts of financial data and analytics that are available at Bloomberg are unmatched in the industry," he says. "As such, it is extremely rewarding to know that most of the models we build are things that provide value to all our customers." One of the challenges of working with financial data is that it is very long-tailed and thus the models must handle those rare, extreme events gracefully.

Accountants and Financial Analysts

Staff that focus on internal financial statements, auditing, forecasting, analysis of business performance, etc. Meet Patrick. With a Bachelor of Arts in philosophy, politics, and economics and a background as a debt capital markets analyst at RBS Securities, Patrick is now a retail finance and strategy manager for Warby Parker in New York City. He is responsible for retail financial planning and analysis and supporting the development of the company's store roll-out strategy. He spends his days deep in Excel managing the stores' profit and losses and KPIs, developing models of future performance, digging into model variance, and analyzing market development. Currently he spends about 60% of his time on reporting and the remainder on analysis, but this is shifting toward analysis as his access, comfort, and skills with the company's business intelligence tools improve.

Data Visualization Specialists

People with a strong design aesthetic who create infographics, dashboards, and other design assets. They may also code in technologies such as JavaScript, CoffeeScript, CSS, and HTML working with data-visualization libraries, such as D3 (a very powerful and beautiful visualization library covered in Scott Murray's *Interactive Data Visualization for the Web* (O'Reilly) and HTML5.

Meet Jim (Jim V in Figure 4-1). After obtaining a master's degree in computer science, specializing in bioinformatics and machine learning, Jim worked for Garmin developing GUIs for its GPS devices and thereafter at a biological research facility analyzing large-scale sequence data. It was there that he discovered D3 and began to blog about it, developing clear, instructive tutorials. He is now a data-visualization engineer and data scientist at Nordstrom's data lab in Seattle. Using a mix of Ruby, some Python, and R (especially the packages ggplot2 and dplyr), he splits his time between supporting personalization and recommendation systems and visualizing data, with the primary audience being employees in other teams.

In larger organizations, you may find additional specialized roles such as those who solely generate reports, or who specialize in using a particular business intelligence tool. Others may focus only on big data technologies, such as Hadoop or Spark.

As you can see, there is a huge amount of overlap of these roles and terms. Most are munging data with some sort of SQL-like language. Some code more than others. Many roles involve building statistical models, often with SAS or R. Most involve a mix of both reporting and analysis.

Analytics Is a Team Sport

Analytics is a team sport. A well-oiled, data-driven organization is going to have both a range of analytical personnel with different roles and also personnel with complementary skills. It needs to consider the "portfolio" of skills in the team and the profile of new hires that would work best to flesh out and strengthen missing or weak areas in that team.

For instance, Figure 4-1 shows the team profile of Nordstrom's data lab in 2013. You can easily spot the strongest mathematicians and statisticians in the team (Elissa, Mark, and Erin), the strongest developers (David and Jason W), and their data-visualization expert, Jim V, profiled earlier. I asked Jason Gowans, the director of the lab, what he thinks about when hiring a new addition. "The first is that we're proponents of the Jeff Bezos two-pizza rule," he said. "Therefore, it's unlikely we'll be much bigger than we currently are. We think that helps us stay focused on what we think are the big opportunities. The second is that each member brings something unique to the team and can help everyone else 'level up.'"

They made a smart move early in the team's history to hire a strong data-visualization guy, something that many teams leave until later. Having beautiful, polished proof-of-concept data products helped the team gain traction and acceptance within the broader organization. "Jim has been a key ingredient in our ability to generate enthusiasm for our work and really bring it to life with his datavisualization skills," Jason said.

Data scientists, often coming from an academic background, are especially T-shaped. When they have two dominant areas, they are termed Pi-shaped. You can think of hiring and team formation as analytics Tetris.

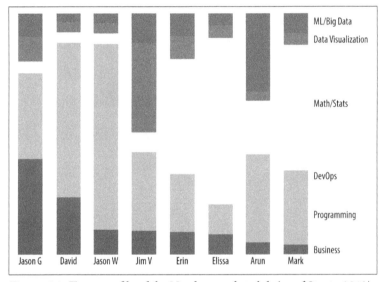

Figure 4-1. Team profile of the Nordstrom data lab (as of Strata 2013). ML = machine learning. Devops is a relatively new term arising from agile software development and represents a mix of IT, system administration, and software engineering.

A 2012 survey of hundreds of self-reporting data personnel by Harris et al. (*http://bit.ly/analyzing-analyzers*) covered five skill groups:

- Business
- Math/operations research
- Machine learning/big data
- Programming
- Statistics

They identified four clusters of roles:

Data business people
> "Quite T-shaped with top skills in Business, and moderate skills elsewhere."

Data researchers
> Deep in statistics and less broad with low rankings in machine learning/big data, business, and programming.

Data developers
> Pi-shaped with strong programming skills and relatively strong machine learning/big data skills and moderate skills in the other three groups.

Data creatives
> The least T-shaped group "who were, on average neither ranked the strongest nor the weakest in any skill group."

Their average profiles are shown in Figure 4-2. It is easy to spot the wide variation among the four types.

These four roles map imprecisely onto the analyst job titles (Table 4-1); organizations with more personnel and complexity may have a greater number of defined roles; smaller operations will likely have fewer people wearing more hats. It's also worth noting that while Harris et al. found data creatives "neither strongest nor weakest in any skill group," they didn't categorize visualization and communication as a skill group, and it is a vital one for a working team. One might also note that as a data-science problem, this is a weakness of surveys: they are limited to the categories that the survey designers envision. In this case, there was domain knowledge to realize that data creatives were part of successful teams, but not exactly clarity about what they added.

Table 4-1. Mapping of the analyst roles listed earlier in this chapter with those of Harris et al. 2013

Data businessperson	Data creative	Data developer	Data researcher
Business analysts	Data-visualization specialists	Data scientists	Statisticians
Data analysts		Data engineers	Quants
Accountants and Financial Analysts			

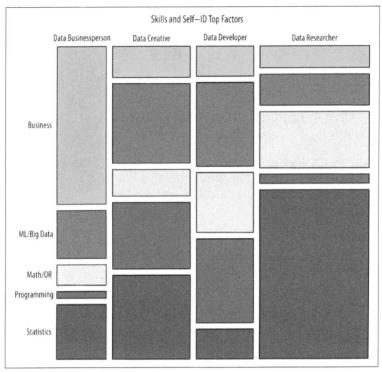

Figure 4-2. The skill profile of the four clusters of respondents (Figure 3-3 from Harris et al., 2013).

Ideally, when hiring, managers have to think at three levels:

Individual level
    Is this person a good fit? Do they possess the skills, potential, and drive that we seek?

Team level
    Does this person complement the rest of the team and fill in missing holes or shore up a weak spot?

Work level
    How does the team profile match the work that is required? That is, what is the team profile that best fits what we are trying to achieve? For instance, work that focuses primarily on financial predictive models may have a different optimal staffing skill set than work focused on optimizing customer service.

Skills and Qualities

What are the traits that make for a great analyst?[2]

Numerate
> They don't have to have a Ph.D. in math or stats, but they should at least be comfortable with descriptive statistics (median, mode, quartiles, etc.; see Chapter 5) and be willing to learn more.

Detail-oriented and methodical
> If these numbers, reports, and analyses are flowing up to senior management to make a major business decision, they had better be correct. The analysts must be of a "measure twice, cut once" ilk.

Appropriately skeptical
> Great analysts cultivate a good "spidey sense" of when something seems wrong in the raw or aggregated data or the analysis itself. First, they will proactively think through the range of values that would make sense. Second, they will proactively question the validity of the data and double-check the source data and the calculations when a metric is higher or lower than expected.

Confident
> Analysts not only need confidence to present their findings to groups of (senior) colleagues, but if the findings are surprising or expose gross inefficiencies, their data and analysis may be brought into question. They have to have confidence in their work to stand by it.

Curious
> Part of an analyst's role is seek actionable insights and so they need to be curious to always be developing hypotheses or questioning potentially interesting aspects of the data.

Good communicators and storytellers
> An analyst's work is worthless if it is not conveyed well to decision makers and business owners who can act upon the recom-

---

2 Stephen Few's *Now You See It* (Analytics Press) has a good discussion of this topic, pp. 19–24.

mendations. They have to tell a compelling, coherent story around the data and the findings. Thus, they must have sharp written, verbal, and data-visualization skills. (More on this in Chapter 7.)

Patient

There is a lot that is outside an analyst's direct control. That includes the accuracy or availability of the raw data source, missing data, changing requirements, or hidden biases in the data revealed only late in an analysis that may mean they have to scrap or redo their analyses. Analysts need patience.

Data lovers

In the same way that many computer programmers just love to code and the domain is almost irrelevant, some people just love data as a resource, a way to make sense of their world and make an impact. They just love to dig in. Hire those people.

Life-learners

This isn't specific to analysts, but those who love to learn, the ones who are always reading the latest articles and textbooks and taking classes to develop their knowledge and skills, will do well.

Pragmatic and business-savvy

You have to focus on the right questions. It can be all to easy to get sucked down a rabbit hole and spend too much time digging into a sub-1% edge case that has no real impact to the business. Like good editors, they have to keep the bigger picture in mind and know when to kill a story and move onto something else that is a better use of time.

I asked Daniel Tunkelang, head of search quality at LinkedIn, what he seeks when hiring analysts:

> I look for three things in data analysts/scientists. First, they need to be smart, creative problem solvers who not only have analytical skills but also know how and when to apply them. Second, they have to be implementers and show that they have both the ability and passion to build solutions using the appropriate tools. Third, they have to have enough product sense, whether it comes from instinct or experience, to navigate in the problem space they'll be working in and ask the right questions.

Ken Rudin, head of analytics at Facebook, says (*http://bit.ly/rudin-big-impact*):

> You can use science and technology and statistics to figure out what the answers are but it is still an art to figure out what the right questions are...It is no longer sufficient to hire people who have a Ph.D. in statistics. You also need to make sure that the people that you have have "business savvy." Business savvy, I believe is becoming one of the most critical assets, one of the most critical skills, for any analyst to have.
>
> How do you figure out if a potential analyst that you are looking at has business savvy? When you interview them, don't focus just on how do we calculate this metric. Give them a case study, a business case study from your own business, and ask them, "in this scenario, what are the metrics you think would be important to look at?" That's how you can get at that.

Just One More Tool

In terms of practical skills, it goes without saying that the majority of analysts around the world use Microsoft's Word, Excel, and PowerPoint as their major workhorses. They are very powerful tools. It is surprising, however, how a few additional tools can make a big difference in terms of productivity.

 This section is meant as a challenge to two primary audiences. If you are an analyst, challenge yourself to learn *just one more tool or utility* in the next month or quarter. If you are a manager of analysts, get them to challenge themselves in this manner. Check in and find out how much of an impact that has had. You will be surprised.

Here are a few areas to consider.

Exploratory Data Analysis and Statistical Modeling

R (*http://www.r-project.org/*) is an increasingly popular environment for statistical computing and it has exceptional data-visualization libraries (such as ggplot2). For instance, you can read in a CSV and visualize the relationship among all possible pairs of variables in just two commands:

```
data<-read.csv(filename.csv);
pairs(data)
```

Figure 4-3 shows the output of those commands. In the second panel of the top row, we can see the relationship between sepal width (x-axis) versus sepal length (y-axis) of iris flowers.

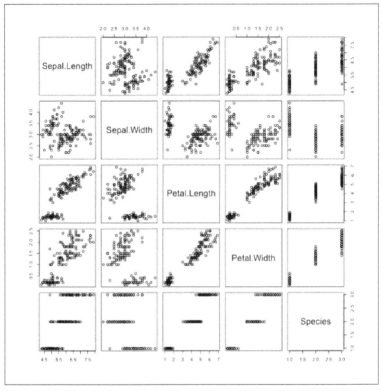

Figure 4-3. This is the output of the command pairs(iris) in R. Iris is a well-known dataset, collected by Edgar Anderson but made famous by the statistician R. A. Fisher, consisting of measurements of 50 samples of three iris flower species (http://bit.ly/wiki-iris-data). The correlations among the variables and the differences among the three species is obvious when you are able to view the relationships holistically like this.

As such, it can be invaluable for rapid exploratory data analysis. (The nonopen SAS and SPSS are popular and powerful, too.) There are about 6,700 packages for all sorts of data types, models, domains, and visualizations, and it is free and open source.[3] If you already know R, then learn a new R package and broaden your skill set.

Database Queries

While Excel can be incredibly powerful, it does have scaling issues: at a certain size of data and number of VLOOKUPS, it can bring your computer to its knees. It is for this reason that SQL is a valuable tool in any analyst's toolkit. SQL is a transferable skill; and while there are some small differences in the language among databases (such as MySQL, PostgreSQL, and Access), it is pretty much standardized, so once you know SQL you can switch among different relational databases easily. You can then query data in a scalable manner (crunch millions of rows), can share queries with colleagues (sharing small text queries and not huge chunks of raw data), and you have a process that is repeatable (you can rerun analyses easily).

There are many books and offline and online courses to help you get started in SQL. One free online course that I would recommend is W3Schools' SQL Tutorial (*http://www.w3schools.com/sql/*) because you can run queries in the browser itself. Another approach to getting started is to install a database on your local machine. Installing and configuring mainstream databases, such as MySQL and PostgreSQL, can be tricky to install. Thus, I would highly recommend starting out with SQLite[4]—a lot of applications on your smartphone are using SQLite to store application data. This is free, almost trivial to install, saves your data to a single transportable file, and will get you up and running writing SQL queries in minutes.

In case you are worried that this is an old technology that will soon be superseded by a shiny new approach, in the O'Reilly 2014 Data Science Salary Survey, King and Magoulas remark "SQL was the most commonly used tool...Even with the rapid influx of new data technology, there is no sign that SQL is going away."

---

3 Great open source tools for analytics can be found in *Data Analysis with Open Source Tools* by P. K. Janert (O'Reilly).

4 One introductory book is *Using SQLite* by J. A. Kreibich (O'Reilly).

File Inspection and Manipulation

If the analytics team must work with large or many raw datafiles, then someone—it doesn't have to be everyone because analytics is a team sport—should pick up some simple Unix command-line skills for file filtering and manipulation. Alternatively, a scripting language, such as Python, will provide those tools and much more.

See Chapter 5 for a fuller discussion.

Example of One More Tool: Counting Lines with the *nix 'wc' Utility

If you know the *nix (i.e., Unix and Linux) command line, you can move on. For everyone else...

Suppose that you receive a 10 MB CSV datafile and need to count the number of records. How would you do that? Open up Excel, scroll down or use CTRL+↓ and see the row number of the last row? Sure, that works. How about if it was a 100 MB file? Excel can just about handle that, but it might take you 10 minutes to achieve. OK, how about 1 GB? That approach is not going to work.

New angle on the problem: what if it were three 10 MB CSV files? Open up Excel three times, once per file. Sure, that works. What if it were 300 files? Hmm, we need another approach.

What if I told you that you could complete all of these problems in a few seconds? The *nix command line is packed full of small, focused utilities that do one particular job and do them very well. **wc** is a utility that does a **w**ord **c**ount, as well as lines, character, and bytes.

Q: But I don't have access to *nix! I run Windows.

A: No problem, just install the free cygwin (*https://www.cygwin.com/*). That gives you the Unix command line in Windows.

Q: But I don't have access to *nix! I run OS X.

A: Macs are Unix under the hood. Go to Applications, open up Utilities, and then click Terminal. Boom! There is your Unix command line.

The format for the command is trivial: `wc -l filename`

`wc` is the word count utility, `-l` (the letter) tells it to count lines rather than words, and `filename` is the filename of your file. Example:

```
$ wc -l weblog_20150302.log
  1704190 weblog_20150302.log
```

(`$` is the prompt; yours may look different.) This shows you that the *weblog* file had 1.7 million rows. To count lines of each file in a directory, just provide a folder name instead of a filename:

```
wc -l mydatafiles/
   123 file1.csv
   456 file2.csv
   579 total
```

Wasn't that easy? It even totals them for you. I use this command all the time as part of my data quality checks to help me estimate how long it will take to load a dataset into a database and to verify that all the data got loaded.

Hopefully, you understand the broader point here: simple utilities that take minutes to learn can dramatically boost an analyst's skill set and productivity.

Which tool or utility to learn depends on your current skill set and its weak spot(s). However, everyone has a weak spot. Take up the challenge.

If you need further incentive, O'Reilly's 2013 Data Science Salary Survey (*http://bit.ly/2013-data-sci-survey*) from attendees from two large Strata conferences in 2012 and 2013 found the following:

> Salaries positively correlated with the number of tools used by respondents. The average respondent selected 10 tools and had a median income of $100k; those using 15 or more tools had a median salary of $130k.

This was more clearly and starkly presented in their 2014 survey (Figure 4-4).

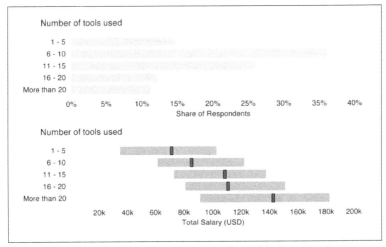

Figure 4-4. The relationship between number of different tools versus data science salary. This is Figure 1-13 of the 2014 O'Reilly Data Science Salary Survey.

In 2013, they further concluded:

> It seems very likely that knowing how to use tools such as R, Python, Hadoop frameworks, D3, and scalable machine learning tools qualifies an analyst for more highly paid positions—more so than knowing SQL, Excel, and RDB [relational database] platforms. We can also deduce that the more tools an analyst knows, the better: if you are thinking of learning a tool from the Hadoop cluster, it's better to learn several.

Finally, the 2014 survey shows about a $15,000 bump for coding versus noncoding analysts. If you are a noncoding analyst, do yourself a favor and learn to code!

Analytics-org Structure

Having considered the types of analyst roles and skills, I now consider how they are organized in the context of the larger organization.

First, let's consider the two common extremes.

Centralized

There is a central analytics team to which all analysts report. There are many advantages. First, the team can standardize skills, training, and tooling, and they can share resources and reduce software license costs. Second, they can more easily promote the use of analytics and advanced analytics within the organization. Third, analysts can communicate easily, learn from or mentor each other, and feel that they are part of a like-minded team. Fourth, there is, or can be, the perception of greater objectivity as their success or rewards are unlikely to be aligned with the success of the projects that they are analyzing. Finally, they can help promote master data sources as single sources of truth. On the downside, they can be somewhat removed from the business owners and their goals, they tend to be very reactive to requests for work[5,6] they can be more bureaucratic. As Piyanka Jain notes, "everything needs to get into the pipeline, and get prioritized, and get resources allocated against it."[7]

Decentralized

A decentralized analytical organization embeds the analysts in individual teams. Those analysts report to those teams and share their goals. In other words, they live the goals, reports, and metrics of those teams. The downside is that they can be somewhat removed from other analysts. There is the potential for redundancy of effort, divergence of tools, skills, metric definitions, and implementation. There can also be a lack of communication and sharing among analysts from different teams. The decentralized model is the most common, accounting for 42% of respondents in one survey, a factor that Davenport et al. (p. 108) consider reflects "analytics immaturity." They do not explicitly clarify or defend that position, but my interpretation is that it is difficult to excel at some of the higher levels analytics, such as an operations research department working on

---

5 "Ken Rudin 'Big Impact from Big Data'," (*http://bit.ly/rudin-big-impact*) October 29, 2013, video clip, YouTube.

6 Davenport, T. H., and J. G. Harris. *Analytics at Work*. Boston: Harvard Business Press, 2007.

7 Jain, P., "To Centralize Analytics or Not, That is the Question," (*http://bit.ly/forbes-centralize*) *Forbes*, February 15, 2013.

hard optimization or predictive problems, without some more centralized coordination, expertise, and oversight.

There are many pros and cons of these two structures (summarized in Table 4-2). Being part of a larger, centralized analyst organization, analysts have more local support, mentorship, and a clearer career path. However, in a decentralized structure, the line of business manager has dedicated resources and presumably a faster turnaround time.

Table 4-2. The pros of centralized versus decentralized analytics structure. (Cons are implicit as the opposite of the pros in the other column.) Greater domain knowledge could go either way (see text for explanation).

Pro	Centralized	Decentralized
Clear career path	✓	
Direct, full-time access		✓
Faster turnaround time		✓
Greater redundancy of domain knowledge	✓	
Standardized toolset and training	✓	
Standardized metrics: numbers that agree	✓	
Less bureaucracy		✓
(Perceived) objectivity	✓	
Greater domain knowledge	?	?

Sixty-three percent more transformed organizations than aspirational organizations (think back to Chapter 1) "use a centralized enterprise unit as the primary source of analytics." As before, there are confounding variables at play—in particular, company size and total number of analysts—because transformed organizations are also more likely to be using analytics in the business units, too.[8]

One should expect that analysts in the decentralized organization would build up greater domain knowledge, such as deeply understanding the voice of the customer data, analytical processes, and metrics. Such concentration of knowledge may represent a risk, however, to the enterprise as a whole if those few individuals leave.

---

8 LaValle, S., M. S. Hopkins, E. Lesser, R. Shockley, and N. Kruschwitz, "Analytics: the New Path to Value," (*http://bit.ly/sloan-big-data*) MIT Sloan Management Review 52, no. 2 (2010): Figure 9.

(In a centralized organization, there will more likely be redundancy of domain knowledge as analysts switch among different lines of business.) This may mean that domain knowledge is actually *less*, on average, in a decentralized structure if those analysts are frequently leaving to be replaced by novices that require multiyear training from scratch.

Interestingly, Jeb Stone[9] argues that in a centralized organization with a few standard technologies,

> to increase value to the organization, an analyst should master these additional technologies, cross-train on these specific lines of business, and approach the level and quality of work already benchmarked by senior analysts. Without a career path, your analysts are highly incented to learn in-demand technology on your dime—whether or not your organization has a need for it—and then jump ship to an employer who will compensate them for that skill. Perhaps even more to the point: rock-star analysts will avoid employers with a decentralized Analytics function, because they know it'll take them longer to come up to speed and that there is likely no performance incentive program specific to their accomplishments.

In an attempt to find a structure that draws as many pros and minimizes the cons, an intermediate form exists, called the hybrid model. This model, such as employed at Facebook, has a centralized analytics team, and thus you have the benefits of standardized training, tooling, and the like, but the analysts physically sit with the different business teams and moreover share those teams' goals. Thus, you have the benefit of close alignment and analytical standards. The downside is that you introduce a situation in which analysts may be reporting to more than one manager, one from the business side and one from the analytics side. This introduces the very real potential of conflicting or confusing messages.

When you have a decentralized model, you need some way to bring the analysts together to develop common skills, to attend training on tooling, discuss data sources, metrics, analyses being worked upon, and so on. One approach, and one that we employ at Warby Parker, is to form an analysts' guild, "an organized group of people who have joined together because they share the same job or interest." It gets analysts from different teams, and in our case from dif-

---

9 Stone, J., "Centralized vs Decentralized Analytics: All You Need To Know," (*http://bit.ly/stone-analytics*) April 22, 2012.

ferent buildings, talking to each other, discussing issues, and doing show and tells. It also allows my data team to provide training on business intelligence tools and statistics.

A guild such as this makes it more matrix-like but does require buy-in from the managers or department heads to which those analysts report and/or from more senior management. Analysts need to be encouraged by their managers to break away from their work to attend and participate in the guild.

Other organizational structures[10,11] more common in larger organizations, include:

Consulting
In some organizations, the centralized model is modified such that analysts are hired out to departments with appropriate chargebacks, in a consultative structure. With poor executive leadership, there is the potential downside that the analysts follow the money or the most vocal executives and that they are not necessarily working on projects that would deliver the most value to the organization.

Functional
A form of serial centralization in which a central group sits within one functional business unit, primarily serving that unit, but may provide some services to other parts of the organization. They may then migrate *en masse* to another business unit as the need arises.

Center of excellence
This is similar to the hybrid structure but on a larger scale and houses a set of analytical experts, such as statisticians, in the central hub. Thus, you have analytics being performed both in the individual units and from central staff.

Table 4-3 summarizes the different organizational structures and lists some example organizations of each type. However, it should be stressed that these labels identify *idealized* structures, and in reality,

---

10 Davenport, T. H., and J. G. Harris. *Analytics at Work*. Boston: Harvard Business Press, 2007.

11 Khalil, E., and K. Wood, "Aligning Data Science – Making Organizational Structures Work," (*http://bit.ly/khalil-aligning*) (Tysons Corner, VA: Booz Allen Hamilton, Inc., 2014).

there are very blurry lines among them, and many intermediate forms exist. For instance, Warby Parker is primarily a decentralized form with analysts reporting to line-of-business managers only, but there are some elements of a center of excellence model with a central data team hosting data scientists and providing some support in terms of advanced analytics (as well as business intelligence tooling, analyst training, and driving standards). That structure, however, is expected to change as the analytics organization matures.

Table 4-3. Summary and examples of the different analytical organization structures

Organizational structure	Analysts report to or share goals with		Examples
	Central analyst org	Business owners	
Centralized	✓		Mars, Expedia, One Kings Lane
Decentralized		✓	PBS, Dallas Mavericks
Hybrid/embedded	✓	✓	Facebook, Ford, Booz Allen Hamilton
Functional	✓		Fidelity
Consulting	✓		eBay, United Airlines
Center of excellence	✓	✓	Capital One, Bank of America

There is no answer as to "What is the best structure?" It depends. It depends upon the organization size and industry. For instance, an analytical center of excellence form makes little sense when there are, say, five analysts. They are more prevalent in organizations with more than 25,000 staff. One form may make the most sense at one point, but as the company scales, it outgrows it and may need a re-org to a more appropriate form.

However, based on an Accenture survey and analysis of more than 700 analysts,[12] Davenport et al. (p. 106) do claim:

> We think the centralized and center of excellence models (or a federated model combining elements of both) offer the greatest potential benefit for organizations ready to take an enterprise approach to analytics. Analysts in a centralized or center of excellence model have significantly higher levels of engagement, job satisfaction, per-

12 Harris, J. G., E. Craig, and H. Egan, "How to Organize Your Analytical Talent," (Dublin: Accenture Institute for High Performance, 2009).

ceived organizational support and resources, and intention to stay than decentralized analysts or those who work in consulting units.[13]

In Chapter 11, we'll discuss where these teams sit in the larger organizational structure and the C-suite executives that they roll up to. Before, that, however, let's consider more closely what analysts do: analyze.

13 Davenport, T. H., Harris, J. G., and Morison, R. *Competing on Analytics*. Boston: Harvard Business Press, 2010.

CHAPTER 5

Data Analysis

If you torture the data long enough, it will confess [to anything].
—Ronald Coase

In the next block of three chapters, I focus on the core activity of data analysts: analysis, focusing on the goals of analysis within the organization and how to do *impactful* analysis.

I'll examine activities such as analyzing data, designing metrics, gaining insights, and presenting or selling those insights, ideas, and recommendations to the decision-makers. Chapter 6 covers the design of metrics and key performance indicators (KPIs), and Chapter 7 focuses on data visualization and storytelling. This first chapter of the trio, however, focuses on analysis itself.

Importantly, it does not cover *how* to perform analysis or statistical inference because there are many better texts available that do that (see Further Reading). Instead, it considers the goal of the analyst: what does it mean for an analyst to analyze? What are they trying to achieve? What tools do they have in their toolkit? I'll bring back the idea of levels of analytics from Chapter 1 and introduce some other perspectives on types of analysis.

The goal here is to highlight the range of statistical and visualization tools that are available to analysts to glean insights from data. A secondary goal is to urge analysts to use the appropriate tools and, where necessary, to learn more sophisticated tools that can provide a deeper level of understanding of the problem at hand.

A fine woodworker making a wooden table needs quality raw materials, such as mahogany hardwood; a range of tools, such as chisels and set-squares, and the skills to know when and how to use and apply those tools. If one of those three is missing, the quality of the end product is greatly diminished. And, so it is with analysis. To obtain the greatest value-producing analytical product, you need the raw materials—high-quality data—and a range of tools, such as different analysis techniques, and the skills to know when and how to apply those analytical tools to bear upon the problem.

What Is Analysis?

It is worth spending a few moments considering the term "analysis." It derives from Greek, meaning to loosen up or unravel (from ἀνά [aná, "on, up"] + λύω [lúō, "I loosen"]). That makes sense, but it is too high-level to help us grasp what it really entails. For a more business-oriented perspective, recall the definition from Chapter 1:

> Transforming data assets into competitive insights, that will drive business decisions and actions using people, processes and technologies.
>
> —Mario Faria

Let's dig a little deeper and dissect that. Hopefully from Chapters 2 and 3, we have some sense of "data assets," but what's an insight?

According to Wikipedia (*http://bit.ly/wiki-insight*):

> Insight is the understanding of a specific cause and effect in a specific context. The term can have several related meanings:
>
> - A piece of information
> - The act or result of understanding the inner nature of things or of seeing intuitively (called noesis in Greek)
> - An introspection
> - The power of acute observation and deduction, penetration, discernment, perception, called intellection or noesis
> - An understanding of cause and effect based on identification of relationships and behaviors within a model, context, or scenario

OK, understanding cause and effect, understanding the inner nature of things, models, etc. That helps.

Information (*http://bit.ly/foldoc-info*), "the result of applying data processing to data, giving it context and meaning," is often used synonymously for data, although technically they are not the same (see box and also "The Differences Between Data, Information, and Knowledge" (*http://bit.ly/data-info-knowledge*)).

Data Versus Information Versus Knowledge

Data is the raw, unprocessed facts about the world. Information is captured, processed data, while knowledge is a set of mental models and beliefs about the world built from information over time.

The current temperature is 44°F. That is a numerical fact. It exists and is true whether or not someone records it or observes it. It just is. However, it is not useful (to anyone other than me) because it is ambiguous. It lacks context. Where? When?

It is 44°F in New York City at 10 a.m. on November 2, 2014. That is more contextualized data. However, it is still a statement of facts with no interpretation.

44°F is much colder than normal. That is information. We have processed the data point, and combined it with other data points to ascertain what is "normal" and where this value stands in relation to that reference point.

44°F is chilly. I'll need my coat. You combine information over time and build up a mental model of what that means. This is knowledge. Of course, those models are all relative; someone in Alaska might consider 44°F in November to be unseasonably warm.

From the depths of information, we can roll back up to the top-level definition of analysis (Figure 5-1). Although the remaining terms, such as "understanding" and "context" are still loaded, hopefully we now have a clearer sense of what analysis entails, at least conceptually.

Given that new level of understanding, let's examine the set of tools that analysts have access to. I'm not referring to software tools, such as Excel or R, but instead in terms of the statistical tools available and the *types* of analysis that one can perform.

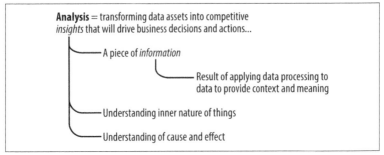

Figure 5-1. Result of a two-level drill down from definition of analysis.

Types of Analysis

Jeffrey Leek, an assistant professor of Biostatistics at Johns Hopkins and co-editor of the simply statistics blog (*http://simplystatistics.org/*), considers that there are six types of analysis,[1] here ordered from simplest to most complex and demanding:

- Descriptive
- Exploratory
- Inferential
- Predictive
- Causal
- Mechanistic

I am going to cover the first five only. The last, mechanistic, I associate more with basic science, research and development, and the term "modeling" more than "analysis." Mechanistic modeling and analysis represents a very deep understanding of a system, which comes from studying a stable system in a very controlled manner with many experiments over many years—hence my association with basic science. This situation doesn't tend to occur within most businesses, with some exceptions, such as R&D departments in pharma and engineering. To be more pithy, if you are involved at the level of mechanistic analysis, the pinnacle of analysis, you probably don't need this book to tell you how to do that kind of work.

If you think back to Chapter 1, your "spidey sense" might now be tingling. There we discussed eight levels of *analytics*. Here we are

---

1 Or at least he considers these six types only in his data analysis course (*http://bit.ly/leek-data-analysis*).

presented with six types of *analysis*, and, there is only one term in common: predictive. What the heck does this mean?

The preceding list comprises types of statistical analysis. Importantly, they can drive multiple levels of analytics. For instance, exploratory data analysis (which we touched upon in Chapter 2) can be used to prepare an ad hoc report (analytics level 2). It could also be used to derive the business logic for an alert (analytics level 4): for example, find the 98th percentile of a distribution and sound an alert if the relevant metric exceeds that level. You can think of levels of analytics as activities using one or more types of statistical analysis with some business rules, constraints, and output format requirements on top of that.

Figure 5-2 attempts to show the mapping between the two lists. The heatmap shows level of analytics on the left and five types of analysis below. The level in each cell is a crude estimate of the amount of effort or time, centered on that type of analysis. For instance, standard reports tend to use descriptive and exploratory analysis but are extremely unlikely to use causal models. At the other end, optimization analytics will certainly build upon descriptive analysis and exploratory data analysis, but their primary focus is on predictive analysis, possibly reaching across to causal analysis.

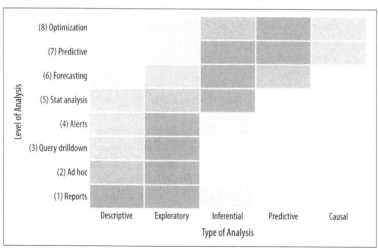

Figure 5-2. Crude mapping between level of analytics (left) and types of analysis (bottom). See detailed explanation in text.

I should clarify one point. There are many other types of quantitative analysis, such as survival analysis, social-network analysis, and time-series analysis. However, each of those is tied to a specific domain or data type, and the analytical tools and approaches within those are *comprised* of these six more fundamental analytical activities and approaches. For instance, in time-series analysis, you might compute the period of a phenomenon (that's descriptive analysis), and then you might plot a variable over time (that's EDA), and finally you might model and predict future values (the predictive analysis). You get the picture. In other words, these six classes are archetypes of analysis. There are also types of analysis that are more logical and qualitative. For instance, root-cause analysis, the "5 whys method" (*http://bit.ly/5-whys-method*) from Toyota and Six Sigma, is a good example.

With that, let's go through each of the five types of analysis.

Glossary

Confused by measure versus dimension versus metric? Don't feel bad. There is a lot of overlap and inconsistencies in their use and little consensus. Here's my take:

Variable
> Something that is prone to change over space, time, or sample units, for example, "Let variable v = velocity of the car" or "Gender is a categorical variable."

Dimension
> A variable. While "variable" is more frequently used by scientists and programmers, dimension is more common in business intelligence. A dimension is a variable to categorize facts and measures and typically is categorical or temporal, but could be rankings, ratings, or integers. For instance, you may wish to plot total sales (measure) versus state (dimension) or year (dimension) or calculate website bounce rate (measure) versus gender (dimension). I like to think of dimensions as the things that are often on the x-axes and measures the things that are on the y-axes in bar and line charts.

Measure
> A measurement of the raw value of an object, such as length, or it can mean a standard unit of scale. However, in business intelligence, it typically refers to a function (e.g., BMI) or

aggregate, such as min, sum, count, or average of measured data. Think of it as pure or derived measurement of something.

Metric
> Function of two or more measures (in the measurement sense of measure), or is simply a measure (in the function sense of measure). Derived measure.

Statistic
> A single measure of some attribute of a sample of values, for example, arithmetic mean = 6.3. It is a function applied to a set of data values that returns a single value. Confusingly, both the function and the final value are the statistic.

Key performance indicator
> This is a measure in a business context where it is associated with a performance goal or target and/or some baseline value (KPIs are covered in the next chapter). That is, it shows performance relative to some business objective or starting point.

Descriptive Analysis

Descriptive analysis is the simplest type of analysis. It describes and summarizes a dataset quantitatively. Importantly, it characterizes the sample of data at hand and does not attempt to describe anything about the population from which it comes. It can often form the data that is displayed in dashboards, such as number of new members this week or booking year to date (see "Dashboards" on page 147).

The natural place to start is a univariate analysis, meaning describing a single variable (column or field) of the data. We discussed the five-number summary in Chapter 2. However, there are many other possible statistics covering areas such as location ("middle" of the data), dispersion (range or spread of data), and shape of the distribution.

The simplest but one of the most important measures is:

Sample size
> The number of data points or records in the sample.

Location metrics include:

Mean (average)
The arithmetic mean of the data: sum of values divided by number of values.

Geometric mean
The geomean, for short, is used to capture the average when there are multiplicative effects at play, such as compound interest over time when rates vary year to year. It is the nth root of the product of the n values. If you receive 8% interest in year 1 and then 6% for three subsequent years, the average interest rate is 6.5%.

Harmonic mean
Arithmetic mean of the reciprocals of the value, typically used for averaging rates. For instance, if you drive to the store at 50 mph but hit traffic on the return and drive at 20 mph, the average speed is not 35 mph but 29 mph.

Median
The 50th percentile.

Mode
The most frequently occurring value.

Dispersion or central tendency measures include:

Minimum
The smallest value in the sample (0th percentile).

Q1
The 25th percentile. The value such that one quarter of the sample has values below this value. Also known as the lower hinge.

Q3
The 75th percentile. Also known as the upper hinge.

Maximum
The largest value in the sample (100th percentile).

Interquartile range
The central 50% of data; that is, Q3 – Q1.

Range

Maximum minus minimum.

Standard deviation

Measure of the dispersion from the arithmetic mean of a sample. It is the square root of variance, and its units are the same as the sample data.

Variance

Another measure of dispersion and is the average squared difference from the arithmetic mean and is the square of standard deviation. Its units are the square of those of the data.

Standard error

Standard deviation divided by the square root of sample size. Measures the expected standard deviation of the sample mean if we were to repeatedly obtain samples of same sample size from same source population.

Gini coefficient

A measure of dispersion originally developed to quantify the degree of inequality in incomes in a population, but which can be used more broadly. Conceptually, it is easiest to view this as the half the average absolute difference between two individuals sampled at random from the population, divided by the average income in the population.

Shape measures include:

Skew

A measure that captures the asymmetry of a distribution. If the distribution has a larger tail on the right compared to the left, it has a positive skew. Conversely for right skew. The number of followers across Twitter users is highly positive skewed (e.g., "An In-Depth Look at the 5% of Most Active Users" (sysomos (*http://bit.ly/sysomos-twitter*)) and "Tweets loud and quiet" (Radar (*http://bit.ly/radar-tweets*)).

Kurtosis

Measure of the sharpness of the peak of a distribution. Highly kurtotic (*http://bit.ly/wiki-kurtosis*) distributions have sharp peaks with fat tails. This can be an important consideration in investing because it means that extreme swings are more common than if the variable was normally distributed.

I would also include the type of distribution as a useful descriptive statistic. For instance, normal (Gaussian), log normal, exponential, and uniform are all common. Knowing the type and thus shape of a distribution can inform you of the characteristics it might have (e.g., that it may generate rare but extreme outlier values), can sometimes provide clues to the generating processes, and typically indicates what other metrics you should gather. For instance, if the distribution is some form of power law, such as the distribution of the number of Twitter followers, you know that you should compute the decay constant as an important characteristic metric.

Not all variables are continuous, of course. Gender and product group, for instance, are both categorical. Thus, descriptive analysis might involve tables of relative frequencies for different categories or contingency tables, such as the following:

Sales by sales region					
Gender	Western	Southern	Central	Eastern	Total
Male	3485	1393	6371	11435	22684
Female	6745	1546	8625	15721	32637
Total	10230	2939	14996	27156	**55321**

The key at this level of analysis is for the analyst to know what to slice and group the data by, and to recognize when something stands out as interesting. For example, in the preceding table, why do women comprise such as larger proportion of sales in the western region?

Moving up to two variables, descriptive analysis can involve measures of association, such as computing a correlation coefficient or covariance.

The goal of descriptive analysis is to describe the key features of the sample numerically. It should shed light on the key numbers that summarize distributions within the data, and it may describe or show the relationships among variables with metrics that describe association, or by tables that cross-tabulate counts.

Some of these simple metrics may prove highly valuable in themselves. You may want to know and track the median order amount or longest duration to resolve a customer case. That is, they may be sufficiently interesting to drive a standard report, ad hoc report, query drill down, or alert (analytics levels 1 to 4) and that alone can provide value to the organization. They may also provide insight, or comfort, regarding data quality. For instance, if the maximum age of a player on a first-person shooter gaming site is 115, either the player entered bad data or the date of birth field was set to a default date of 1900 (or you have a *very* cool great grandma)—simple min, max, ranges, and histograms can help with that.

Finally, descriptive analysis is typically the first step on the ladder—a chance to get a sense of the data—to more deeper analysis.

Exploratory Analysis

Descriptive analysis is a very important first step. However, numerical summaries can only get you so far. One problem is that you are condensing a large number of values down to a few summary numbers. Unsurprisingly, different samples with different distributions, shapes, and properties can result in the same summary statistics.

In Figure 5-3, the two samples have the same mean value of 100 but have very different distributions.

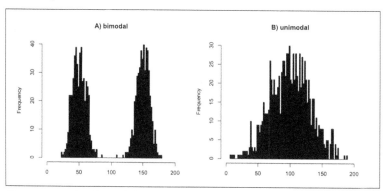

Figure 5-3. A) a bimodal distribution and b) a unimodal distribution, both of which have the same mean value of ~100.

Now that seems kind of unsurprising. We have a simple single summary statistic: mean of a single variable. There are lots of possible "solutions" or samples that could result in that summary statistic value.

What is far more surprising, however, is the following. Suppose that you were told that you had *four* bivariate (2D) samples with variables x and y with the following statistics:

Property	Value
Sample size in each case	11
Mean of x in each case	9
Sample variance of x in each case	11
Mean of y in each case	7.5
Sample variance of y in each case	4.122 or 4.127
Correlation between x and y in each case	0.816
Linear regression in each case	$y = 3.00 + 0.500x$

That's a highly constrained system. Those four samples have got to look fairly similar, don't they? As you can see from Figure 5-4, far from it.

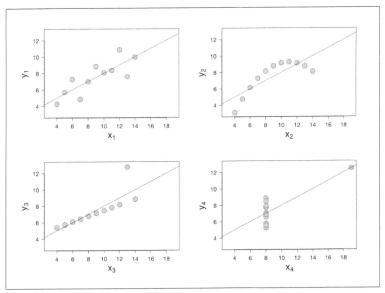

Figure 5-4. Anscombe's quartet. Each of these four samples has the same mean x, mean y, variance of x, variance of y, correlation, and regression line (at least to two decimal places). Figure from http:// bit.ly/anscombes-quartet.

This is known as Anscombe's quartet[2] after statistician Francis Anscombe, who devised this in 1973. In those early days of statistical computing, his motivation for the quartet was against the existing doctrine of the day in which textbooks on statistical method and statistical software applications claimed that (page 17):

1. numerical calculations are exact, but graphs are rough,

2. for any particular kind of statistical data, there is just one set of calculations constituting a correct statistical analysis,

3. performing intricate calculations is virtuous whereas looking at the data is cheating.

Anscombe went on to say:

> Most kinds of statistical calculations rest on assumptions about the behavior of the data. Those assumptions may be false, and then the calculations may be misleading. We ought always to try and check whether the assumptions are reasonably correct; and if they are wrong we ought to be able to perceive in what ways they are wrong. Graphs are very valuable for these purposes.

Using graphics to examine and visualize data is called exploratory data analysis (hereafter, EDA), and was championed and promoted by John Tukey and his heavily influential 1977 book, *Exploratory Data Analysis* (Pearson). If done well, graphs help us see the bigger picture of a data set, and help us spot obvious or unusual patterns— something that our brains are innately good at. Those are often where insights start to come from. Why is there a kink in that curve? At what point are we seeing diminishing returns from marketing spend?

EDA allows us to challenge or confirm our assumptions about the data. This is why I mentioned R's `pairs()` command in Chapter 2 about data quality. We often have pretty good expectations of what unclean data might look like, such as outliers, missing data, and other anomalies, perhaps more so than our expectations of what clean data might look like.

As we study and gain greater experience with a domain, we develop our intuition of what factors and possible relations at are play. EDA, with its broad suite of ways to view the data points and relation-

---

2 Anscombe, F. J., "Graphs in statistical analysis," *American Statistician* 27 (1973): 17–21.

ships, provides us a range of lenses with which to study a system. That, in turn, helps an analyst to come up with new hypotheses of what might be happening and, if you understand which variables you can control, which levers you have to work with in the system to drive the metrics, such as revenue or conversion, in the desired direction. EDA can also highlight gaps in our knowledge and help determine which experiments might make sense to run to fill in those gaps.

For univariate data, where the data is continuous (real numbers) or discrete (integers), common graphical types include stem-and-leaf plots (Figure 5-5), histograms (Figure 5-6), and box plots (Figure 5-7).

Stem	Leaf
1	0 3 6
2	1 6 7 8
3	5 5 6
4	1 1 5 6 9
5	0 3 6 8

Figure 5-5. A stem-and-leaf plot.

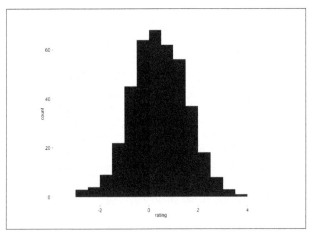

Figure 5-6. A histogram.

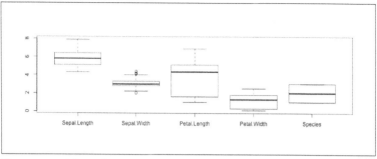

Figure 5-7. A box plot.

If a histogram is scaled so that its area equals 1, this is a probability density function (PDF). Another useful way to view the same data is to plot the cumulative probability, called the cumulative density function (CDF). That can highlight interesting points of the distribution, including central data points.

Figures 5-8, 5-9, and 5-10 show the common graphical types for univariate categorical variables.

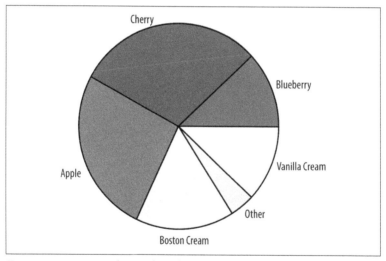

Figure 5-8. A pie or donut chart.[3]

---

3 Donuts: tasty to eat. Donut charts: just don't do it. Use a pie or bar chart instead.

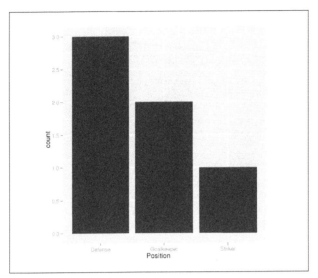

Figure 5-9. A bar chart.

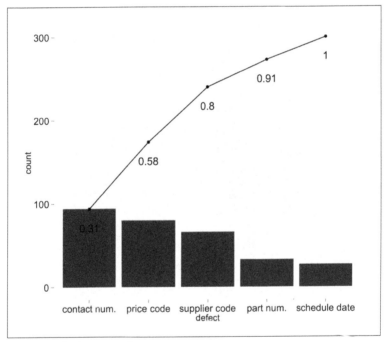

Figure 5-10. A pareto chart.

For two variables, there is a larger array of common types:

	Continuous or discrete	Categorical
Categorical	• Box plot • Area chart • Range chart • Table chart	• Spider/radar chart • Stacked bar chart • Funnel chart
Continuous or discrete	• Scatter plot • Line graph • Polar plot • Maps & Voronoi diagram • Density plot • Contour plot	• Same as top left

(See also Figure 7-5.)

For examining three variables at once, there is a whole slew of graphic types. Some are more traditional, generic, and common (surface, bubble plots, 3D scatter) while other have specialized purposes (see the D3 gallery (*http://bit.ly/d3-viz*)).

Where one variable is time (such as years) or categorical, another approach can be to use "small multiples" where you create a lattice of one- or two-dimensional plots (Figure 5-11).

Don't restrict yourself to one or two types. All of these chart types exist for a reason. Study their strengths and weaknesses, and use whatever type will show any interesting signals, trends, or patterns to best effect. (We'll return to some aspects of this in Chapter 7.)

Where possible and appropriate, use a command, such as a `pairs()`, to autogenerate plots of different combinations of variables that your eye can rapidly scan to look for interesting features or oddities that deserve greater investigation.

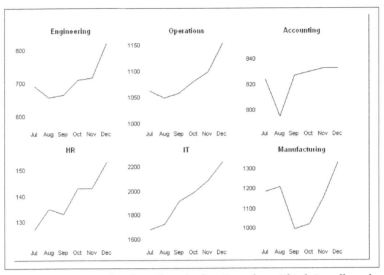

Figure 5-11. Example of small multiples. From http://bit.ly/small-mult.

Inferential Analysis

Descriptive analysis and EDA come under the broad umbrella of descriptive statistics—they *describe* properties of the data sample at hand. We now switch to the other main branch: statistical inference. As the name implies, the goal is to *infer* some information—which might be parameters, distributions, or relationships—about the broader population from which the sample came. It also sets the stage for hypothesis testing in which we design and run experiments to test and analyze our understanding of the underlying mechanisms.

Because this is not a statistics textbook, this section will only give a cursory overview of the sorts of questions one can ask, the classes of insights that might be generated, and the added value that can be obtained by using inferential analysis. If you need an introductory text, I would highly recommend the free *OpenIntro Statistics* (*http://bit.ly/openintro-stat*).

Why do we need inference? We typically infer metrics about the population from a sample because data collection is too expensive, impractical, or even impossible to obtain all data. Consider an exit poll for a presidential election. It is unrealistic to poll 125 million voters. Instead, we want to get a good representative sample and make an accurate inference about what the results would have been had we polled everyone. Also, if you are running quality checks on your manufacturing process and it involves *destructive* testing, then clearly it is impossible to test everything because you would have nothing left to sell.

Another reason for inference is to provide an objective framework for evaluating differences and results. Suppose that you ran a surprise and delight campaign (*http://bit.ly/surprise-and-delight*). You select 1,000 customers with some common criteria, such as that they must have made two purchases in the last year and are members of your loyalty program. You send half of them (the test group) a surprise gift with a note saying "Just because we love our customers, here is a little thank you," and the other half (the control group) get nothing. You evaluate the number of purchases over the next three months, and your descriptive analysis shows that the test group spent $3.36 more per month on average than the control group. What does that mean? It sounds good, but how reliable is that value? Would we likely see a similar value if we ran the experiment again, or is this difference just by chance? Maybe it is swayed by a single customer who purchased one large order? Statistical inference allows us to provide an estimate of likelihood that we saw that difference by chance alone if there were no real difference in the underlying purchasing behavior.

Imagine handing that result to a decision maker. With descriptive analysis alone, you can only state the result: "We found this difference of $3.36/month, it's in the right direction, and it seems what we might expect.'" However, with inferential analysis, you would be able to make a far stronger case: "We found this difference of $3.36/month, and there is only a 2.3% chance that that we would have seen such as result if there were no real underlying difference. The data strongly suggest this is a real effect of the campaign.'" Or, conversely, "We saw this difference, but there is a 27% chance that it was a chance effect. In all likelihood there is no real impact from that campaign, at least on that metric." From both an analyst's and decision maker's perspective, inferential analysis provides greater value and impact to the organization.

The types of questions that one can answer with statistical inference include (but are not limited to):

Standard error, confidence intervals, and margin of error

How much confidence can I have in this particular sample mean or sample proportion? How much might it vary due to chance if I were to repeat the experiment?

Expected mean of single sample

Is this sample mean significantly different from my expected value?

Difference of means from two samples

Are the means from these two samples significantly different from each other? (More technically: what is the likelihood that we would observe this difference of means, or greater, if the null hypothesis were true that there is no difference in the population means for the two samples?)

Sample size calculations and power analysis

What is the minimum sample size I will need, given what I currently know about the process, to achieve a certain level of confidence in the data? These types of statistical tools are important for planning A/B testing, covered in Chapter 8.

Distributions

Is the distribution of values in this sample consistent with a normal (bell-shaped) distribution? Do these two samples likely have the same underlying distribution?

Regression

Suppose that I conducted a well-designed experiment in which I systematically varied one (independent) variable while controlling as much as possible for all others factors, and then I fitted a regression (trend) line. How much confidence can I have in that trend line? How much is it likely to vary (in both gradient and intercept) if I were to repeat the experiment many times?

Goodness of fit and association

Given a categorical variable (say, product category), do the frequencies or counts (say, purchases) match a set of expected relative frequencies? Is there a relationship among two variables, one of which is categorical?

Even though this is a very brief overview, hopefully you can see the potential value in the set of tools that statistical inference provides. It allows one to design experiments and analyze data more objectively, hopefully reducing false positives from chance effects.

Predictive Analysis

Prediction is very difficult, especially about the future.
—attributed to Niels Bohr

Predictive analysis builds upon inferential analysis. The goal is to learn about relationships among variables from an existing training dataset and develop a statistical model that can predict values of attributes for new, incomplete, or future data points.

At first blush, this sounds like voodoo magic. After all, we have no idea when the next big earthquake will destroy San Francisco (the "big one" is overdue), precisely when and where hurricanes will form next season, or the price of Apple's stock on Monday morning (if I could do that, I wouldn't be writing this book). It is true that we are indeed unable to predict features about these extreme, complex, or chaotic phenomena—"black swans"[4]—well. However, many aspects of business and other domains have sufficient signal that predictive analysis can work well. For instance, Nate Silver was able to predict all 2008 US Senate races and winners in 49 out of 50 states in that year's presidential elections.

In retail, there can be strong sales patterns. Figure 5-12 (upper blue curve) shows a very clear and predictable pattern of annual sales of sunglasses, peaking in June–July with troughs in November and January (presumably, the little subpeaks each December are holiday sales). A similar pattern, but translated six months, are sales of gloves with peaks each December. Predictive analysis can then be used to generate *forecasts*, that is, future predictions in a time series, which in turn can be used to generate plans of when to manufacture or buy goods, how many to make or buy, when to have them shipped to stores, and so on.

As well as time series, predictive analysis can also make predictions about which *class* an object might fall into. For instance, given a person's salary information, credit card purchase history, and history of paying (or not paying) bills, we can predict their credit risk. Or,

---

4 Taleb, N. N., *The Black Swan. The Impact of the Improbable* (New York: Penguin Press, 2007).

given a set of tweets that contain a short movie review, each of which has been labeled by a human as being positive ("I loved this movie.") or negative ("This movie sucked."), we can develop a model that will predict the sentiment—positive or negative—for new tweets, such as "The movie's special effects were awesome," that the model was not trained upon.

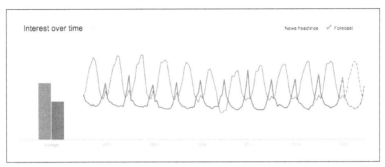

Figure 5-12. Google Trends showing predictable, seasonal patterns of interest in sunglasses (upper, blue) and gloves (lower, red) from 2004–2014 and forecasting out one year to 2015.

The applications of predictive analysis are enormous with huge impacts. Following are a few examples.

Predictions that form the basis of a service per se:

Dating apps
Good recommendations of who to date can lead to greater customer satisfaction.

Stock prediction software (caveat emptor!)
By tracking movements in stock prices and identifying patterns, algorithms can attempt to buy low, sell high, and maximize returns.

Predictions that provide enhanced service to the customer:

Spam filters
Recognizing and filtering out spam ("Buy ViaGRa onLine") versus nonspam ("Your meeting with the CEO") messages leads to clean inboxes and happier users.

Content apps
Good recommendations of what to watch (Netflix) leads to higher retention and lower churn.

Social networking

LinkedIn's "People You May Know" increases the user's network effect and provides both the user greater value and the service more valuable data.

Predictions that can drive higher conversion and basket sizes:

Cross sell and upsell

Even simple association-based recommendations, such as "Customers Who Bought the Frozen DVD Also Bought The Little Mermaid" (Amazon) leads to higher sales and, for some, makes holiday shopping quicker and easier.

Ads and coupons

Learning and individual's history and predicting an individual's state, interest, or intent can drive more relevant display ads or effective supermarket coupons (such as from Tesco, which we will discuss in more detail later).

Predictions that drive a better strategy:

Bank approval

Predicting who will default on mortgages and baking those insights into the approval processes can decrease risk.

Predictive policing

Predicting crime hotspots and so when and where to send police patrols.

Demand forecasting

Predicting future website or service traffic, such as tweets sent during the Super Bowl, can lead to a proactive, preemptive ramping up of servers to meet demand and keep the service running (fewer "fail whales").

Political campaigning

Predicting individual voter's intention (vote/not vote, Democrat/Republican/Undecided) well and rescoring nightly based on new data, led to finer and better targeted efforts (media, calls for campaign contributions, and door knocking) and contributed greatly to success in the Obama presidential campaigns.

This is just a small sample. For an excellent overview of predictive analytics and a more comprehensive list, see John Siegel's book, *Predictive Analytics* (John Wiley & Sons), especially Tables 1–9.

So how do we perform such analysis? There is a whole slew of approaches and tools. The simplest possible model is to predict that tomorrow will be the same as today. That can work well for some slowly changing phenomena, such as weather in Southern California, but not for volatile systems, such as stock prices. Regression is the broadest family of tools. Within that, however, are a number of variants (lasso, ridge, robust, etc.) to deal with different characteristics of the data. Of particular interest and power is logistic regression that can be used to predict classes. For instance, spam/not spam used to be mostly predicted with a Naive Bayes predictor, but nowadays, logistic regression is more common. Other techniques and what come under the term "machine learning" include neural networks; tree-based approaches, such as classification and regression trees; random forests; support vector machines; and k-nearest neighbors.

While powerful, predictive analysis is not necessarily difficult. One of the hardest steps is to obtain a good, clean dataset. When developing a classifier, that often means manually curating a corpus of data; for instance, labeling a set of tweets as positive or negative, which can be especially laborious. Once you have that in place, though, with a good library, such as scikit-learn (*http://scikit-learn.org/stable/*), implementing a basic model can involve literally a few lines of code. To obtain a *good* model, however, often requires more effort and iteration and a process called feature engineering. Features are the model's inputs. They can involve basic raw data that you have collected, such as order amount, simple derived variables, such as "Is order date on a weekend? Yes/No," as well as more complex abstract features, such as the "similarity score" between two movies. Thinking up features is as much an art as a science and can rely on domain knowledge.

Finally, predictive analysis doesn't necessarily require large amounts of data. Nate Silver's 2008 presidential predictions input data was only 188,000 (see Oliver Grisel's presentation (*http://bit.ly/grisel-predictive*) for evidence of that and a good short overview of predictive analysis). What was key was that it involved a large number of different sources and polls, each wrong and biased in some way, but collectively they averaged out to be close to reality. There is evidence, at least for certain classes of problems, that having large(r) amounts of data lets you get away with simple models[5] (see Appendix A).

All in all, predictive analysis is a powerful weapon in a data-driven organization's arsenal.

Causal Analysis

We have probably all heard the maxim: correlation does not imply causation.[6] If you collect some data and then do some EDA to look for interesting relationships among variables, you'll probably find something. Even if there is a very strong correlation between two variables, it does not mean that one causes the other. (For instance, HDL cholesterol inversely correlates with rates of heart disease: the more of this "good" cholesterol, the better. However, HDL-increasing drugs don't lower heart disease. Why? HDL is a byproduct of healthy heart, not a cause.) Thus, such post hoc analyses have strong limitations. If you really want to understand a system and know for sure what levers you have available to influence focal variables and metrics, then you need to develop a causal model.

As in the surprise-and-delight example earlier, the idea is to run one or a series of experiments in which you control as much as possible and ideally change just one small thing. Thus, you might run an experiment in an email campaign to your customers in which you test the email subject line. If everything is the same (same email content, sent at same time, etc.) and the only thing different between the control and the treatment is the subject line, and you see a significantly higher open rate, then you have strong evidence and can conclude that the higher open rate is due to the effect of that subject line, that the subject line is the causal factor.

This experiment is somewhat limited because while it provides good evidence of the influence of the subject line, it is not clear which word of phrase resonates with the customers. For that, you would need to run more experiments. Let's take a more quantitative example: the time at which you send an email can make a big difference

---

5 Fortuny, E. J. de, D. Martens, and F. Provost, Predictive Modeling with Big Data: Is Bigger Really Better?" (*http://bit.ly/defortuny-predictive*) *Big Data* 1, no. 4 (2013): 215–226.

6 If you are not convinced, check out the spurious correlations (*http://www.tylervi gen.com/*), such as US cheese consumption correlates with number of people who died by becoming tangled in their bedsheets.

to open rates. For that you can do a controlled experiment with multiple treatments (send batch at 8:00 a.m., send batch at 9:00 a.m., send batch at 10:00 a.m., etc.) and examine how email send time causes a change in open rates. You will be able to predict (interpolate) what open rates would be if you were to send email at 8:30 a.m.

What Can You Do?

Analysts: You should be striving to both "sharpen your saw" as well as obtain more tools for your toolkit. You will become a more effective and valued analyst, and it is an investment in yourself and your career. Evaluate the statistical and visualization skills that you currently use. How can they be improved? For instance, would learning R enable you to do EDA more quickly and in a more reproducible manner? Would an additional, higher-level type of analytical approach provide greater insights and impact to your project? What would it take to learn that skill?

Management: Keep an eye out for situations where additional analytical types might provide better insights and impact to the organization. If stock outs are a problem in your supply chain, would predictive models help? Can you do more experiments that will deepen the institutional knowledge of causal factors? Push analysts to develop their skills and openly support them with training, mentorship, and time to hone their skills and enhance the analytics org. Let them experiment with other software tools that might provide new types of insights or let them do their work more quickly and easily.

Such experiments provide a causal, deeper understanding of the system that be used for predictions and can help plan campaigns and other changes to enhance the metrics that one is trying to drive. They can also form the basis of the simulation models that can be used to optimize the system. For instance, one can simulate a supply chain and study the effects of how differing replenishment triggers and rules can affect the chance of stock outs or the total shipping and warehousing costs. These types of activities are in the bottom-right of Davenport's matrix in Table 1-2 and are the highest levels of analytics. Given the controlled scientific manner in which the knowledge is assembled over time and the power that such models hold, such causal models are what Jeffrey Leek calls the "gold standard" for data analysis.

In a business, all of this analysis and modeling activity is not for the general interest for the analysts or more senior managers; it is with the goal of driving the core metrics, such as email open rates, conversion metrics, and ultimately revenue. Thus, it is crucial that those metrics are the correct ones to be aiming for and that they are designed well. If not, then you could be optimizing for the wrong thing. Given the importance of good metric design, I will now cover that topic in the next chapter.

CHAPTER 6

Metric Design

> *If you don't know where you're going,*
> *you'll probably end up somewhere else.*
> —Yogi Berra

> *Count what is countable, measure what is measurable,*
> *and what is not measurable, make measurable.*
> —Galileo Galilei

A data-driven organization needs to set out a clear strategy, that is, a direction that the business is heading, and then determine a set of top-level metrics—key performance indictors (KPIs)—to track whether the business is indeed heading in the right direction and to monitor progress and success. Responsibility for driving those top-level KPIs flows down to divisions or business units where they may define additional KPIs specific for that business unit. Ultimately, this ends up a set of operational and diagnostic metrics that monitor tasks, programs, tests, and projects that drives the KPIs.

Given this, it is imperative that metrics are designed well. They should act as true, accurate compasses. You don't want to be following a *strategic* metric that indicates you are heading in the desired southeast direction, when your true heading is actually northeast, or an *operational* metric that indicates mobile conversion is increasing at 5% per annum when it is, in fact, flat. You don't want to be watching a faulty *diagnostic* metric that fails to inform you as early as it could that your website is on the verge of crashing. Metrics are also the outputs from experiments and A/B tests which, if instrumented well, will inform causal analysis and that, as we discussed in the previous chapter, provide the greatest raw material for data-driven insights and strategies. David Skok (*http://bit.ly/skok-designing*) sums this up well:

> One way to look at how companies work is to imagine them as a machine that has Outputs, and Levers that you, the management team, can pull to affect its behavior. Weak management teams have only a limited understanding of how their machines work, and what levers are available to affect performance. The better the management team, the better they will understand how that machine works, and how they can optimize its performance (what levers they can pull). When we look to design metrics, we are looking to deepen our understanding of the machinery, and how it works. Well designed metrics will automatically drive behavior to optimize output from the machine.

In this chapter, I will cover the design of metrics. I start out with general considerations and then focus on KPIs more specifically. I will, however, only lightly touch on how you choose metrics because a full discussion is beyond the scope of this book, and a number of robust frameworks cover this important stage, such as balanced scorecard, TQM, performance prism, and tableau du bord.

Metric Design

There are several considerations when choosing or designing a metric. In an ideal world, metrics should exhibit a number of traits.

Simple

Design a metric to be "as simple as it can be, but not simpler" (Einstein).

Which of these would be easier to explain to a colleague?

Customer: A person with whom there has been an exchange of monies from the sale of one of our products.

Customer: A person who has purchased a product from us,

- Excluding gift card purchases
- Excluding those who returned their item for a full refund within 45 days
- Including anyone who redeemed a gift card

You get the point.

Simple metrics are, by definition, simple to define, which in turn means they are:

- Simpler to convey to others: there is less chance of confusion
- Simpler to implement: they are more likely to be calculated correctly
- More likely to be comparable to other teams or organizations

Of course, there are many reasons why one might legitimately want to add on additional business logic and edge cases to create a more complex metric. You may need to filter out sources of bias or extremal edge cases. Or, you may need a metric that explicitly tracks a particular biased subsample, such as the subset of customer cases that cost you the most to resolve.

You have to take each case on its merits, but try to avoid adding additional complexity for rare edge cases that add little to the overall business value and insight of that metric.

Bottom line: don't make metrics unnecessarily complex.

Standardized

Match standard metric definitions wherever possible. For instance, if there is a standard, well-defined metric for website bounce rate, then use it unless there is a very good reason to define and implement a home-grown variant. If the retail industry uses exits to measure foot traffic at stores, use that metric and not enters, even if they might be highly numerically or conceptually comparable. For instance, to track monthly active users, Facebook only includes people logged in, whereas Yelp considers both those logged in as well as guests.

Being standardized will generate less confusion, especially for colleagues joining your teams from other organizations. It will also make it easier to compare your metrics with others in the same sector, that is, to make use of competitor knowledge and to benchmark your organization's performance.

More important is to make sure that the metric is standardized within your organization. I have seen confusion when different teams think that they are using the same definition and may talk about it in the same terms, but in reality, the implementation in their team's spreadsheets or systems have in fact diverged from one another. Their numbers don't match, and arguments ensue.

Best practice is to have a centralized, automated, documented, versioned single source of truth that different teams draw from. You'll be able to incorporate analyses and insights from others, comfortable that you are comparing like for like. As such, this makes it easier to build up a repository of analyses and an institutional knowledge of the causal factors about the business (or market) that the organization can trust, use, and build upon.

Bottom line: use standard metrics unless you have very good reasons to deviate from them. If they are unconventional, document how and why they are nonstandard.

Accurate

Metrics should be accurate. That is, their mean numerical value should be close to the true underlying mean value (or population mean; see Figure 6-1). If you compare this to archery, it is the equivalent of an arrow being on target.

Consider the checkout amount from Amazon purchases. The mean checkout amount *excluding book purchases* is an inaccurate measure of the average checkout amounts for all purchases. It is biased. In Chapter 2, we mentioned some examples of missing data bias. For instance, the average customer happiness doesn't capture the true happiness if those unsatisfied customers subject to slow shipping are more likely to submit their surveys late and miss the cutoff date, or not submit it at all. We have a sample that biases the happiness metric up, away from the true, lower value.

When designing metrics, try to think about possible sources of bias in both the data itself and in the metric. In Chapter 2, we discussed some sources of bias in the raw data collection. From the metric's perspective, think carefully about any conditions that filter subsets of the data in or out or any hidden or stale "fudge factors."

Imagine a sharpshooter at a shooting range, firing a rifle at a distant target and using a scope to help him see. There is a constant breeze blowing the bullet off target; thus, he turns a knob on the side of the scope to adjust the (mis)alignment of the scope and the barrel—the "fudge factor"—to account for the wind. If the wind drops or picks up, however, that scope alignment is stale and will no longer help get the bullet on the target. Conditions change, and you have to keep your models and any fudge factors up to date.

The same is true in business. At Warby Parker, we use electronic devices to count the foot traffic in and out of our retail stores. One use of such data is to compute our retail conversion metric, the proportion of people who enter the store that purchase something. At one location, staff can only access the stock and break rooms by going through the main entrance, and this extra staff traffic inflated the traffic count, decreasing the conversion metric. It was a biased metric. We remedied this with a statistical model that estimated, for a given day of week and given level of busyness, the proportion of traffic that was staff versus customers as a correction factor. This resulted in a much more realistic conversion metric. The concern is that such models can become stale as business conditions change; for instance, customers may be more motivated to purchase during the holidays. Either the model has to be recalibrated periodically, or, as we are now trialing, use superior technology that can identify staff explicitly and exclude them from the traffic counts.

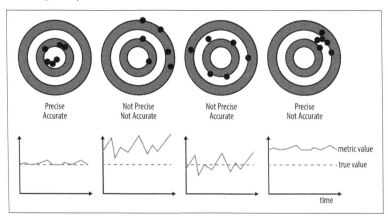

Figure 6-1. Precision (being stable or clustered) and accuracy (being on target) with illustrative example in two-dimensional data. Inaccurate metrics have a bias such that their mean differs from the true mean in a systemic way. Precision captures the variability: how much the mean value would differ if you were to repeat the experiment multiple times and collect new samples of the same size.

Precise

Metrics should be precise. That is, they should return similar values if repeated with the same conditions—if you compare this to archery, it is the equivalent of a set of arrows being close to each other.

One tool or lever you have to control precision is sample size. The larger the sample size, the smaller is the standard error. The relationship is not linear, however. Because standard error of the mean equals the standard deviation divided by the square root of the sample size, to halve the standard error, we need to *quadruple* the sample size.

We can visualize the combination of accuracy and precision in Figure 6-1. Unless you have some validated reference data, you are not always going to know whether your metrics are inaccurate. However, you will likely soon discover if your metrics are imprecise (unstable).

Bottom line: strive for accurate and precise metrics, and consider the costs and benefits of larger samples.

Relative Versus Absolute

An important consideration is deciding whether to use absolute or relative metrics. That choice can generate metrics that paint a very different picture of the same scenario.

Imagine an organization that has a membership structure, and 25% are considered VIPs (say, they have purchased more than $1,000 of product.) Six months later, only 17% are VIPs. Yikes, what happened? Did they abandon? How can we turn the business around? However, if, during that period, the company had a laser focus on driving new customers, then the total number of members may have increased (orange block in Figure 6-2), and the number of VIPs may have stayed the same, but the proportion of VIPs will be lower. In fact, it is possible that there could have been gains in the number of VIPs while still showing a decrease in proportion.

Conversely, suppose after six months we see a significant increase in number and proportion of VIPs. That might indicate a healthy increasing customer base, but it could actually be static if the company focused only on driving returning customers and increasing repeat purchase rate (Figure 6-2 lower). (In many companies, this second scenario of increasing repeat purchases is highly preferable to new customer growth because the cost of acquisition of new customers is so high.)

As can be seen, the choice of absolute (number of VIPs) or relative (proportion of VIPs) metrics can lead to very different interpretations.

Bottom line: Think through what you want to have happen in the underlying data, and choose the metric to be absolute or relative so that it will appropriately track that change.

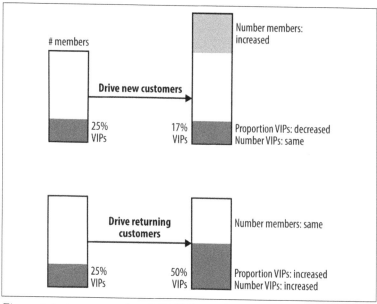

Figure 6-2. A company has 25% VIPs. In the top scenario, the company focuses on driving new customers (orange block). This leads to more members, same number of VIPs, and lower proportion of VIPs. In the lower scenario, the company focuses on driving returning customers. The proportion and number of VIPs are both higher but without any change in total number of members.

Robust

Define   metrics that are statistically "robust," that is, they are relatively insensitive to individual extremal values.

Consider this example from the *San Francisco Chronicle* (*http://bit.ly/sfc-tech-wage*):

> The average tech wage on the mid-Peninsula (San Mateo County) last year was $291,497... A likely explanation for the distortion: Facebook chief executive Mark Zuckerberg took only a dollar in salary but reaped $3.3 billion exercising Facebook stock options in 2013... if you remove $3.3 billion from the total, you end up with an average tech wage of roughly $210,000.

Using average here is inappropriate given the high degree of positive skew of the salary data. The average is increased significantly (more than 35%) by a single outlier value. In this case, a median is a far better choice because it is robust to high-valued outliers and better captures the location or middle of the data.

It should be noted that there are times when you want to design a metric that is specifically sensitive to boundary values. Peak load on a website is meant to capture the rare maximal values encountered.

You can estimate or visualize robustness by resampling. Take a sub-set of the data and compute your metric. Repeat many times (with replacement) to get a set of metric values and plot their distribution. Is it more variable than you might expect or desire?

Bottom line: use exploratory data analysis (such as histograms and bivariate scatter plots) to get a feel for the data, and use those to guide the choice of appropriate robust metrics and measures.

Direct

Try to choose metrics that directly measure the underlying process that you are trying to drive. That is, it is not always possible to measure or quantify everything, and you may have to choose a *proxy*, or an indirect measure, in its place.

Cathy O'Neil (*http://bit.ly/data-skeptic*) provides a nice example of how student test scores are a proxy for teaching quality. The further the distance between the underlying process and the proxy (or layers of proxies), the less useful and the more misleading the measure can be. You can end up optimizing the proxy, which might be somewhat orthogonal to what you really want to drive and optimize.

Another example comes from Susan Webber (*http://bit.ly/webber-metrics*), who discusses Coca Cola's testing and introduction of New Coke in the 1980s. They ran user tests that showed very positive results, even compared to regular Coke. When it launched, however, the product tanked. Why? Users found it too sweet. The problem is that testing involved "sip tests," and we tolerate greater sweetness in sips than in gulps. Had they tested a "normal" user experience (chugging down a mouthful on a hot day), they would have been able to optimize for the real-world taste, experience, and preference.

Bottom line: where possible, instrument your systems and processes as much as possible and at the lowest level possible to try to avoid proxies. Don't always take the easy way out, and use the data that you happen to have. Focus on the data you should be collecting and using that if it would better serve your needs.

Key Performance Indicators

Key performance indicators (KPIs), also known as key success indicators (KSIs), are the suite of highest-level measures linked to the company's strategic objectives. They help define and track the direction that the business is going and help it meets its goals. As mentioned earlier, these are the metrics that help keep the ship going in the right direction.

Avinash Kaushik (*http://bit.ly/kaushik-kpi*), a well-known commentator and teacher of web analytics, defines them as

> Measures that help you understand how you are doing against your objectives.

He stresses the "bookends" of the definition: measures and objectives, as KPIs bind these two key pieces together. Examples of KPIs include "increase brand awareness by 10%" or "double the number of active users by year end" or "increase online conversion by 5% in Q2."

It is critical that KPIs:

Are clearly defined
You don't want any confusion or ambiguity about a core metric that the organization as a whole is trying to drive. You need a clear metric definition, a clear target value, and a clear or standard timeframe (typically, year end).

Are measurable
KPIs have to be quantifiable. You must be able to measure progress numerically over time. In other words, there should be a

needle that can be moved and not a binary metric. As DJ Patil, US Chief Data Scientist, says in his book, Building Data Science Teams (*http://bit.ly/data-sci-teams*) (O'Reilly), "I've found that the strongest data-driven organizations all live by the motto, 'If you can't measure it, you can't fix it.'"

Have targets

"Increase revenue" is a poorly defined KPI because it has no numerical target. If the organization increases revenue by just $5, staff can claim that the target is met and stop trying. Conversely, if the target is too much of a stretch or impossible to achieve, such as "increase revenue 5,000%," it will not be taken seriously, or people will soon give up, resigned to suffer whatever consequences may ensue. KPIs should be achievable but at a stretch with hard work.

Are visible

KPIs need to be visible to at least those responsible for driving them but, ideally, broader than that. Staff need to have feedback and have a clear sense of whether their efforts are paying off, or they need to change tack and try something different. For instance, Warby Parker's strategic metrics and KPIs are visible to all staff and are reviewed regularly (at least quarterly) with all staff during all-hands meetings.

Reflect what the organization is trying to achieve

It is too easy to fall into the trap of tracking what can be easily measured, such as reponse time to answer calls in a customer center, when the true objective might be to increase customer satisfaction. As the saying goes, "we make important what we can measure."[1] That might require new processes to collect data and measure progress and success. Do the extra work, and influence what you truly want to impact.

Like goals, KPIs should be SMART (*http://bit.ly/smart-criteria*):

- **S**pecific
- **M**easurable
- **A**chievable

---

1 Feinberg, R. A., I-S. Kim, L. Hokama, K. de Ruyter, and C. Keen, "Operational deteminants of caller satisfaction in the call center," *Int. J. Service Industry Management* 11, no. 2 (2000): 131–141.

- Result-oriented
- Time-bound

Or, perhaps, more pertinently, SMARTER, by the addition of Evaluated and Reviewed (or Rewarded).

KPI Examples

Bernard Marr (*http://bit.ly/marr-75-kpis*) has identified 75 common KPIs.[2]. They include areas such as financial performance and understanding customers (Table 6-1).

Table 6-1. A subset of common KPIs found in businesses from Bernard Marr

Financial performance	Understanding customers
• Net profit	• Net Promoter Score (NPS)
• Net profit margin	• Customer retention rate
• Gross profit margin	• Customer satisfaction index
• Operating profit margin	• Customer profitability score
• EBITDA	• Customer lifetime value (CLV)
• Revenue growth rate	• Customer turnover rate
• Total shareholder return (TSR)	• Customer engagement
• Economic value added (EVA)	• Customer complaints
• Return on investment (ROI)	
• Return on capital employed (ROCE)	
• Return on assets (ROA)	
• Return on equity (ROE)	
• Debt-to-equity (D/E) ratio	
• Cash conversion cycle (CCC)	
• Working capital ratio	
• Operating expense ratio (OER)	
• CAPEX to sales ratio	
• Price earnings ratio (P/E ratio)	

However, every business needs to choose and tailor its set of KPIs for its sector, its particular business model, its lifecycle stage, and its particular objectives. For instance, Warby Parker's strategic objectives and KPIs show almost no overlap with Marr's list. There is nothing wrong with the list—it covers most typical businesses and

---

2 Marr, B. *Key Performance Indicators (KPI): The 75 measures every manager needs to know.* London: Financial Times Press, 2012.

their needs—it just doesn't capture that each business is unique. Warby Parker has a strong social mission—we distribute a pair of glasses to someone in need for every pair that we sell. Thus, unsurprisingly, we have strategic objectives and KPIs associated with our Do Good program because that is what we want to focus on driving further. We design and manufacture our own glasses, and so we have KPIs focused on improving that aspect of the business, too.

What I am driving at is that there is no cookie-cutter set of KPIs that a business should use. They require very careful, deliberate thought from senior management and other stakeholders about where to direct the business and the attention and effort of all staff over the course of the next year.

Kaplan and Norton's balanced scorecard approach[3] tries to ensure that the suite of KPIs provide a coherent view of the organization across four areas: financial, customer, internal business process, and learning and growth. They liken it to flying an airplane.[4] To be able to fly a plane and get to your destination, a pilot needs to keep stock of fuel, airspeed, altitude, compass, external conditions, and so on *simultaneously*. You can't make one flight focusing solely on optimizing fuel consumption and then plan to focus only on altitude on a later flight. One should view that complete instrumentation as a single strategy.

If you've peeked into the cockpit of a commercial airplane, you will see dozens, if not hundreds, of dials, meters, and levers. The reality, however, is that the pilot and co-pilot are only regularly monitoring a tiny core subset. (If you've ever flown a glider or sailplane, as I used to do, you'll soon realize the essence of what is needed: altimeter, compass, air speed indicator, and variometer. That's it.) Compass: important. Light on in the galley: not so much. What you will find are many warning lights; a pilot will, of course, respond immediately if they go off, but in "normal" mode, he or she can pretty much forget about them. In other words, a organization will indeed need dashboards and alerts to monitor the hundreds or thousands of operational and diagnostic metrics, but tracking those can be

---

3 Kaplan, R. S., and D. P. Norton. *The Balanced Scorecard: Translating Strategy into Action*. Harvard Business Review Press, Boston: Harvard Business Preview Press, 1996.

4 Kaplan, R. S., and D. P. Norton, "Linking the Balanced Scorecard to Strategy," *California Management Review* 39, no. 1 (1996): 53–79.

delegated down. Those dashboards and metrics may be highly localized to individual units or teams, but the KPIs are special: a small set of metrics that should be highly visible to all.

So, how many KPIs do you need?

How Many KPIs?

KPIs will tend to cover all majors areas of the business and any parts of the business that are the particular strategic focus for that period, typically a year. A business might have a handful (4–5) of "perspectives" or stakeholder groups. These might, but don't have to be aligned with C-suite members. Thus, a "perspective" might be finance oveseen by the CFO, technology strategic objectives managed by the CTO/CIO team, marketing objectives owned by the CMO, and so on. Bob Champagne (*http://bit.ly/champagne-kpis*) suggests that within each of those might be 2–5 strategic objectives, and each objective might be associated with 1–3 KPIs. However, the total number of KPIs should be at the lower end of the $5 \times (2-5) \times (1-3)$ product. He suggests 20–30 maximum, and one of the commenters to his post remarks "twenty is plenty." Kaplan and Norton cite 16–25.

If you do have too many KPIs, staff are going to have divided focus, will try to multitask, and will become less effective. For instance, a small company can't expand its product line and increase customer satisfaction and increase revenue and expand internationally all at the same time. It's too much. Staff will become exhausted and are being set up to fail. Instead, focus should be directed to a smaller, more coherent set of goals, objectives, and KPIs that everyone can understand and get behind.

KPI Definitions and Targets

If KPIs are to be SMART, they must be both specific and measurable. This means that one should avoid generic, ambiguous, and ill-defined verbs such as "improve" and "enhance" or nouns or adjectives such as "the best," "leading," or "quality." Stacey Barr (*http://bit.ly/barr-jargon*), a performance measurement specialist, calls these "weasel words." Instead, she recommends taking a vague goal, such as "to transform the performance of our customers," having a conversation to dig into those weasel words, and understanding and replacing them with more sensory-specific language, such as "when our customers work with us, they can achieve their business targets much sooner." With that, it then becomes easier to define more tangible, concrete metrics to achieve that goal, such as "reduce average time to reach their targets" or "increase percentage of targets reached within target date."

Earlier I mentioned "double the number of active users by year end" as an example KPI. This is a case where it is very important to have clear definitions. "Active" is especially open to interpretation. In an online gaming company, that could mean users who have simply logged in within the last 30 days, or who have played a certain minimum number of games or spent a minimum number of hours gaming. Those need to be set out unambiguously at the time that these KPIs and their targets are set.

So what are some good and bad KPI targets? Maria Micallef[5] provides some excellent examples.

Good targets:

- "We will reduce the number of missed household bin [trash] collections by 5% by next year."
- "We will increase the number of customers from Italy by 20 per cent before the end of 2011."

Each of these has a clear, specific metric (assuming that the concepts of "missed" and "customers" are unambiguous or well set out), and they are clearly measurable and time bound. How about bad targets?

Bad targets:

- "We aim to have the best transport service in the region."
- "We will improve the way that we handle complaints."
- "We will answer 75 per cent of all complaints within 5 days."

Let's dissect these.

The issue with the first is obvious: what does "best" mean?

The second is clear, too: improve how?

The third, however, is especially interesting: "Answer 75 per cent of all complaints." That seems specific. "Within 5 days" is clear and

---

5 Micallef, M., "Key Performance Indicators for Business Excellence." (*http://bit.ly/micallef-kpis*)

time-bounded. In fact, assuming that this is achievable, it appears to meet all the criteria of SMART or SMARTER KPIs. What's the issue with it?

The problem lies with the other 25% of complaints. What of them? As Micallef states, this is a "poor target if the remaining 25 per cent take 3 months to answer." One thing that you have to design against in your metrics is to avoid staff gaming the system or knowingly or unknowingly taking advantage of "loopholes" such as these and meeting targets, while at the same time the organization is not actually reaching the intended strategic objective.[1] In this case, bad word of mouth from those 25% could be enough to tear a company's reputation to shreds.

In these last two chapters, I've covered KPIs that define what the organization is trying to achieve, what to consider when designing good diagnostic and operational metrics (which are the things that the organization is going to track and try to optimize), and I've covered the types of analysis that can't be brought to bear upon those data. The next step in the analytics value chain is to package up those insights, findings, and recommendations and present them to peers, management, and decision makers. That is, you need to tell a story with that data, which is the subject of the next chapter.

---

1 See Kerr (1975) (*http://bit.ly/kerr-folly*) for examples of "fouled up" incentive programs, one cause of which is "fascination with an 'objective' criterion: managers seek to establish simple quantifiable standard against which to measure and reward performance. Such efforts may be successful in highly predictable within an organization, but are likely to cause goal displacement when applied anywhere else."

CHAPTER 7

Storytelling with Data

*When you've got a good visualization, people get it right away and you
get a conversation going. You get feedback. It accelerates productivity. It's
far better than talking on the phone or sending email. You instantly
convey the same idea to many minds.*

—Ofer Mendelevitch[1]

In the previous two chapters, I covered types of analysis, ranging
from descriptive to causal, and the design of metrics including the
especially important subset, KPIs. In this chapter, we move further
along the analytics value chain: packaging up the findings, insights,
and recommendations to present to the decision makers and other
stakeholders, to increase the quality of discussion and decision making at every level.

This chapter is a relatively high-level overview of the process and
objective of communicating analytics output in a data-driven organization—the *why* and the *what* of communicating data rather than
the *how*. I'll cover the prerequisites; that is, what you need to think
about before you even start preparing a presentation or visualization. To be more concrete, I will also cover a chart chooser and data-
visualization checklist, letting those two, and the source references
more or less speak for themselves. That will leave space to cover
presentation-level remarks, such as overall structure and focusing
the message.

---

1 Cited in *Data Visualization: A New Language for Storytelling* by Mike Barlow (O'Reilly).

Storytelling

"Every dataset, every database, every spreadsheet has a story to tell," says Stuart Frankel, CEO of Narrative Science. An analyst's job is to find that story, or at least find the story that matters to the organization, interpret it, and communicate it. Moreover, they have to tell an accurate, empirically supported story. If they don't, people will construct one themselves from their own, weak data. In *Analytics at Work*, Davenport et al. (p. 138–139) tell of an executive at a hospital system who claimed that a major influencer of patient satisfaction and perception of quality was the taste of food. When the analysts went to work to verify this claim, they found that food was the worst factor in a suite of more than 30 predictors. The executive's claim couldn't be further from the truth. The reason for this mismatch? The executive had talked to *two* patients who had complained about the food. That executive's story was purely anecdotal, whereas the analysts' work was based on representative data and objective statistical analysis.

Given that, colloquially, "story" can be can be meant as an anecdote, what do I mean by the term in this context, that is, presentation in a data-driven organization?

Take a look at Figure 7-1. Anything strike you as unusual or interesting?

Obviously, 2009 was a rollercoaster year for Twitter with a huge jump in account signup rate and a significant dropoff throughout the year. (However, this is still a positive rate, and the user base continued to grow.) There is actually a rich story in this one curve. The first jump we notice (around March 2007) was buzz around the South by Southwest Interactive conference, in which the service first got noticed by early adopters and usage tripled. The flattening after the second jump (around May 2008) is where Twitter actively started blacklisting spammers. 2009 was a key year in which the service tipped into the mainstream; for instance, in April, at the start of the downward slope of the main peak, Ashton Kutcher challenged CNN to see who would become the first to reach 1 million followers (Ashton won, just, by half an hour), and Oprah Winfrey tweeted for the first time and did so on air. This curve, for Australian accounts, show similarities but also differences with that for the US. For instance, the last jump, in 2013, corresponds to the run-up to an

Australian federal election. Thus, there is a national story in here, too.

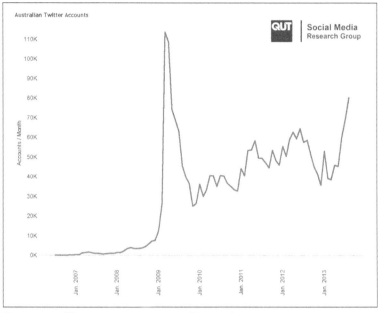

Figure 7-1. New account creation of Australian twitter accounts versus time. From http://bit.ly/aus-twitter.

Thus, "story" is meant to capture the key findings, features, or patterns in data, to convey what caused them where possible, and, looking forward, to spell out the implications and recommendations to the organization. To Stephen Few, "Data visualization is the use of visual representations to explore, analyze, and present quantitative data." I view storytelling here as an additional interpretative layer, a narrative structure, on top of the data visualization. Figure 7-1 *plus* the narrative is more insightful and revealing than Figure 7-1 alone. The two have to be closely matched. You need the optimal visualization to reveal the pattern during analysis and then also to show the evidence or pattern to the final audience, and you also need the correct, accurate, and valid narrative to interpret those findings and implications.

Ideally, in this case, you would put the salient points into the plot itself and so enhance the narrative directly and make it more self-contained (Figure 7-2).

Finding a story and interpreting it involves a range of analytical techniques that typically will include exploratory data analysis, that is to say, data visualization with charts and tables (Chapter 5). While this chapter focuses on data visualization, it is not an introduction to the subject. I certainly could not do it justice, and there are many great books that do. I would recommend starting with the gold standards: the works of Edward Tufte (*Envisioning Information*, *Visual Explanations*, and *The Visual Display of Quantitative Information* [Graphics Press]). *The Visual Display* especially will get you in the mindset of a visual designer and critic. This is the book in which Tufte introduced the valuable concepts of chartjunk and data-to-ink ratios, both of which are explained later.

For more practical, introductory texts, I really like Stephen Few's *Now You See It* (Analytics Press), which focuses more on data visualization for quantitative data exploration and analysis; and *Show Me The Numbers* (Analytics Press), which focuses more on presentation. For web-based visualizations, try Scott Murray's *Interactive Data Visualization* (O'Reilly). This chapter is also not a style guide; for that, I would heartily recommend Dona Wong's *The Wall Street Journal Guide to Information Graphics* (W. W. Norton & Company).

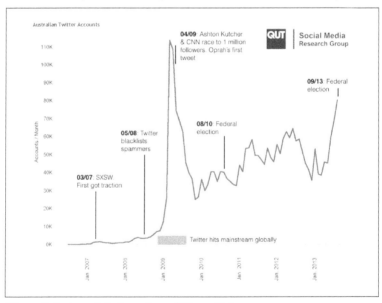

Figure 7-2. Annotated version of Figure 7-1.

First Steps

When starting to think about the best way to present some data, information, and analysis, there are three questions to consider:

- What are you trying to achieve?
- Who is your audience?
- What's your medium?

These are essential for narrowing down the type of presentation, style, and level of technical material that will get your message across and have the greatest impact. Only after these three have been nailed down can you reasonably think about the more practical aspects of how you are going to structure the content and format it visually.

What Are You Trying to Achieve?

What is your objective? Why are you putting this presentation or report together? What do you hope to achieve? Presumably, this will have been set out before you do your analysis, but you must have a clear understanding of why you are presenting these data or findings, what you have concluded, and what you want to happen.

For instance, if this is a descriptive analysis only, the objective may be for the reader to gain a greater understanding of the system, to grasp the behaviors, magnitudes, and variabilities of key components; that is, it is just a knowledge share. Alternatively, if this is an analysis of an A/B test, the objective may be to summarize how well the different treatments fared against the control, the confidence in the results, and the potential increased revenue assuming that the lift is real. In this case, the ultimate objective is likely to get a decision, a green light to roll this treatment feature out to 100% of users in production. Those two are very different analyses with different objectives and will require a different presentation style.

Let's take the latter example, A/B test results, and examine it more closely. In this case, the analyst should have done the analysis, come to a conclusion about the meaning and confidence of the results, and made a recommendation: we should roll this feature out. The presentation should make the recommendation and also provide the supporting evidence: this is how we set up the experiment, these are the metrics of interest, this is what we found, here is some ambiguity that we encountered, and this is why we came to the final conclusion.

Who Is Your Audience?

The next question to consider is the audience. How data literate are they? How technical are they? What expectations do they have? What's their level of interest and motivation? How busy are they?

In a sense, an analyst needs to meet his or her objective *despite* the audience. For the analyst, this may have been his or her primary focus for days or weeks. To the audience, however, this may be just one of 10 decisions that they make today, especially if they are in the C-suite. The analyst should have a sound understanding of the statistical techniques employed, whereas the audience more than likely will not. The analyst will have been immersed in data, code, and statistics, whereas the receiver only cares about the business decision and impact. The analyst or presenter has to take all of this into consideration and structure the material to maximize the impact.

For instance, if you realistically only have two minutes of your C-suite's time, you need to be short, crisp, and precise: "I recommend taking this course of action because it will drive $1 million incremental revenue over the next year." For others, such as presenting to fellow data scientists and statisticians in an hour-long deep dive, they may want as much technical detail as possible; they may want to pore over the test statistics, degrees of freedom, confidence intervals, density plots, and the like.

CFOs are very comfortable poring over dense matrices of financial metrics. (Whether that's actually their preferred mode to consume data is another matter.) A broader audience, however, such at an all-hands meeting, may need only the very highest level and most non-technical key takeaways. You have to decide what is appropriate and tailor your material accordingly.

What's Your Medium?

The last question is to determine the medium that you will use. That is, should you use a written report; a visual presentation, such as PowerPoint; a dashboard; or an infographic.

This is partially tied to the previous question. That is, if you are presenting at an all-hands meeting, you essentially have a choice of a visual presentation or a verbal presentation. For the CFO, you may need to provide a written report to incorporate a suite of tables to cover the breadth of views he or she needs and expects, or you may need to present a PowerPoint deck to a set of managers.

That decision, in combination with your determination of their level of interest and the amount of time they are likely to invest to consume your analysis, will determine the depth and level of detail contained with the presentation as well as the size. If you've got just three minutes to present to the C-suite, you don't want a 37-slide PowerPoint presentation with lots of technical detail. PowerPoint might be appropriate, but it likely can only be two or three slides.

Importantly, you can't copy visuals from one medium to another as is and expect them to be optimal. For instance, copying a dense table from that written report and pasting it into a PowerPoint slide for the all-hands meeting is just not going to work well. You have to tailor each slide, chart, and table for the medium at hand.

Sell, Sell, Sell!

A well-designed experiment, well-chosen metrics, and above all, a carefully and clearly defined question provide the greatest chance of seeing the dominant patterns in the data and answering those questions. The analyst's job is to find and illustrate the clearest, cleanest, and most relevant patterns, and to interpret them and translate them back to the impact upon the business. However, it is still potentially only one interpretation of the data out of many. Others may see the same data but come at it with different biases, objectives, or domain experience. Thus, to Sebastian Guttierez, a data-visualization expert, the role of an analyst presenting data through visualization is as a salesman. He told me, "You are trying to sell something: we should increase our budget, we should change our database, we should get more logs... At the end of the day, you have a message...I view sharing data or data visualization with non-data scientists or non-data analysts much more like a marketing exercise."

What are they selling? At least two things. First, if there are multiple interpretations, analysts must select and promote the most objective, logical, and *parsimonious* interpretation and demonstrate why they take this particular view. Second, if they've gone through all the effort to gather data, clean it, load it, understand and analyze it, perhaps build a model, and they've found something significant, something that can be used to impact the business, they want the potential impact that they have found to be realized. They should want to sell the *action*—what we should do—and the *outcome*—what will result if we do. (We will return to this theme in Chapter 9.) In other words, analysts should not be passive presenters of data, information, and findings but instead active salesmen of those ideas. Moreover, as Sebastian remarked, when you take a marketing perspective, and you have a message that you need to communicate, that should prompt you as an analyst to get more data if that is needed to provide a richer, more compelling fact-based story.

Importantly, the culture should be structured so that analysts are incentivized to have maximum impact. Ken Rudin, head of analytics at Facebook and previously at Zynga, exemplifies this:

> "Analytics is about impact…In our company [Zynga], if you have brilliant insight and you did great research and no one changes, you get zero credit."

Data Visualization

Now that we have a better understanding of what storytelling means and an analyst's role and motivations, let's switch gears and touch upon a few of the mechanics of data visualization. As mentioned at the beginning, this chapter is not meant to be a comprehensive guide or text on the subject. I'm going to provide a few pointers and tie those to some general remarks, typical errors that I see, and, yes, some of my pet peeves.

Assuming that an analyst has chosen appropriate metrics, appropriate dimensions (i.e., how the data has been sliced, say by month or by sales channel) and has found some interesting and significant pattern in those data, he next needs to select a way to present the data. In some cases, that might be a data table, but typically it will involve a chart.

Choosing a Chart

An analyst has a lot of choice in terms of chart types. The appropriate type of chart or visualization depends upon the type of variables (continuous, discrete, categorical, or ordinal), how many variables or factors one wants to incorporate into a single chart, and even the data values themselves. For instance, stacked bar charts can work well with two categories of data but fail miserably with a larger number (Figure 7-3).

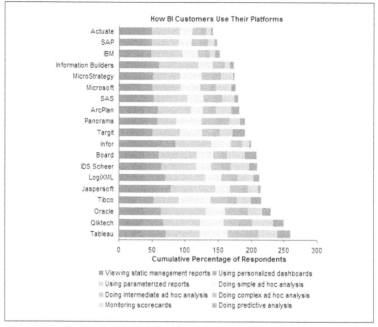

Figure 7-3. Example of a stacked bar chart (showing how BI customers use BI products) with a reasonably large number of categories (eight). The leftmost category is most easily compared among platforms because it is all aligned along the y-axis. For other categories, however, it becomes very hard to interpret because those data points vary in both width and offset. For example, how does the rightmost category vary among platforms? From Jon Peltier (http://bit.ly/peltier-stacked).

For comparison, Figure 7-3 is another view of that same data, one that is more easily comparable among platforms but at the expense of losing sense of the total cumulative percentage of respondents (i.e., total bar width in Figure 7-3).

Selecting a chart type is central in terms of the ability to get the story across to the viewer. So, how does one choose when there are so many? One way to categorize the many different chart types is to focus on four types of reason for that chart:

Comparisons
For example, how cohorts compare, how something changes with time

Distribution
To show the variability of a set of data

Relationships
To show correlations or associations among variables

Comparisons
To show how data is divided among two or more categories

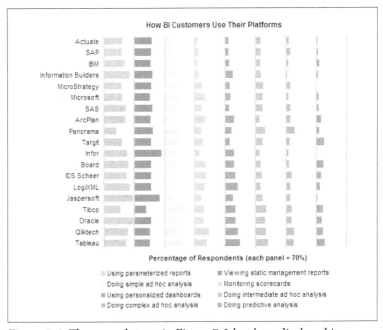

Figure 7-4. The same data as in Figure 7-3 but here displayed in a panel bar chart. Here, within-category comparisons are far easier to interpret. From Jon Peltier (http://bit.ly/peltier-stacked).

Figure 7-5 shows an example of the different types of charts and how they relate to those four objectives and guides. That figure covers the most common chart types, but there are many others. For instance, this doesn't cover social network or geospatial data. A more comprehensive diagram of chart types can be found in the Graphic Continuum (*http://bit.ly/graphic-continuum*), but that is too large and detailed to be reproducible and readable on a single page of this book. I would also suggest viewing the gallery of D3 visualizations (*http://bit.ly/d3-viz*). D3 is a popular JavaScript library that can be used for interesting, interactive, and more experimental or specialized visualizations.

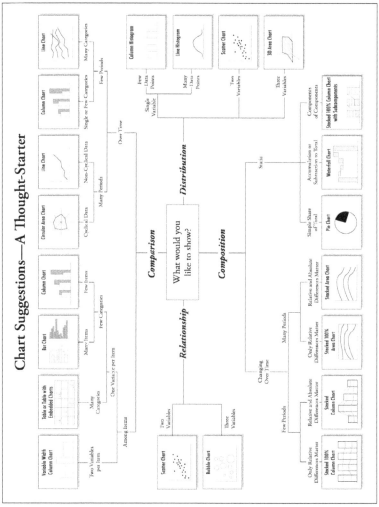

Figure 7-5. There are many types of charts, each of which is designed to meet a particular task. Choose the appropriate one to meet your needs. Created by Andrew Abela (http://bit.ly/abela-choosing). Reproduced with permission.

As you can see, for a given dataset, different chart types can be appropriate and yet work in different ways, each providing a different lens highlighting different characteristics of the data. The key is to experiment, to try out different ones. Search the "design space" to find the view that tells the strongest story but remains honest and objective. (For instance, don't truncate y-axes to distort the gradient of a line graph.[2])

Designing Elements of the Chart

Choosing a chart is a relatively easy task because it is a constrained choice (although it doesn't stop people from making inappropriate choices). However, it is just the beginning. The following box shows a checklist of a number of components that you should both consider and check your visual with a critical eye. Going through each of those items in detail is beyond the scope of this book. This is meant more as a signpost to get you started. I will, instead, refer you to the experts and the references given at the start of the chapter.

While many of the items in this checklist may seem obvious, it is surprising how many charts violate one or more of these criteria, leading to a suboptimal, less-effective visual.

Data Visualization Checklist

A data visualization has many components, each of which needs careful consideration. A single bad choice, such as low contrast colors, tiny font size, or the inappropriate chart choice, can render the whole visualization ugly, off-putting, and useless. The items in the following list are the headings from a very useful checklist from Stephanie Evergreen. See the complete checklist (*http://bit.ly/evergreen-checklist*) for full details about each line item.

Text
- 6-12 word descriptive title is left-justified in upper left corner.
- Subtitle and/or annotations provide additional information.
- Text size is hierarchical and readable.
- Text is horizontal.
- Data are labeled directly.
- Labels are used sparingly.

---

2 Fox, J., "The Rise of the Y-Axis-Zero Fundamentalists," (*http://bit.ly/fox-y-axis*) December 14, 2014.

Arrangement	• Proportions are accurate.
	• Data are intentionally ordered.
	• Axis intervals are equidistant.
	• Graph is two dimensional.
	• Display is free from decoration.
Color	• Color scheme is intentional.
	• Color is used to highlight key patterns.
	• Color is legible when printed in black and white.
	• Color is legible for people with colorblindness.
	• Text sufficiently contrasts background.
Lines	• Gridlines, if present, are muted.
	• Graph does not have border line.
	• Axes do not have unnecessary tick marks.
	• Graph has one horizontal and one vertical axis.
Overall	• Graph highlights significant finding or conclusion.
	• The type of graph is appropriate for data.
	• Graph has appropriate level of precision.
	• Contextualized or comparison data are present.
	• Individual chart elements work together to reinforce the overarching takeaway message.

Focusing the message

The purpose of creating a visual is to convey a message clearly. You have a number of "weapons" in the arsenal, such as fonts, gridlines, and orientation. Another is the use of highlight colors. One approach to focus the message and reader is to show only the data of interest. However, that can lead to data out of context. For instance, imagine that a chart showed that Japan generated 260 terawatt hours of power in 2009. Is that a lot? I have no idea. However, another approach is keep the focal data within context but use highlight color (Figure 7-6). Our eyes instantly pick out the Japan row through the use of the bold label and lighter color. However, the shape of the surrounding bars put its generation in context: it is high but less than one-third that of US production.

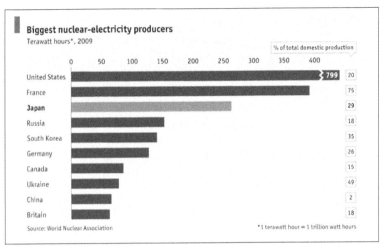

Figure 7-6. Example of good use of highlighting. For the Japan row, the label is emboldened and the bar is lighter, thus making it stand out yet remain in context. From http://bit.ly/economist-nuclear.

That was an example of adding to the chart to strengthen the message. Now for the opposite. You must avoid what Stephanie Evergreen calls going "Martha Stewart" on your chart, that is to say, overdecorating it. Keep it simple. You need to strip away any clutter, any excesses, to let the data and its message shine through.

Edward Tufte coined the term chartjunk to cover these visual distractions: "Chartjunk refers to all visual elements in charts and graphs that are not necessary to comprehend the information represented on the graph, or that distract the viewer from this information." Tufte takes it to an extreme, proffering a minimalist approach. I prefer Robert Kosara's more modern and pragmatic definition (*http://bit.ly/kosara-chartjunk*): "any element of a chart that does not contribute to clarifying the intended message." Kosara recognizes that you sometimes may need to add elements to the chart to highlight specific components to strengthen the core message or story.

It is at this juncture that many data visualization books pick on *USA Today* to exemplify chartjunk (including Tufte).[3] Instead, I will pick on the new gold standard: the NSA PRISM slides (Figure 7-7).

In Figure 7-7, we see a timeline of when different tech companies became part of the PRISM data-collection program. That's the core message, but it is diluted by lots of additional visual components. There are 11 logos at top. They relate to the yellow circles but not with a 1:1 match (there are only 9 yellow blobs) and are placed in an unstructured mass. They distract the reader. In addition, there is the NSA division logo as well as the program logo. Finally, there is the green arrow. What does that convey, and what does up mean? These are all chartjunk.

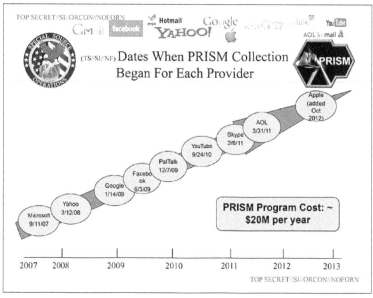

Figure 7-7. A chartjunk-ridden slide from the NSA PRISM program (http://bit.ly/nsa-prism-slides).

---

3 Do a Google image search for chartjunk, and you will see many *USA Today* examples. However, I would also suggest that the *New York Times Magazine*'s Analysis column is full of egregious examples, too.

Such embellishments draw your attention away from the core point in two ways:

- It gives viewers other things to spend time looking at and thinking about.
- It is harder for viewers to work out which is the thing that they should be looking at. They don't know where to focus.

Figure 7-8 shows one possible rework of that slide. This was created by Emiland De Cubber. Here, the slide is stripped down to the essentials: these are the companies and the dates at which they became part of the program. Nine logos and nine dates. Your eye can almost instantly survey the landscape, counting the number of companies per time point (1,1,3,1,2,1) and then on a second pass glance at the logos to see what those companies are. It is not perfect, but it is a significantly more effective visual than the original.

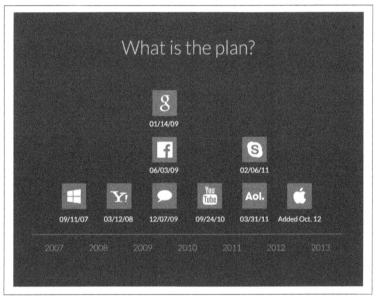

Figure 7-8. A rework of the PRISM slide by Emiland De Cubber (http://bit.ly/decubber-nsa-prism))

Organizing your data

The primary decision of how the data is organized within a chart will be determined by the chart choice and vice versa. Within the constraint of that chart choice there are still high-level structural choices, such as whether to set a bar chart horizontally or vertically. What I find fascinating is that even after this level, there are subtle changes in how the data is organized that can impact the message significantly.

Figure 7-9 shows average annual salary in UK government jobs by pay grade, broken out by gender.

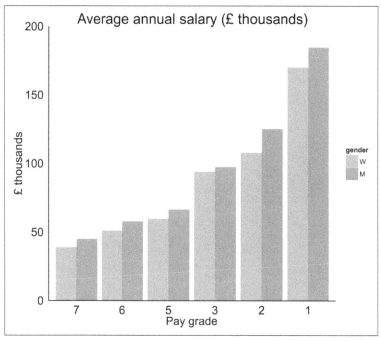

Figure 7-9. Average annual salary (in £ thousands) of UK government jobs by pay grade (lower numbers are more senior) and by gender. Data from http://bit.ly/bbc-pay-gap.

The chart looks OK. We have a clear title and axis labels. Pay grades are on the x-axis increase with seniority from left to right (although, confusingly, the pay grade number decreases with seniority), as one would expect, given our Western, left-to-right cultural bias. The y-axis looks good, too. There is no truncation. The choice of £25,000 increments seems appropriate. One does have a lot of choice with colors. Here I used blue (most often associated with boys) and the complementary color, orange, for women. These are good choices. There is nothing fundamentally wrong with this chart.

Now look what happens when you swap the order of male and female bars within each pay grade (Figure 7-10).

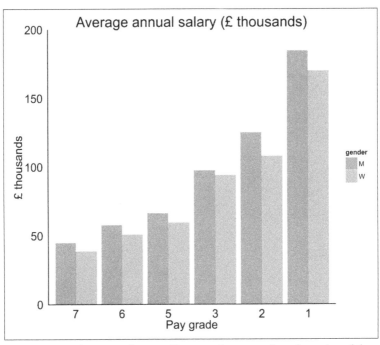

Figure 7-10. The same chart as Figure 7-9, except that the order of the genders within each pay grade is reversed. Does the pay inequality seem stronger?

The difference is remarkable. These are the same data, same axes, same box plots with the same color scheme. Yet this one small change completely changes how one perceives the gender inequality. [4] The central story, the inequality, is much more visible. There was nothing wrong with the first version; this second one is just enhanced.

This example demonstrates clearly, I think, that you really have to experiment with each and every chart that you create, that you have to train yourself to have a very critical eye. That comes with exposure and practice dissecting examples such as these. Thus, I would strongly recommend all analysts to pick up some of the books mentioned at the start of the chapter, study Kaiser Fung's trifecta

---

4 As Stephen Few explains it, our brain is wired to look for patterns, and we prefer simpler, smoother curves. From a computational perspective, they would be easier to encode. The second version, which is more jagged, commands our attention because we have to work harder to categorize its shape.

checkup (*http://bit.ly/fung-trifecta*), attend a data visualization class, and above all, practice. Examine the charts in the *Wall Street Journal*, *New York Times*, and *The Economist*, all of which set a very high bar. What makes them work, and where do they fail? (And they do fail at times.) Compare the charts in /r/dataisbeautiful/ (*http://bit.ly/r-data-beautiful*) versus r/dataisugly (*http://bit.ly/r-data-ugly*). What makes them beautiful and ugly, respectively? Ask yourself how would you do it differently.

Delivery

In this section, I dip into ways of delivering insights. First, I briefly cover infographics, which have become especially popular with marketing departments in recent years. Second, I cover the far more important topic of dashboards. As mentioned at the start of this book, many organizations believe that they are data-driven because they have lots of dashboards. They are certainly useful and prevalent. I'll cover several types of dashboards and discuss their utility (or not) in decision making.

Infographics

In a data-driven business context, I'm not a huge fan of infographics, meant in the modern sense of flashy, colorful visuals peppered with a few facts, typically created by designers rather than analysts. I find that they have a very low data-to-ink ratio (a term coined by Tufte) to capture the information density of a visual. In fact, most infographics have both lots of chartjunk and sparse data. For instance, Figure 7-11 is a fun and visually appealing display of brain size in different-sized animals.

But a more dense way of presenting that exact same data would be a bar chart or table:

Animal	Weight in grams (pounds)
Sperm whale	7,800 (17.2)
Dolphin	1,600 (3.5)
Human (adult)	1,400 (3)
...	...
Frog	0.24 (0.008oz)

Figure 7-11. Big Thinkers infographic from Rogers and Blechman (2014) Information Graphics: Animal Kingdom. Big Picture Press.

However, what is most interesting, the true story, is the ratio of brain size to body size. Thus, a chart that brings in that other dimension reveals one of the amazing findings out of comparative biology, a strong scaling law. Figure 7-12 shows brain size relative to body size decreases with increasing body size.[5]

I've deliberately chosen an extreme example here to make a point. The Big Thinkers infographic was part of a children's book and so was designed to be fun, informative, and memorable. It achieves its goal admirably. Generally, however, a data-driven organization will have little use for such infographics internally and certainly not for any decision making. Having said that, they do have their place. My team recently used one to give a "year in review" of our work at an all-hands meeting. The audience was diverse and mostly nontechnical, and the point was a quick scan of some of the year's highlights. Thus, the infographic format worked well in that situation, and it can also be useful to communicate externally to the public.

---

5 Both axes are logarithmic. It is not obvious at first glance but the x-axis has intervals of 100x while the y-axis has intervals of only 10x, so this is a very steep curve. Take the squirrel. That is about 10 gram brain/1 kilogram body. The whale, however, is about 10,000/10,000, which is only 1 gram brain/1 kilogram body. Note humans and dolphins, which are both far from the line, so they have relatively large brains *for their body size*, but still less (~5x) than a mouse.

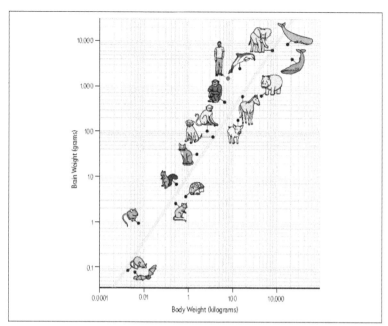

Figure 7-12. Brain size versus body weight. (Note the axes, both logarithmic but with 100× intervals on the x-axis but only 10× on the y-axis.) From Dongen, P.A.M. 1998. Brain Size in Vertebrates. In: The Central Nervous System of Vertebrates, Vol 3. Ed. by R. Nieuwenhuys et al., Springer.

Interestingly, recent research (*http://bit.ly/borkin-memorable*) found that chartjunk, pictograms, color, and contrast—all of which are prominent in infographics—made charts memorable. You were more likely to remember having seen the chart before. However, to reiterate the core message: the goal is communication to drive action. Decision makers need high-quality information that allows them not just to see and remember the point, but to evaluate it and be sure that the decision being made is right.

The viewer should understand the central point(s) that the data shows quickly and easily. Chartjunk hinders that.

Dashboards

Many organizations mistakenly measure their data-drivenness by the number of reports and dashboards they produce. Dashboards are very useful and can support a range of activities, such as providing an interface for data discovery and query drill down, alerts, and an accessible view or "face" to forecasts and predictive models.

We can think of dashboards as falling into three categories:

- Executive or strategic
- Analytical
- Operational

Executive dashboards (Figure 7-13) provide a very high-level view of the organization and typically focus on the scorecard (the KPIs and their targets). The dashboard should provide a quick and easy view as to whether the organization is meeting its targets and whether there is anything to be concerned about. In short, it should capture the pulse of the organization at the 50,000-foot level. The primary audience is senior management, but an enlightened data-driven organization will provide much broader access.

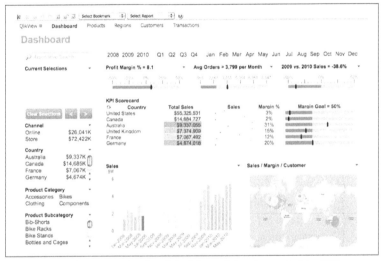

Figure 7-13. An executive-level dashboard, implemented in Qlik-View, showing sales KPIs versus region. Image from http://bit.ly/imaps-qlikview.

Analytical dashboards (Figure 7-14) take a lower level view, capturing key trends and metrics within one unit or particular facet of the business, such as the sales pipeline, marketing, or supply chain. Typically, these will be interactive, allowing the user to drill down into any unusual trends and outliers and to do data discovery work.

Their users are typically the analytics org and the managers of the business units.

Finally, operational dashboards (Figure 7-15) provide lower latency, more detailed views of very specific parts of the business, such as real time sales, web traffic, or customer service cases and phone call queues. Those typically have more of an alerting role for issues and are also used in a more responsive manner by staff who can take immediate actions, such as spin up more servers, switch staff from one task to another to reduce a backlog, or sell stock.

Figure 7-14. An example of an analytical dashboard for website visitors from Google Analytics.

With all of these types, the dashboards should be targeted. There should be a clear sense of who the users are and what they need to see. As in the previous section, the KISS principle (*http://bit.ly/kiss-principle*) (Keep it simple, Stupid!) applies: there should be a clear use case and compelling reason for each and every chart or number that appears in the dashboard. In other words, resist the temptation to add more and more views. As the dashboard becomes cluttered, it will become harder to read and to interpret and will become less effective. Less is more.

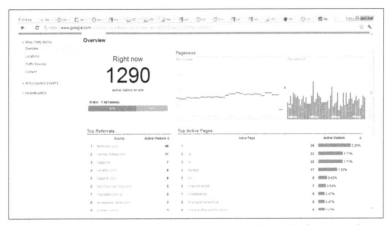

Figure 7-15. An example of an operational dashboard. This one, also from Google Analytics but showing a more detailed view than Figure 7-14, provides a near real-time view of website activity: where they are coming from, which pages they are going to, and at what rate. From http://bit.ly/naren-analytics.

However, as DJ Patil and Hilary Mason (*http://bit.ly/data-driven-report*) suggest, it can make sense to have multiple dashboards covering the same data but for different timescales or audiences. For instance, at One Kings Lane, the customer service associates answering the phones could view an operational dashboard on a wall-mounted monitor that showed key metrics, such as real-time call volume, response time, and case resolution. Their manager had access to that as well a more detailed analytical dashboard in which she could slice data by group, by individual, and by case type. In addition, the top-level metrics fed into the executive dashboards that senior management viewed throughout the day. Each of those was tailored to the target audience and use case.

In the context of this book, it is useful to examine whether dashboards are really used for decision making. As mentioned previously, operational dashboards show changes in (near) real time and are often configured to alert the end user to issues, who can then decide to act appropriately. For instance, if call center volume increases, a manager can direct resources from other tasks to help deal with the spike. However, analytical and executive dashboards, or at least their top-level views, are unlikely to be the sole information used for important decisions. One recent report (*http://bit.ly/aberdeen-holistic*) remarks:

> It is rare that a report or dashboard containing insightful information is the ultimate end only driver of a critical decision. More often than not, the end-user will find they ask the inevitable question, "why?" Why are sales down 30% in the northeast region? Why did sell-through of widget a skyrocket in Q4? With interactive drill-down capabilities that holistic BI users [i.e., tools in a data-driven organization] provide, these vital follow-up questions can be asked and answered in a timely way.

I will cover decision making in more detail in Chapter 9.

Monitoring use

A dashboard may have no value anyway, but it certainly cannot have any value if no one views it (even when viewed, it may have no value if no one changes because of it or takes action upon it). In a 2011 interview with Kevin Rose, Jack Dorsey (*http://bit.ly/rose-dorsey*), cofounder of Twitter and CEO of Square, mentioned an interesting idea that I hadn't heard before:

> We have a dashboard in Square and we have a metric "how many times do people actually look at that dashboard to see how the company is doing?" That speaks to how much people care about how the company is doing.

Of course, a data-driven org can instrument more than dashboard use. If reports are emailed to stakeholders from a server, you can probably turn on email read receipts and track open rate. Avinash Kaushik (*http://bit.ly/kaushik-empowering*) goes further and suggests "all automated reports are turned off on a random day/week/month each quarter to assess use/value."

Summary

This has been somewhat of a whirlwind tour of storytelling and data visualization. Once again, I refer you to the experts. What I hope to have conveyed is the importance of getting this right in a data-driven organization. A lot of work goes into getting to the point of having an analysis performed or an insight obtained; and too often, shoddy presentations bury what are interesting and important stories. Data presentation and visualization skills can be learned and honed by anyone and everyone and it is a really good investment for the analytics org.

In 1657, Blaise Pascal, the famous French mathematician and physicist, wrote in *Lettres Provinciales* (translated), "I have made this longer than usual because I have not had time to make it shorter." His point, of course, is that it requires time and effort to edit, to distill content down to its core, to convey the minimal, pertinent information to impart an idea. And so it is with data visualization and storytelling.

Stephanie Evergreen considers that the goals of presenting data are:

- To persuade others
- To frame thinking
- To drive to action

To do any of those, you need to remove chartjunk, to let the viewer know where to focus. However, you also need to make the viewer think as little as possible. Importantly, this doesn't mean dumb down the content.

First, start with a very clear understanding of the question that you are trying to answer, and a clear expectation of the audience, including their expectations and needs.

Second, choose your visual carefully so that it is both appropriate to the data and to maximize the signal that shines through.

Third, have one key message per visual, table, or slide. Feed the viewer in bite-sized chunks. In De Cubber's rework of the PRISM slides, he placed the timeline of data collection in one slide and the simple, single number of the $20 million price tag in a separate slide. In this way, both are easily consumed. I often see large financial data tables. They are typically crammed with data, a suite of financial metrics for each month over the last year with actuals and budgets, and month over month and year over year comparisons, and so on. There are many stories in that data, but they are all buried. Maybe one or two cells are highlighted, but your eye has to swim against a tide of cells to get to the row and column header cells to obtain the context. Instead, I would suggest that an analyst determines the story that she needs to tell and pick out those information morsels in individual slides. Boil it down to just the key information and interpretation. Give them a Michelin-star experience with a series of amuse-bouches.

Fourth, add useful signposts such as title, axis labels, and highlight colors (see the earlier checklist) to provide the necessary context.

Further, format them to make them easily consumable. For instance, avoid requiring viewers to tilt their heads to read vertical text or having to squint to read text with tiny fonts.

Fifth, remove any mental steps or calculations that the viewer would need to perform to make the connection or obtain the underlying message in the data. One example is having a legend far away from the bars of a bar chart and requiring the viewer to do what Stephanie calls "mental gymnastics" to associate the label, and hence meaning, to the bars and their values. Another example hen comparing bars, this time from Stephen Few, is what he calls deviation analysis. Imagine a bar chart showing actual versus budget for a set of departments. If the core message is the delta between each pair, then you are asking the viewers to mentally compute the difference. An approach that makes it quicker and easier to consume is to do the math for them and show the set of deltas and not the original pairs of bars. Focus on what you want to show, what you want the viewers to take away from the visuals, and then put yourself in the shoes of the viewers: what do they need to do to receive that message? Strip away any tasks that require effort on the part of the viewer.

If you do all of these—lead the viewer/reader through a single or series of simple pieces of information and insights—you will have a more direct and compelling visual that conveys your core message effectively and unambiguously.

This concludes the trio of chapters around metrics, analysis, and presentation, which are the "meat" of an analyst's role. In the next chapter, I cover an important aspect of a data-driven organization's culture, which is testing. That is, setting up a more "Prove it!" culture in which ideas are tested under real circumstances with real customers, thereby providing the most direct possible evidence about the impact of a proposed change or new feature.

CHAPTER 8

A/B Testing

He who consistently uses #abtesting to make data-driven decisions
has invariably been humbled by the poor success rate of ideas.
—Ron Kohavi

I've come to terms with the fact that the point of experiments, data, and
testing, isn't for me to be right...I needed the information from these
tests to get to the right answer, eventually.
—PJ McCormick[1]

It was 1998, and Greg Linden, one of Amazon's early engineers, had
an idea. Why not create recommendations on checkout? Supermarkets put candy at the checkout aisle to stimulate impulse buys. That
works. Why not peek into the Amazon.com cart and make personalized, relevant recommendations that the customer might appreciate? He hacked up a prototype, got it working, and showed it
around. The rest of the story is best told in his own words:

> While the reaction was positive, there was some concern. In particular, a marketing senior vice-president was dead set against it. His
> main objection was that it might distract people away from checking out—it is true that it is much easier and more common to see
> customers abandon their cart at the register in online retail—and
> he rallied others to his cause.

---

1 "PJ McCormick, Challenging Data Driven Design, WarmGun 2013," (*http://bit.ly/*
mccormick-challenging) November 27, 2013, video clip, YouTube.

At this point, I was told I was forbidden to work on this any further. I was told Amazon was not ready to launch this feature. It should have stopped there.

Instead, I prepared the feature for an online test. I believed in shopping cart recommendations. I wanted to measure the sales impact.

I heard the SVP was angry when he discovered I was pushing out a test. But, even for top executives, it was hard to block a test. Measurement is good. The only good argument against testing would be that the negative impact might be so severe that Amazon couldn't afford it, a difficult claim to make. The test rolled out.

The results were clear. Not only did it win, but the feature won by such a wide margin that not having it live was costing Amazon a noticeable chunk of change. With new urgency, shopping cart recommendations launched.

Greg was lucky. Not so much because it worked (that is, of course, significant), but because even back then Amazon had enough testing infrastructure and data-driven culture for him to be able to roll out a test. He was able to prove its value, roll it out, and impact the bottom line.

In many situations, especially those that are novel, our intuition or gut instinct is poor. We are often surprised by results. Don't believe me? Let's look at a few quick examples from online experiments. The first is a call to action in an ad. In terms of click-through rate (CTR), which won, and by how much?

- Get $10 off the first purchase. Book online now!
- Get an additional $10 off. Book online now.

The answer is that the second version won with a CTR double that of the first version.[2] OK, how about the pair in Figure 8-1? (Can you even spot the difference?) Which won and by how much?

The version at left, grammatically correct by the addition of a single comma, won by 8%.

---

[2] Gabbert, A., "The Importance of A/B Testing: 24 Marketing Experts on Their Most Surprising A/B Test," (*http://bit.ly/ws-ab-testing*) September 25, 2012.

<table>
<tr><td>How to Write a Book, Fast</td><td>How to Write a Book Fast</td></tr>
<tr><td>14 Days from Start to Finish</td><td>14 Days from Start to Finish</td></tr>
<tr><td>Unique, Step By Step Program</td><td>Unique. Step By Step Program</td></tr>
<tr><td>Write-A-Book-Faster.com</td><td>Write-A-Book-Faster.com</td></tr>
</table>

Figure 8-1. Which of these versions performed better in terms of CTR? The grammatically correct version on the left had an 8% higher CTR (4.4% versus 4.12%). Ibid.

Finally, the last example (Figure 8-2) consists of two almost identical versions of a page except in the right, all the form fields are optional. That version led to a 31% higher conversion rate. Moreover, the quality of those leads was *higher*.

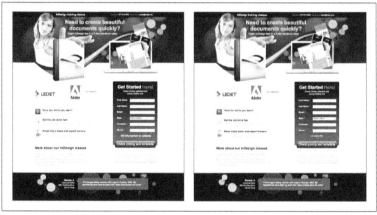

Figure 8-2. In the version at left, all form fields are optional while in the version at right, all fields are required. The former led to 31% higher conversions, and moreover had higher quality leads. Image from http://bit.ly/optional-vs-required, copyright protected.

In all these examples, it would have been hard to predict which won, harder to predict by how much, and hard to predict the impact on other metrics. This is why well-designed experimentation is so valuable. It switches the conversation from "I think..." to "The data shows..." Thus, this is an invaluable component of a data-driven organization.

Let's put this into perspective. In Chapter 5, we covered types of analysis, including causal analysis, the effective pinnacle at least in terms of a typical business. Controlled experimentation, the application of the scientific method or "data scientific methods,"[3] is the direct way to get at those causal relationships.

The three examples discussed were instances of a type of experiment called an A/B test. The following is a crude description of such a test. There are many missing caveats and details that I will fill in later in this chapter, but this lays out the basic idea. In an A/B test, you set up a control, such as current state of your website (the A-variant). You send half your website traffic to that version. Those visitors are the "A" group. The other half are sent to another version of the site with some change, say the checkout button says "purchase" rather than "buy now" (the B-variant). Those visitors are the "B" group. You determine what you are testing, the success metric: say, does the button text impact average revenue per visitor? You run the experiment for a predetermined number of days or weeks, and then you run a statistical analysis. You analyze whether there was a statistically significant difference in the focal behavior—in this example, revenue per visitor—between the A-group and the B-group. If there is a difference, what's the cause? Well, if everything was controlled (i.e., was the same except for this one small change), there are two possibilities. It could be due to random chance, which can happen if the sample size is too small (i.e., the experiment is "under-powered"). Alternatively, the change between the A- and B-variant was the causal factor. The data shows that this feature caused this change in behavior.

Because active, objective experimentation and the cultural implications that go with it are such a crucial aspect of a data-driven organization, this chapter will overview what A/B testing is. It will encompass both the more common "classical" frequentist approach as well as the more modern Bayesian approach, both of which I'll describe. I'll detail how to implement tests, covering best practices of how to do it and how not to do it. In addition to the examples described earlier, I'll provide a number of examples that will highlight why we need it and the significant impact that it can make to a business. With that, let's get started.

---

3 Patil, DJ, and H. Mason. *Data Driven: Creating a Data Culture*. Sebastopol, CA: O'Reilly, 2015.

Why A/B Test?

As mentioned, our intuition can be very poor (something that is touched upon in greater detail in Chapter 9). Even domain experts get it wrong more often that they would like to admit. In his book *A/B Testing: The Most Powerful Way To Turn Clicks Into Customers* (Wiley & Sons), Dan Siroker, CEO and cofounder of the A/B testing platform Optimizely, tells of his time during the 2008 Obama campaign. They set out to optimize the supporter signup page, the hook designed to gather people's emails. The original page was a "Get involved" static image with a red button that said "SIGN UP." The team thought that videos of the most powerful speeches would outperform that static image. After testing various static images and different videos, they discovered that "*every* video dramatically underperformed *every* image." The best combination of image and signup button text (the best was "LEARN MORE") improved signups by 40.6%. That translated to 2.8 more million email subscribers, 280,000 more volunteers, and a staggering additional $57 million dollars in donations. You often just can't tell in advance what will work—humans are just messy, fickle, and unpredictable—and by how much. However, with results like this, it is easy to see that this can convey significant competitive advantage and inform you about your actual users, customers, and prospects in a direct, tangible way.

Moreover, online testing is relatively cheap and easy. It doesn't necessarily take a lot of development or creative time to create a new version of a button that says "LEARN MORE" rather than "SIGN UP." It is also not permanent. If you try something and it doesn't work, roll back to the original, and you've learned a lesson about your customers. It is relatively low risk.

You can also test just about everything. Whatever your industry, there are always optimizations to be made and lessons to be learned. The Obama campaign team tested very heavily. They tested email subject lines, email content, timing and frequency of email sends, all aspects of the website, even the scripts that volunteers used to talk to potential donors. As this last example shows, such testing is not restricted to the online world. A second offline example is the "surprise and delight" marketing campaigns that some companies engage in where they send, out of the blue, a gift to some subset of customers. Those should be run as carefully crafted experiments. One can compare metrics such as return rate, lifetime value, or even positive social media word of mouth (such as tweets) between those who received the gift and, importantly, a comparable set of customers who did not. In all these cases, they should be treated with exactly the same degree of scientific rigor and structured in the same manner as an online A/B experiment.

One of the nice things about A/B testing is that you don't have to have an *a priori* causal explanation of why something should work; you just need to test, explore, and find those improvements that make a positive impact. Kohavi remarks that at Amazon, half of the experiments failed to show improvements, and at Microsoft, it was two thirds.[3] You don't need every experiment to work in order to win in the long term. A single improvement can make a huge difference to the bottom line.

How To: Best Practices in A/B Testing

With that background into the appeal and benefit of A/B testing, let us switch gears and look at details and best practices of how to do it well.

Before the Experiment

In this section, I cover a number of aspects of experimental design, that is, what should be done before the experiments runs. The first, and most important, aspect is to define your success metrics. I then cover something called A/A tests, which are important for testing your apparatus but can also be used to generate a few false positives and inform your bosses and colleagues about statistical significance and the importance of a sufficiently large sample size. I then cover a detailed A/B test plan (what are we testing, who is part of the test, what analyses will be performed, etc.). Finally, I cover a crucial aspect, and typically the #1 question asked by beginners: what is the required sample size?

---

3 Kohavi, R., "Planning, Running, and Analyzing Controlled Experiments on the Web," (*http://bit.ly/kohavi-planning*), June 2012.

Success metrics

Best practice: clearly define the success metrics before the test starts.

It is important to have a clear understanding of the objective and the treatment(s). Why are we doing this? It is especially important to define the key metrics, sometimes called the "overall evaluation criterion," before the test starts. What defines success? If you don't, you may be tempted to instrument the test as much as possible, and collect lots of data, but when it comes to analysis, there is strong chance of "fishing," which is statistically testing everything and jumping on significant results. Worse, there is a chance of cherry picking, which is just reporting the metrics and results that look good. These approaches are only going to get you into trouble and are not going to deliver long-term value to the organization.

A/A tests

Best practice: run A/A tests.

If A represents the control group, then, as you might imagine, an A/A test pits a control group against another control group, both of which are encountering the same website experience. What, you might ask, is the value of that? There are several benefits.

First, you can use it to test and keep tabs on your testing infrastructure and assignment processes. If you set your system to split traffic 50/50 but you encounter very different samples sizes in the two groups, then it indicates that something is wrong in the assignment process.

Second, if you see comparable samples sizes but very different performance metrics, that can indicate a problem in event tracking, analytics, or reporting. However, we should expect to see significant differences in A/A tests about 5% of the time, assuming that you use the standard 5% significance level. Thus, differences in A/A tests are to be expected. What you need to track is, over the course of many A/A tests, whether you are seeing significant differences at a *rate* greater than your significance level. If so, that can indicate an issue. However, Georgi Georgiev (*http://bit.ly/georgiev-tests*) makes a good point that "Even if you only need 500 or a 100 A/A tests to observe statistically significant deviations from the expected results, it's still a huge waste of money. Simply because impressions, clicks and visitors aren't for free, not to mention what you could have been doing with that traffic." You should be running lots and lots of A/B tests, constantly innovating. However, if you don't have a constant stream and there is testing downtime, you may as well run A/A tests.

Third, you can use the results of the test to estimate the variability of your metric in your control. In some sample size calculations, such as when testing the mean of a value (say, average basket size or time on site), you will need that value to compute the sample size.

Finally, the Nelio A/B Testing blog (*http://bit.ly/nelio-aa-testing*) remarks that there is a cultural, educational benefit to running A/A tests. For those organizations, end users, and decision makers new to A/B testing, especially those that are less well versed in the underlying probability and statistical theory, it serves a useful lesson. Don't jump the gun in an A/B test and assume that a treatment must be better than the control even when results are significant. A statistically significant result can still occur from chance effects alone, and the greatest evidence of that is an A/A test.

A/B test plan

Best practice: think through the whole test before you run it.

There is a lot to think about when setting up a test. I would suggest that organizations starting to ramp up an A/B testing culture ask the stakeholders to think through all of the following before the test runs. You don't want discussions on the success metrics after the test is live. You don't want anyone gaming the system during analysis. Front load all the discussion and agreement.

Goal:

- What is the goal of this test?

Ownership:

- Who is the primary business owner?
- Who is in charge of implementation?
- Who is the business analyst?

Experimental design:

- What are the treatments and control (i.e., the experiences)?
- What are your control and treatment groups (i.e., the people)?

- What are your null and alternative hypotheses?[3]
- What metrics will be tracked?
- When is the period for discussion and feedback?
- When will the test start?
- Is there a burn-in period? If so, at what date do you consider the experiment started for analytical purposes?
- How long will the test run?
- How was the sample size determined?

Analysis:

- Who will perform the analysis? (Ideally, there will be a separation between those who create the experiment and those who evaluate it.)
- What analysis will be performed?
- When will the analysis start?
- When will the analysis be complete?
- What software will be used to perform the analysis?

Output:

- How will the results be communicated?
- How will the final decision be made?

This seems a long list, but as you run more and more tests, some of these answers will become standardized. For instance, the answers might be, "We always use R for analysis," or "It is Sarah's job to perform the statistical analysis." This set of questions will get internalized into the culture, and the process will become more automated and streamlined until it is second nature.

As I've described it so far, the experimental procedure and analysis is very clean, almost clinical and robotic—test A versus B, whichever wins, roll it out. If it were like this, it would be completely data-driven. However, the world is more complex that. There are other factors at play. First, results are not always clear-cut. There can be ambiguity. Maybe the treatment's metric was consistently higher

---

3 Null hypothesis is your base assumption that there is no difference (e.g., click-through rate (CTR) of control = CTR of treatment). The alternative hypothesis is what you fall back on if you reject the null hypothesis. This can be one of three types: CTR control != CTR treatment; CTR control > CTR treatment; or CTR control < CTR treatment. Stick to a two-sided alternative (i.e., !=) unless you have very good reasons to choose a directional alternative (i.e., > or <).

throughout the test but not significantly so; maybe there was a trade-off between factors (say, sales volume and conversion); or maybe, during analysis, you discovered a possible element of bias. All of these can muddy the analysis and interpretation. Such ambiguity is reality. Second, an individual experiment doesn't necessarily capture a longer-term strategy being played out. PJ McCormick (*http://bit.ly/mccormick-challenging*) discusses an example of this at Amazon. He describes an A/B test where the control, the current experience, was a tiny product image so small the user could not see the product well. The treatment was simply a larger product image. No-brainer, you would think. The smaller image, the one so small you could not see what you were clicking on, won out! Instead, they decided to go with the larger product image. Why?

> We launched the larger version because customers could see the product. It was a better experience. Furthermore, it aligns where we want to take our experience in the long term. It aligns with our vision. Data can't think long term for you. It doesn't make decisions. It is information that you need to inform your thinking. But if you make knee-jerk reactions without thinking more about what these numbers mean, and then balancing that with the long term vision that you have for your product, or for your users, you're going to make the wrong decisions.[3]

(Decision making is the subject of the next chapter.)

Sample size

Best practice: use a sample-size calculator.

By far the most common question I am asked concerning A/B tests is, "How long do I need to run this for?" My typical answer is, "I don't know, we'll have to calculate it using a sample-size calculator."

 This section is a little more technical than others, and those terrified of statistics can safely skip this section. The bottom line is that you need to calculate the minimal sample sizes using a simple, online statistical tool, and you need to stick to those sample sizes. You can't cut experiments off early and expect meaningful results.

---

[3] This does beg the question: why test? If a test outcome is not going to drive an action, is this a valuable use of time and effort?

The reason that it is not simple to answer is that there are multiple effects that we are trying to optimize.

Imagine that we run a typical A/B test. There are four possible scenarios:

There is no actual, underlying difference between the control and treatment, and:

1. We conclude *correctly* that there is no difference.
2. We conclude *incorrectly* that there is a difference. This is a false positive.

Or, there is an actual difference between the control and treatment:

3. We conclude *incorrectly* that there is no difference. This is a false negative.
4. We conclude *correctly* that there is a difference.

This is summarized here:

		Truth	
		No difference	*Is a difference*
Your findings	*No difference*	1) Correct	3) False negative
	Is a difference	2) False positive	4) Correct

We want to try to maximize our chance of making the correct conclusion (1 or 4) and minimize the chance of making either a false positive (2) or false negative (3).

We have two levers that we can use.

The first lever is the more obvious sample size. If you were running an exit poll for a presidential election, you would be more confident in your results if you asked 500,000 voters than if you asked 5,000. Likewise in an A/B test. Having a larger sample size increases your "power," a statistical term, to detect a difference if there is a difference. Looking back to our four possibilities, if there is an underlying difference, larger samples reduce the chance of false negatives (i.e., more likely to conclude 4 than 3). Typically, we use a power of 0.8. That means we will be 80% likely to detect a difference if there is a difference. Keep this in mind, and we'll come back to it in just a second.

The second lever we have is statistical significance, typically set at 5%.[3] (For massive scale, a good approach is to pick $p \leq 10^{-4}$.) This means the acceptable chance of making a false positive if there is no actual difference between treatment and control. Imagine that we had an unbiased coin, but we did not know whether it was unbiased or not. We toss it 10 times, and it comes up heads 10 times. That seems highly biased toward heads. However, an unbiased coin could still come up with 10 heads but only 1 in 1,024 times, or about 0.1%. If we conclude it was biased, we do so at a risk of being wrong of 0.1%. That seems an acceptable risk. Next, imagine we decide that if we see 8, 9, or 10 heads, or the opposite extreme 0, 1, or 2 heads, we will conclude it is biased. That has a chance of being wrong of about 11%. That seems too risky. The point is that we need to strike a balance between the strength of evidence that the treatment does have a real effect versus the chance that we are just observing random effects (given there is no underlying difference).

OK, armed with our criteria of power = 0.8 and significance level = 0.05, we head to a sample-size calculator (Figure 8-3). Here you enter those two values (see bottom of the figure), but you also need to provide some additional information. In this sample-size calculator (one optimized for conversion events, such as checkout for website visit), it asks for the baseline conversion rate. This means the current rate in your control. It also asks what is the minimum detectable effect. This means if there is a really big underlying effect of the treatment, say 7%, you are probably going to spot it straight away, and you can get away with a small sample size. If you want to detect a smaller difference, say 1%, then you are going to need a larger sample size to be really sure you have a real effect and not chance effects. For 10% conversion rate and 1% difference, you are going to need 28,616 subjects: 14,313 in the control and the same number in the treatment.

There are different sample-size calculators for different situations. For instance, if you are comparing means, say, average basket size in the control versus the treatment, there is a similar calculator but with slightly different input requirements, such as baseline variability. See *http://bit.ly/brant-calculator*.

---

3 Why 5%? It is most associated with a single sentence in a 1925 paper from R. A. Fisher, but in reality, the story starts with F. W. Bessel in 1818. I summarized the story on my blog (*http://bit.ly/anderson-bessel*).

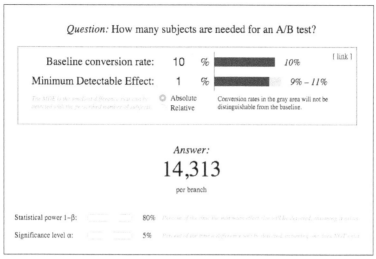

Figure 8-3. A sample-size calculator for conversion events, from http://bit.ly/miller-calculator.

You can use average daily traffic divided by the total sample size to get an estimate of the number of days to run the experiment.

I should stress that these sample sizes are *minimal* sample sizes. Suppose that your sample size calculation and traffic rates indicated that you needed to run your experiment for four days. If you happen to have lower than average traffic over those four days, you must continue the experiment until those minimal sample sizes are met. If you don't extend the experiment or if you cut any experiment off early, you are going to underpower your experiment. This will result in an elevated false negative rate: you are not able to detect differences that exist. Moreover, if you do see a positive result, it increases the chance that it is not real (see "Most Winning A/B Test Results Are Illusory" (*http://bit.ly/goodson-winning*)). That is a really important effect. You'll see a positive effect, you celebrate, roll that treatment feature out to production, but then fail to see a lift. You've wasted time, effort, and trust.

We now have our sample sizes. Or do we? If you ran the experiment for four days, from Monday to Thursday, would you expect the same effect, the same demographics of visitors and online behavior than if you ran it from Friday to Monday? In many cases, no, they differ. There is a day-of-the-week effect; weekend visitors and behavior are often different from weekdays. Thus, if the sample-size calculator says four days, it is often advised to run it for seven days to capture a complete week. If the sample size calculator says 25 days, run it for four weeks.

As you can see, determining sample size is important. If you try to get away with a smaller-than-necessary sample size, you are likely to be subject to false results, ones that indicate an effect but that will fail to materialize extra revenue. Or you will fail to identify real treatment effects and thus lose out on potential revenue. Clearly, both of these are undesirable. Finally, the underlying math of those sample size calculators is tricky. It is hard to estimate well without these. Use the tools available.

Running the Experiment

Assuming that you have the treatments implemented and the site instrumented to collect the data that you need, the issues of assigning individuals and starting and stopping the test still remain.

Assignment

Best practice: roll treatment out to 50% of eligible users and ensure constancy.

In assigning individuals to groups, the first question to address is which visitors are eligible to be in the experiment at all. It is possible that some visitors may be excluded from the experiment completely. That is, for many A/B tests, one's source population is the complete website traffic, or all visitors. However, you may be interested only in a certain subset of the visitors. Those might be returning customers only, or customers from a particular geography or demographic, or only those in a particular membership tier. It depends on the treatment and its target audience. Those entry criteria need to be well defined.

That subset represents the totality of who could be sent to the control or treatment. The next question is to address how many of those should be sent to the treatment. Ideally, one splits the traffic 50/50, but that is not always the case. Kohavi et al. (*http://bit.ly/kohavi-controlled*) remark that "one common practice among novice experimenters is to run new variants for only a small percentage of users." They suggest that these practitioners do so acting in a risk-averse manner, to limit exposure if there is a problem with the treatment. However, they argue that this is bad practice because experiments will have to run longer. Tests have to meet a minimum sample size in both the control and treatment, and so if traffic to the treatment is limited to, say, only 10%, clearly it is going to take significantly longer to reach that required sample size. They suggest that one should "ramp up" the experiment, increasing the proportion of traffic sent to the treatment over time (discussed later) to limit risk but ultimately reach 50% traffic being diverted to the treatment.

There must be a reliable mechanism to assign visitors to the control or to the treatment. That is, users must be assigned to the control (or treatment) both randomly and consistently. In terms of random, there should be no bias. Assuming a desired 50/50 split, they should be equally likely to end up in each variant. One approach is to use a good random-number generator, preassign users to a variant, and store which variant they belong to in some database table or perhaps a cookie. The UI can then serve up the correct experience based on a database lookup on login. This can work well in sites where all users are authenticated. Another approach is to assign users on the fly. However, we require that the user is consistently assigned to the same variant on multiple visits to the site. Thus, for that, we require a deterministic assignment process. For instance, one could apply a mod or suitable hash function to each customer's ID. (Kohavi et al. discuss different protocols for consistent assignment in detail.) Providing a consistent experience for the user is important. Having a user switch variants will be confusing for them and muddy the data and its analysis.

Even with consistent experience, confusion can arise. Imagine an *existing* customer who is assigned to the treatment and is arriving at the modified site for the first time. He has expectations from his last visit, and it can take him longer to navigate the new experience. However, a new visitor has no such expectations and can be less confused. Such so-called "primacy effects" can be significant and is something to dig into during analysis.

Starting the test

Best practice: ramp up the users to 50%.

When you start a test, you can flip the switch and divert 50% of your traffic to the treatment. The problem is that if there are any major software bugs, and you present customers with a mangled, broken experience, you are likely to drive those customers away, and you've exposed 50% of your site traffic to that experience. Instead, you can take a more risk-averse approach and do a slower ramp up, monitoring the metrics carefully. Ronny Kohavi (*http://bit.ly/kohavi-controlled-tutorial*) suggests the following schedule:

- 1% in treatment for 4 hours.
- 5% in treatment for 4 hours (i.e., switch an additional 4% from control to treatment).
- 20% in treatment for 4 hours.
- 50 % in treatment for the remainder of experiment.

Of course, if you do see an issue, it is important that there is an abort button that can be hit, a way to kill the experiment immediately and divert all the traffic back to the control.

When do you stop?

Best practice: run the experiment until minimal sample size has been achieved, or longer.

I went through the section on determining sample size in detail because it has significant consequences. If you underpower an experiment, you are going to increase the error rate. You will overlook real, positive treatment effects that could drive incremental revenue, and you will mistake chance effects as treatments effects (i.e., you will roll out a feature that has no real impact). In short, you will be subject to more false negatives and false positives. Never cut short an experiment because things are looking good for a treatment.

It is very unfortunate that many of the A/B testing vendors encourage users to run experiments until significance is achieved. *Never run a test like this!* (Can you tell that I view this as being really really important?) Citing four vendors, Martin Goodson (*http://bit.ly/goodson-winning*) remarks, "Some software for A/B testing is designed in such a way that it's natural to constantly monitor the results of a test, stopping the test as soon as a significant result is achieved. Alarmingly, false positives can comprise as much as 80% of winning test results when tests are performed in this way." (See also "How Not To Run An A/B Test" (*http://bit.ly/miller-how-not*).)

Once you have ramped up the experiment and you are confident that there are no egregious issues, the best advice is to do it the Ronco way: "Set it and forget it." Monitor sample sizes over time but not the evaluation metrics.

Other Approaches

Here I briefly touch upon two other approaches that can be used in addition to or instead of simple A/B or A/A testing.

Multivariate Testing

So far, I have discussed paired (two sample) tests only, one control with either one treatment (A/B) or another control (A/A). That experimental design is very simple yet very effective. However, there are some drawbacks. Recall the Obama campaign story earlier where they tested different submit button text and different images. Because they had five different button texts and at least six different images, there were at least thirty different combinations. To test all those combinations sequentially means thirty times as long as a single A/B test. It is for this reason that multivariate tests are sometimes used.

Also known as multivariable or factorial tests, these tests run different combinations (or "recipes") simultaneously. Thus, group 1 will be exposed to image1 and text1, group 2 to image2 and text2, all the way to group 30, exposed to image6 and text5.

What are the pros and cons of such a design? If you have sufficiently high traffic and can afford to split it among the different combinations, you can run the tests in parallel and thus in a shorter duration. (YouTube, which obviously has huge traffic, conducted an experiment (*http://bit.ly/yt-multivariate*) in 2009 involving a staggering 1,024 combinations. The best combination resulted in a 15% increase in signups.) You can also test so-called interaction effects. Maybe a larger submit button does better than a normal-sized button, and a red submit button does better than a blue button, but when you combine the two, a large red submit button does amazingly well, better than large alone and better than red alone.

Not all combinations will make sense and can or should be tested. Imagine the first factor to be tested was making a checkout button red (current state) versus black (treatment). Now imagine the second factor was having the button text black (current state) versus white (treatment). This generates four combinations, but the black/black combination is just not going to work. Or, as Kohavi et al. suggest, on a product page, a larger product image plus additional product information may be a poor combination because it pushes the purchase button too far down the page, below the fold. These effects should be caught at the design stage and should not be tested.

Even when you have a complete set of combinations that make sense, it is possible to get away with running a subset of those combinations. These are known as partial or fractional factorial experiments. They consist of a very carefully selected subset of combinations that allow one to get at a reasonable estimate of the main effects as well as the interaction effects. However, they are more complex to design and don't provide the level of information that a full multivariate design or sequential set of A/B tests provide. If you do run multivariate tests, favor exploring more factors (i.e, different types of things to tests such as images and button text) than levels (number of different variants within a factor, for example, five different button texts). Also, you will need to go "all in" and roll this out to 100% of your traffic to maximize sample size and statistical power.

Analysis of multivariate test results is, unsurprisingly, more complex. One needs more advanced statistical tools (such as analysis of variance or ANOVA) compared to A/B tests, and it is harder to visualize the results.

In summary, multivariate testing allows you to explore "design space" or other aspects of your business more rapidly and also test for interaction effects (although Kohavi et al. argue that they are not that prevalent). However, this increased power comes at a cost of increased complexity of setting up, running, and analyzing tests and is only viable with sufficiently high traffic to retain statistical power.

Bayesian Bandits

The A/B testing approach described so far in this chapter, and which is more common and popular "in the wild," comes under classical or "frequentist" statistics. However, there is another approach—one that has increased in popularity over recent years as computational power has increased—called Bayesian statistics (*http://bit.ly/parker-bayesian*).

In a frequentist approach, one starts with a hypothesis, say that the click-through rate of the control experience is the same as the click-through rate of the experiment experience. You gather data and essentially ask, "What is the likelihood of seeing these results (or more extreme) if that hypothesis were true and we ran this experiment many, many times?" It assumes that the state of the world is constant, that we draw probabilistically from a distribution but that distribution and its parameters don't change over time.

A Bayesian approach is different. It starts with a prior belief. What do I know about this system? Maybe you have never tested this type of treatment before, so you start with a simple naive guess. Maybe you've done a previous experiment with a similar treatment. You are allowed to use that information as a starting point. Your prior beliefs are actually not that important because you will update these over time as you gather more evidence. Even if it is wrong, it should evolve toward the correct state of the world. That is the key difference from frequentism. Each piece of data collected—a view, sale, or a click—is additional evidence that you should incorporate into your knowledge. It is very iterative. Moreover, instead of asking, "Is there a difference?," it asks, "Which is the better out of the control or treatment?"; and that, ultimately, is what the business wants to know.

If you were wondering about the term "bandits," it comes from making an analogy with slot machines, also called one-armed bandits. The idea here is that we have multiple bandits (the control and treatments), each of which has a different payout frequency (underlying click-through rate). We want to determine the best bandit (highest click-through rate) but only can do so by a series of pulls (exposures). Because each pays out stochastically, we have to balance pulling potentially poorer-performing bandits to get more information versus pulling only on what we think is the best bandit to maximize payoff.

The system will change the proportion of users seeing the better experience over time. Crudely, we might start out with a 50% control and 50% treatment. Let's suppose that the treatment is *really* good (we are seeing lots more clicks per treatment view than per control view), so the system decreases the proportion going to the control and increases those going to the treatment. So now we have 40% control and 60% treatment. We continue to see great performance in the treatment, so we up its percentage—now it's 30% control and 70% treatment, and so on. This has two impacts. First, we don't need to run any analysis to understand which is better. We can look at the relative proportions. Second, because we run the better experience longer, we realize or benefit from that increased lift immediately. (In statistical terms, we don't have the "regret" or loss of running the known poorer experience for the duration of an experiment.)

Unlike the frequentist approach, we are allowed to peek and observe the changing system over time, and there is no fixed duration; we can run and run the experiment indefinitely. In fact, we can throw in new treatments, remove treatments, and modify treatments, all of which are not allowed in a frequentist approach. We keep running it or provide some stopping criterion: if treatment is 5% better than control, declare it the winner and divert 100% of traffic to it.

Obviously I have glossed over a lot of mathematical details, the meat of which is the update rule, or how the probabilities are changed. The system is actually designed to go through a period of *exploration*, where you try out all the different controls and treatments with the relative frequencies, and then *exploitation*, where you hit the current winner hard (which minimizes the regret). This Bayesian approach will also suffer the same issues as the frequentist approach: a winning streak for the treatment could be due to a fundamental better rate, or it could be due to chance effects. If it were due to chance, then later treatment exposures would likely generate a lower click-through rate, and the treatment proportion would be ratcheted down by the update rule. This does mean that such a system cannot guarantee consistency of experience per user, or at least for returning users.

The Bayesian approach is gaining popularity, but slowly. It is much harder to explain in nontechnical terms how the system operates under the hood, but it is much easier to interpret the results. Unlike the frequentist approach, you don't have to spell out a test duration but instead you define a stopping criterion, which is easier to determine from a business perspective. I also wonder whether part of the reason for the slow adoption is the comfort with an algorithm making modifications and determining the website experience. That is, the Bayesian update rule is essentially in charge, actively changing the proportion of treatments seen by users, and evolving that over time. It takes a very data-driven organization to trust that process, which for many on the business side represents a magic black box.

Cultural Implications

Having gone through the more technical material of best practices, and how to run tests well to maximize the impact, I now want to step back and consider the cultural implications of a great testing culture within a data-driven organization.

Scott Cook (*http://bit.ly/fc-cook*), founder of Intuit, considers that A/B testing shifts the culture from "decisions by persuasion to decisions by experiment." It is a very anti-ego philosophy. Instead of the HiPPOs (highest paid person's opinion; covered in more detail in the next chapter) ruling the roost, there is a more democratic shift from higher-level decisions to lower-level hypothesis generation. He suggests that "you enable your most junior people to test their best ideas." Good ideas and a fresh perspective can come from everywhere. You'll get more ideas, better ideas, and a sense of participation, ownership, and engagement. As I advocated in a blog post (*http://bit.ly/anderson-create*) (the origin of this book, in fact), "let the interns speak."

Siroker and Koomen argue that this ego-liberation allows an organization to push boundaries and be more innovative. "It eliminates the requirement for everyone involved to be a know-it-all," they say. "When people feel comfortable saying, 'I don't know, but let's run an experiment,' they're more inclined to take risks by trying things outside the norm." Scott Cook clearly agrees. He says that with experimentation, "you get surprises more often, and surprises are a key source of innovation. You only get a surprise when you are trying something and the result is different than you expected, so the sooner you run the experiment, the sooner you are likely to find a surprise, and the surprise is the market speaking to you, telling you something you didn't know."

Siroker and Koomen also suggest that meetings can be shorter. They cite Jarred Colli, a former senior product marketing manager at Rocket Lawyer, who claims "Where previously, people would argue over what kind of headlines you use or what kind of picture, and you would spend hours drilling down on some stupid detail, now we don't have those conversations anymore, since we'll test all that stuff. We'll figure what is best." Again, you eliminate the battle of the egos, you eliminate the need to generate theories and instead focus on ideas, ideas that might just work and make a difference. While the majority of ideas don't make a difference, or they move the needle in the wrong direction, you only need one or two hits to make a huge impact. Recall the $57 million that came from optimizing the Obama campaign signup page. That's a huge return. While impressive, that probably pales into comparison with the lifetime value of

Greg Linden's Amazon.com checkout recommender. Bing recently tested whether increasing the number of links in featured ads improved results. That test result (*http://bit.ly/forbes-massive*), that two or more links are better than one, is supposedly worth $100 million *annually*. That wasn't luck. They run 300 experiments concurrently per day. Google is running thousands of experiments at any one time. You have to be in it to win it. As the joke has it: A/B testing actually stands for *always be testing*.

CHAPTER 9

Decision Making

In a significant minority of organizations senior management take decisions behind closed doors for opaque reasons and, should those decisions turn out to be the wrong ones, are not held accountable. This is a disturbing state of affairs.
—Economist Intelligence Unit[3]

There is no mystique about decision-making. It's a teachable and learnable skill for which almost everyone has potential.
—Sydney Finkelstein (ibid.)

Warning: bad joke alert.

What's the most data-driven animal? An adder (*http://bit.ly/wiki-adder*). (Insert groan here.)

What's the least data-driven animal? A HiPPO. This is much more serious. HiPPO, "highest paid person's opinion" (Figure 9-1), a term coined by Avinash Kaushik, is the antithesis of data-drivenness. You all know them. They're the expert with decades of experience. They don't care what the data says, especially when it's wrong, and they are going to stick to their plan because they know best. And, besides, they're the boss, as the Financial Times explains:[4]

---

3 Economist Intelligence Unit, "Decisive Action: how businesses make decisions and how they could do it better" (*http://bit.ly/decisive-action*) (London: Economist Intelligence Unit, 2014).

4 Lynch, M., "Is your HiPPO holding you back?" (*http://bit.ly/fts-hippo*) *Financial Times*, September 14, 2009.

HiPPOs can be deadly for businesses, because they base their decisions on ill-understood metrics at best, or on pure guesswork. With no intelligent tools to derive meaning from the full spectrum of customer interactions and evaluate the how, when, where and why behind actions, the HiPPO approach can be crippling for businesses.

This chapter covers the link in the analytics value chain that perhaps is least discussed: the decision-making step itself. An organization can have quality, timely, and relevant data and skilled analysts who do great work and generate masterful reports and models with carefully crafted and presented insights and recommendations. However, if that report sits on a desk, or unopened in an inbox, or the decision maker has already made up his mind what action he's going to take regardless of what the data shows, then it is all for naught.

Figure 9-1. Let data drive decisions, not HiPPOs. (c) Illustration by Tom Fishburne. Reproduced with permission.

This chapter covers a number of questions related to the decision-making step. I first cover how decisions are made. Are they typically data-driven or are they HiPPO-driven? I then examine what we really mean by data-driven. How does data-driven compare to the related terms "data-informed" and "data-influenced"? Next, I detail what makes decision making hard, covering aspects such as data, culture, and cognitive biases (irrational or illogical thinking). Having set out the raft of challenges, and at the risk of having depressed the reader, I then switch gears to focus on a suite of solutions and suggestions to improve fact-based decision making, all of which are positioned under the framework of the Fogg behavioral model.

How Are Decisions Made?

It's bad. As much as organizations like to think that they are data-driven, intuition still rules the roost. Here's some data: intuition and personal experience rank as the top two factors in a 2012 report from Accenture (n = 600; Figure 9-2).

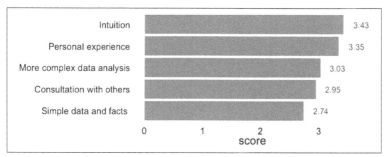

Figure 9-2. Factors used in senior management decisions. After figure 5 of "Analytics in Action: Breakthroughs and Barriers on the Journey to ROI." (http://bit.ly/accenture-analytics) Accenture.

In a 2014 survey of 1,135 senior executives conducted by the Economist Intelligence Unit (*http://bit.ly/pwc-2014-data-survey*), we see the same picture (Figure 9-3): intuition (30%) and experience (28%) together swamp an analytical approach (29%).

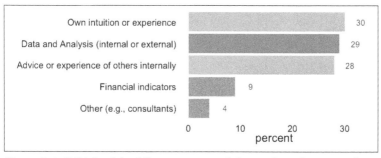

Figure 9-3. Which of the following inputs did you place the most reliance on for your last big decision?

In yet another survey (*http://bit.ly/gyro-only-human*) of more than 700 senior executives, 61% agree that when making decisions, human insights must precede hard analytics, and 62% say it is often necessary or even preferable to rely on gut feelings and soft factors.

Finally, from IBM's survey (*http://bit.ly/ibm-survey-decisions*) of 225 business leaders worldwide, intuition and experience, again, topped the list. See Table 9-1.

Table 9-1. To what extent do you make business decisions based on the following factors?

Factor	Frequently	Always	Total
Personal experience and intuition	54%	25%	79%
Analytically derived	43%	19%	62%
Collective experience	43%	9%	52%

As can be seen from these four reports, there is a pretty consistent picture.

I did, however, find one report where data-driven won out (Figure 9-4). This was another 2014 report by the Economist Intelligence Unit (*http://bit.ly/decisive-action*) (n = 174).

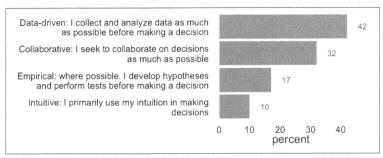

Figure 9-4. Which of the following best describes your personal approach to making significant management decisions?

(See also figure 7 of "Analytics: a blueprint for value." (*http://bit.ly/ analytics-blueprint*) IBM.)

What's driving this? Why does it appear that subjective experience and intuition win out over a more objective, analytical approach? Crudely, we can say that there are at least three drivers: the data itself, culture, and finally that three-pound lump of goo between your ears, the brain. Later, I touch on these three areas to examine some of the root causes of issues with decision making. With a better grasp of the issues at hand, the following section will cover some potential remedies and approaches.

First, let's touch upon whether we can, in fact, be objective when making decisions. Won't intuition always play a part? What, in fact, do we really mean by data-driven at this stage of the analytics chain?

Data-Driven, -Informed, or -Influenced?

Throughout this book, I have used the term "data-driven." I covered a high-level overview of the concept in Chapter 1, and most of the book considers the data component in some way. However, it is worth considering the second component, "driven," briefly here. Are we ever really driven by data? Are other terms, as others have argued, such as data-informed or data-influenced more appropriate?

Scott Berkun raises some really interesting points in a great post entitled "The Dangers of Faith in Data" (*http://bit.ly/berkun-dangers*).[3] He argues: "No team or organization is Data-driven. Data is non conscious: it is merely a list of stupid, dead numbers. Data doesn't have a brain and therefore can't drive or lead anything."

If you think of "driven" in the sense of a driving a car—the data says turn left, your organization turns left—then most of the the time, this does not make sense for any organization, unless...they have reached some of the higher levels of analytics (Chapters 2 and 5). If you have situations that are regular and predictable and you have developed really good predictive models, then absolutely you should have decisions that are data-driven in the sense that they are automatic. For instance, consider just-in-time replenishment processes in manufacturing. You can create an automated process where a predictive algorithm is monitoring sales and stock levels and sends out purchase orders to minimize stock outs, but at the same time minimizes inventory levels. Or, consider automated trading systems where algorithms are trading real stocks with real money autonomously. In scenarios like these, you essentially have taken the decision maker out of the situation but algorithm and data are, in fact,

---

3 I think that this post would make for a great brown bag discussion with colleagues in the analytics org. The post is clearly provocative, debatable in parts, but also contains some very perceptive and valid points, which should make for stimulating discussion.

making real choices that impact their organizations. I agree with Scott that most of the time, this is not what data-driven does or can mean.

However, that is not the only meaning of "driven." One of the dictionary definitions includes the sense "cause (something abstract) to happen or develop," with the example, "The consumer has been driving the economy for a number of years." Clearly, consumers are not sitting in their living rooms with a joystick actively controlling metrics such as inflation, but their actions are indeed a driving force. Their purchases, the credit card debt that they take on, and the amount that they save are all forces, in combination with other factors, including the interpretation of the information by the chair of the Federal Reserve, that shape the economy. For instance, by monitoring key metrics such as unemployment, consumer spending, and home ownership, Ben Bernanke was motivated to keep interest rates low to stimulate the economy. He wasn't forced to do it, the data didn't put a gun to his head, but the trends in those key metrics, plus his skills and experience in monetary policy, really drove those decisions. (Similarly, I think that the surveys in the previous section were not pitting intuition versus data, but instead *intuition alone*; i.e., in the absence of any recent data. This is in contrast to an analytical approach in which data was collected, analyzed, and used in combination with a decision maker's experience and knowledge to drive a decision.) I tend to think about data-driven in this sense. Scott continues, "At best you want to be data influenced, where (living) decision makers have good data available that they can use to help answer good questions about what they're doing, how well it's being done and what perhaps they should be doing in the future." I whole-heartedly agree, except that I think that data-driven can take on the same sense, although data-influenced is perhaps a more explicit term.

Knapp et al. (*http://bit.ly/knapp-leadership*) prefer the term "data-informed," at least in the context of educational leadership. "We find the term data-informed leadership a more useful concept...The term broadens the scope of thinking and action in two productive ways. First, shifting to the concept of data-informed leadership escapes the occasional deterministic implication of data 'driving' action." (This harks back to the earlier car example.) They continue, "Second, the concept presumes that data are useful for more in the practice of leadership than making decisions per se...data may prompt questions and deliberation more than they point to specific decision options." In other words, they argue that data can inform decisions in same sense as Scott argues for "data-*influenced*," and data can help raise questions and inform what is going on in the organization, in the sense of KPIs, reports, and alerts. They also quote Bernhardt, who says "True data-driven decision making is only partly about data. A clear and shared vision and leadership play major roles in data-decision making."

All three of these terms are sensible and acceptable. "Influence" sounds, to me at least, the weakest and most passive and "driven" the strongest and most active. Whether it is the best term or not, the latter is the one that has stuck; at time of writing, the number of results from Google searches for "data-influenced" is 16,000, for "data-informed" it is greater at a 170,000, but this is dwarfed by the 11.5 *million* for "data-driven." Thus, rightly or wrongly, data-driven is the most popular term, the one that has the widest adoption, and is the one that I therefore use in the book.

What Makes Decision Making Hard?

In this section, we are going to cover factors that hinder data-driven decision making and that promote decisions primarily based on experience and gut.

Data

As mentioned earlier (Chapter 2), data has to be timely, relevant, and trustworthy. If it is not, decision makers have limited options. They can postpone the decision, get more data, or they can steam ahead and make the decision anyway with whatever data and tools they might possess, which typically might come down to experience only.

What are some of the potential issues with data?

Data quality and lack of trust

Returning to one of the earlier surveys (*http://bit.ly/pwc-2014-data-survey*) in the chapter, data itself is a real and primary problem for decision makers: "Across the sample, the main impediment to making greater use of this asset for decision making is the quality, accuracy, or completeness of data."

Harvard Business Review (*http://bit.ly/hbr-confident*) states that "51% have had the necessary information to feel confident about their business decisions in the past six months. And this group is reaping the rewards—it is more confident with high risk decisions and feels prepared to make critical business decisions in a timely manner." That's great, but what about the 49% that don't have necessary data to be confident? In another survey (*http://bit.ly/ibm-survey-decisions*), one in three have made major decisions with incomplete information or information that they don't trust. This can only be fixed by data leadership that invests in data management and data quality programs.

Volume

For others, it is not the lack of data but the opposite: the sheer volume of data. They can't keep up. That same HBR paper states, "More than half of respondents said both internal and external data needed for decision-making is increasing more quickly than their companies can process." In that case, focus on a subset of data, pare it down to what's most important, aggregate, and automate—and if necessary, hire more data engineers.

Sifting signal from the noise

Volume presents other issues, too. The more data you collect, the more signal you'll get, and along with that, more noise. It becomes harder and harder to work out what is truly relevant. This is especially a problem with big data in which everything, including the kitchen sink, is encouraged to be recorded and stored. The amount of relevant data will become diluted, and it is hard for analysts to determine the signal from the noise.

Having a very specific and well-defined question, versus general data mining hoping to find something significant and insightful, will help here. However, even then it may be hard to know where to draw the line of what might be useful. "Too much evidence can be as bad as too little—you can drown in detail," said Gerard Hodgkinson, professor of strategic management at Warwick Business School (Decisive Action report).

Paul Andreassen (1988)[3] ran an experiment with a group of MIT business students whereby they selected a portfolio of stock investments. The students were split into two groups. The low-information group (*http://bit.ly/fc-tmi*) had limited information access and only knew whether the stock had gone up or down. The high-information group had access to changes in stock price but also access to a normal stream of financial news from newspapers, radio, TV, etc. The two groups were then allowed to trade. Which group fared better? Surprisingly, the answer is the low-information group, who earned twice as much. The high-information group was exposed to a larger number of potential signals, rumors, and gossip and overly fixated on irrelevancies. They chased noise for signals and traded more often. (This is called information bias.) For instance, traders fixate on recent stock value highs or lows, which by definition are extremal, and use those as an anchor (discussed in more detail later). Consequently, this makes them more likely to sell or buy, respectively.

For nonfinancial examples, see Barry Schwartz's *Paradox of Choice* (Harper Perennial), which contains many examples in which too many options and too much data overwhelms us and can lead to "analytical paralysis."

Those are just some of the problems with data. From a large sample of executives, "Fewer than 44% of employees say they know where to find the information they need for their day-to-day work." Even if they do find it, it might not contain all they need, or the quality might not be sufficient. Unsurprisingly, "If given the option of good-enough data now or perfect data later, most executives choose the former, confident that they can apply judgment to bridge the gaps."[4] Therein lies the problem.

Culture

Another major aspect inhibiting data-driven decision making is the existing culture of the organization. (Culture, probably the most

---

3 Mussweiler, T., and K. Schneller, "'What goes up must come down'—how charts influence decisions to buy and sell stocks," *Journal of Behavioral Finance* 4, no. 3 (2003): 121–130.

4 Shah, S., A. Horne, A., and J. Capellá, "Good data won't guarantee good decisions," *Harvard Business Review* 90, no. 4 (2012): 23-5.

influential aspect of a data-driven organization, will be covered as the primary focus of Chapter 10.)

Intuition is valued

Senior managers, the decision makers, are typically hired for their abilities to think at the strategic level. That often means their ability to create a vision, implement it, see it through to fruition and remove barriers, irrespective of what the data says. Intuition is respected. Intuition is often hired for. Heck, Jack Welch's—the highly revered and influential former CEO of General Electric— biography is called *Straight from the Gut*. (To be fair, Welch was data-driven and promoted Six Sigma.)

Lack of data literacy

Another significant issue is that many senior managers are not data literate. That is, it has been many years or decades since they took a statistics class, if they ever took one at all. It is not part of the curriculum of an MBA, and executive coaches don't teach it. This illiteracy is highly unfortunate because they are the final line of defense. They are the ones taking this set of aggregated data and interpreting the insights and findings from the analysts and evaluating the degree of evidence, risk, and impact that is going to move the organization forward.

Together, these two factors mean that HiPPOs are not an unusual occurrence and often have a certain amount of power.

Lack of accountability

When you combine intuition and lack of data illiteracy with a third factor, a lack of accountability, the combination is deadly. In one survey (Figure 9-5), 41% report that poor decision makers will not progress within the organization—meaning that the majority, 59%, *will* progress—and 19% of respondents say that decision makers at their organization are not held accountable for their decisions at all. In addition, 64% say that information about who made certain decisions is only available to senior management.

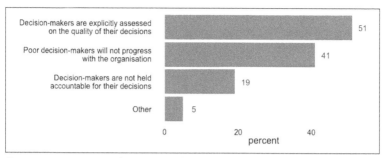

Figure 9-5. How are decision-makers held accountable for their decisions at your organization? From: "Decisive Action: how businesses make decisions and how they could do it better." (http://bit.ly/decisive-action) Economist Intelligence Unit.

This means that half of those managers are not assessed on the quality of their decisions, and they are not held accountable. If you are not very quantitatively minded, then why wouldn't you be a HiPPO?

Accountability has to exist at the analyst level, too. (Recall Ken Rudin: "Analytics is about impact…In our company [Zynga], if you have brilliant insight and you did great research and no one changes, you get zero credit.") Analysts have to sell their ideas to the decision makers. Part of that pitch should be the strength of evidence. They have to be honest about sample sizes, margin of errors, and confidence intervals, but they may have to do that by interpreting that into language that the decision makers can understand.

The Cognitive Barriers

The previous section covered the lack of accountability, lack of skills, and some of the culture around intuition. However, there is another huge barrier to effective data-based decision making, one that favors (bad) intuition: our brain.

The uncomfortable truth is that we are far-from-perfect decision makers. We don't always approach problems in the most objective manner, often bringing stale experience and latching onto irrelevant details. This leads to flawed, illogical thinking and decisions. These influences and mechanisms are called cognitive biases. For a whirlwind tour, see Rolf Dobelli's *The Art of Thinking Clearly* or view this list (*http://bit.ly/wiki-cognitive-bias*).

In human cognition, decision making occurs in two main ways: a fast, involuntary, unconscious manner, called System 1 by Nobel Prize winner Daniel Kahneman, and a slower, more deliberate manner, called System 2. System 1 is our "gut" or intuition, while System 2 is conscious, deliberate thought and the one that we use for deeper, mathematical analysis.

Let's examine why we can't always trust our gut:[3]

We are inconsistent
> When presented with the same evidence at different times, we come to different conclusions; and when different people are presented with the same evidence, we can come to different conclusions.[4]

We remember things that didn't happen
> Our intuition is based on a subconscious collection of data points, some of which are wrong. In a fascinating story about eye witnesses recalling events that did not happen, the *New York Times* (*http://bit.ly/nyt-memory*) suggests that "our memory is made of bits of true facts, surrounded by holes that we Spackle over with guesses and beliefs."

We are not as good as we think we are
> In Kahneman's terms, we have an "illusion of validity." Here's a simple (embarrassing) example. Answer this as quickly as you can:

> A bat and ball together cost $1.10.
> The bat costs a dollar more than the ball.
> How much does the ball cost?

> If you are like most people, including me, you said $0.10...and you would be wrong. The answer is $0.05. Our intuitive System 1 answer is incorrect—and our System 2 is too lazy is too check

---

3 Much of this comes from Kahneman's 2011 book *Thinking, Fast and Slow* (Farrar, Straus and Giroux), which I would highly recommend. If you don't have time to read that book, at least read the wonderful review article Kahneman, D., and G. Klein, "Conditions for intuitive expertise: A failure to disagree," *American Psychologist* 64, no. 6 (2009): 515–526. See also McAfee, A., "The Future of Decision Making: Less Intuition, More Evidence," (*http://bit.ly/hbr-future*), Harvard Business Review, January 7, 2010.

4 Frick, W., "What to Do When People Draw Different Conclusions From the Same Data," (*http://bit.ly/frick-different*) Harvard Business Review, March 31, 2015.

—but if we switch to active System 2 thinking, you can both easily get the correct answer bat = \$1.05 and ball = \$0.05, and verify that it is correct: \$1.05 + \$0.05 = \$1.10 and \$1.05 - \$0.05 = \$1.0. (If you got this wrong, don't feel too bad about it. The error rate among undergrads in top US schools such as MIT, Princeton, and Harvard is 50% and is as high as 90% in lower-ranked schools.)

We won't give up bad data

We internalize facts, build up mental models, and then when new evidence contradicts those facts, we are very resistant to changing our model or accepting the new data. Brendan Nyhan and Jason Reifler from Dartmouth ran some experiments in which subjects read mock news articles that included either a misleading claim from a politician, or a misleading claim and a correction. Interestingly, they found that "individuals who receive unwelcome information [i.e., corrections that went against their beliefs] may not simply resist challenges to their views. Instead, they may come to support their original opinion even more strongly – what we call a 'backfire effect' (*http:// bit.ly/nyhan-corrections*)." They quote Mark Twain, who quips, "It ain't what you don't know that gets you into trouble. It's what you know for sure that just ain't so." In other words, the misinformed are far more dangerous than the uninformed; misinformation is sticky. "Knowledge actually doesn't make our misinformation better, sometimes it can't make our misinformation worse," said Shankar Vendantam (*http://bit.ly/ strata2014-keynote*), author of *The Hidden Brain* (Spiegel & Grau), speaking at 2014 Strata+Hadoop World in New York.

We anchor on irrelevant data

If you've ever bought a car, no doubt you've seen the "official" sticker price pasted on the window. If you are sensible, you've probably haggled with the dealer—who groaned, hummed, and hawed and had to talk to his boss—down to a lower price. With that reduction, you probably felt that you got a good deal. The problem is that that sticker price is bullshit. It is a psychological trick to get you to think in relative terms and compare the current best offer against a higher value rather than focusing on the absolute amount or on other direct evidence. You "anchor" or latch on to that value as a reference point.

In this case, the official sticker price is not unreasonable, so you don't feel hoodwinked. However, completely irrelevant numbers can act as anchors and cause us to make bad judgments. Amos Tversky and Daniel Kahneman (1974) conducted an experiment in which they spun a wheel of fortune containing the numbers 0 to 100, but which unbeknownst to the experimental subjects was rigged to land on 10 or 65 only. For each subject, they spun the wheel, waited for it to stop, and then asked them whether the number of African countries within the United Nations countries was higher or lower than that value (this is the anchoring step). They then asked them to estimate the actual percentage. Those that landed on 10 estimated the proportion of African nations at 25% percent, while those that landed at 65 estimated at 45%, a change in 20% from a seemingly "random" irrelevant spin.

We get tired and hungry

Our decisions are affected by other internal, extraneous factors, such as hunger, mood, and energy. In a remarkable 2011 analysis,[3] the rulings of eight Jewish-Israeli judges, who sit on two parole boards, were tracked. Danzinger et al. monitored the 1,112 rulings that the judges made over 50 days within a 10-month period and, importantly, they also tracked when the judges stopped for a mid-morning break and snack (40 minutes on average) and also for lunch (an hour). The status quo, the easiest decision to make, was to deny parole. A harder task was to grant parole. That took longer to deliberate (5 minutes versus 7 minutes, respectively) and longer to write out the ruling (47 words versus 90 words). The percentage of favorable rulings (granting parole) started out at 65% at the start of the day and decreased to almost 0% before their mid-morning break. Afterwards, it jumped back up to 65% and steadily decreased to zero again before lunch. Guess what? After lunch it jumped back up to 65% and decreased steadily toward the end of the session. (The results could not be explained by race, gravity of offense, time served, or other factors.) The authors could not control whether it was the act of taking a break or it was glucose spike from eating that caused the difference, but it is clear that extra-

3 Danzinger, S., J. Levav, and L. Avnaim-Pesso, "Extraneous factors in judicial decisions," *Proc. Natl. Acad. Sci.* 108 (2011): 6889–6892.

neous factors affected their decision making. The authors conclude "Indeed, the caricature that justice is what the judge ate for breakfast might be an appropriate caricature for human decisionmaking in general."

I've listed a few cognitive biases that we suffer. There are many more (see earlier references). Other important biases that could impair our judgments:

Survivorship bias

We consider the data that "survives" to be sampled as being representative of the population. If you read technology blogs such as *Techcrunch*, *Re/Code*, or *O'Reilly Radar*, you get bombarded by successful startups, inflated funding rounds, and exits. Starting a startup seems like a sure thing. What you don't read about is the vast majority of startups that don't get off the ground, and of those that do, the 97% or so that don't make an exit. We focus on the survivors.

Confirmation bias

Related to "We won't give up bad data" from earlier is a bias that seeks or prefers data that confirms what we think that we know. Although Einstein joked, "If the facts don't fit the theory, change the facts," research is finding that is exactly what the left hemisphere of our brain may do (again, see Shankar Vendatam's keynote (*http://bit.ly/strata2014-keynote*)).

Recency bias

We recall and focus on recent data more than older data.[3] In most cases, that is the right thing to do, but not always. Imagine a stock market that is tanking where there is a clear downward, sustained trend. Just because it ticked upwards slightly yesterday doesn't mean it has hit bottom. When you have a stochastic, volatile environment, you have to expand the time horizon to get a sense of overall trend because the short timescale (high frequency) data provide relatively little and unreliable information.

---

3 I've noticed that when radio stations compile listener-voted greatest hits of all time, the top 20 or so are dominated by hits within the last year. This is the recency bias at work. Customers are subject to this bias, too: they too are swayed more by recent interactions, and if that is bad interaction, it can wash out multiple great interactions before that. You are only as good as your last performance.

Friend or foe bias

When someone tells you information, you first judge whether the person is on your side—whether they are friend or foe, a competitor or cooperator—and then decide whether to believe that information. That is, "audiences view trustworthiness as the motivation to be truthful."[3]

Where Does Intuition Work?

There are of course scenarios where intuition can and does work well. Oft-cited examples include well-trained firefighters who have an innate sense of when a building is becoming dangerous and get the crew out, or neonatal ICU nurses who can tell before the doctors and before clinical test results come back whether an infant is developing a fever or complications, or chess grandmasters who are able to sense the other player's strategy and evaluate what seems like an inordinate amount of moves and counter-moves. This type of performant intuition can only develop in "valid" environments in which cues and signals are reliable and consistent. Thus, this works in a neonatal unit where the patient spends many days or weeks in the same place interacting with the same staff, but it can't work in a volatile environment, such as a stock exchange.

It also takes a long time to develop such intuition. While the 10,000-hour rule has largely been discredited,[4] it is true at some level that practice makes perfect. Few business decision makers will have sufficient time in a small, consistent domain to become a true expert. We may switch careers five to seven times on average (although no one really knows the number for sure), and we often switch roles and domains within organizations. Gone are the days where you join a firm and stay there for the bulk of your career. In other words, I think that in business at least we now more frequently reset the expert counter.

---

3 Fiske, S. T., and C. Dupree, "Gaining trust as well as respect in communicating to motivated audiences about science topics," (*http://bit.ly/fiske-trust*) PNAS 111, no. 4 (2014): 13593–13597.

4 Macnamara, B. N., D. Z. Hambrick, and F. L. Oswald, "Deliberate practice and performance in music, games, sports, education, and professions: a meta analysis," *Psychological Science* 25 (2014): 1608–1618.

Intuition can have immense value if used as a "gut check." If data doesn't match what one might expect, then it can be a clear signal that one should double check the data. I mentioned this in Chapter 2 where I suggested that if one develops expectations of what data or values should be, it can be used as part of the data quality control processes. The "Decisive Action" report states "Intuition can act as warning sign there may be something wrong with the way that the data have been collected or analyzed. This allows leaders to check that the data on which they are basing their decisions are valid."

I am encouraged by the response to the following question: "When taking a decision, if the available data contradicted your gut feeling, what would you do?" 57% said that they would reanalyze the data, and 30% would collect more. Only 10% said that they would go ahead with the existing data (Figure 9-6).

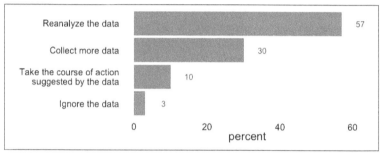

Figure 9-6. When taking a decision, if the available data contradicted your gut feeling, what would you do? From the "Decisive Action" report.

Solutions

Are you depressed yet? The preceding discussion seems to paint a pretty grim picture. Let's now switch tone and move to a solutions-oriented perspective. What can be done to create a more data-driven decision-making practice?

I am going to frame this section in terms of the Fogg Behavioral Model (*http://bit.ly/fogg-behavioral*). If the brain is the source of so many issues with intuition-based decisions, let's get into the head to understand how we can motivate and shape decisions and behaviors.

Criminal investigations often focus on whether the suspect had the means, motive, and opportunity to conduct the crime. If even if one of those three is missing, US criminal law is unlikely to convict. The Fogg Behavior Model is very similar to this triad. It attempts to model the suite of conditions for someone to perform a task by assuming that:

- They must be sufficiently motivated.
- They have the ability to perform the task.
- They have been triggered somehow to perform the task.

The question at hand is, how can we create the right conditions to favor more data-driven decision making over intuitive decision making? Let's examine this through the eyes of the Fogg model.

Motivation

The first condition is motivation. What can create greater motivation to use data or at least improve the decision-making processes (which presumably will involve being more data-driven)?

Fogg lists three motivators:

Pleasure/pain
  A primitive, immediate motivator.

Hope/fear
  A more anticipatory motivator.

Social acceptance/rejection
  "Facebook gains its power to motivate and ultimately influence users mostly because of this motivator," says Fogg.

Some ways that Fogg's three motivators play out in the business world include pride (encourage staff to do a great job for their own benefit), pleasure from recognition, praise, and promotion for doing a good job; and conversely, fear of demotion or being fired for a bad job.

Naively, I thought that money should have been included as a motivator, especially in a business context where end-of-year financial bonuses are tied to job and company performance. Surprisingly, however, it turns out that in tasks that require complex or creative thinking, not only is money not a poor motivator, but it actually leads to *decreased* performance (*http://bit.ly/rsa-motivate*).

Incentives and accountability

I mentioned the lack of accountability earlier. That has to be addressed and fixed. One way, of course, is to tie performance and outcomes back to a quantitative measure, such as sales, signups, or profit. It may often be the case anyway, but focus on ROI or the overall downstream effect and impact. If someone has made a bad decision, it should be reflected in the metrics. Design incentives to get the right behavior and associated culture in place.

Prove it!

Rather than rely on gut, engender a more "prove it" culture in which ideas are challenged until clear evidence is presented, such through A/B tests, proof of concepts, or simulation.

Transparency

Foster more open and transparent culture where who the decision makers are, what decisions they made, and the outcomes of those decisions are more readily available and interpretable. By making both the decision and outcome more visible through presentations, documentation, or through dashboards, you kick in the social-acceptance motivator.

Ability

Fogg lists six aspects that affect someone's ability to perform a task:

Time
> One has more ability to perform a quick task than a long task.

Money
> One has more ability to perform a cheap task than an expensive task.

Physical effort
> One has more ability to perform a task that takes less physical effort than one that is demanding.

Mental cycles
> One has more ability to perform a less brain-taxing task than one that is mentally challenging.

Social deviance
> One has more ability to perform a task that is socially acceptable than one that is unpopular.

Non-routine
> One has greater ability to perform a routine task than one that is non-routine.

With this framework, it becomes relative easy to start to see how we can lower the barriers to making good decisions. I'll highlight the six abilities addressed in square brackets in the remaining discussion.

Tie actions to outcomes

Analysts can make decisions easier (mental cycles) for decision makers and so help them make them more quickly (time) by framing their findings and recommendations well, showing why it matters, and focusing on impact. Yes, present the evidence, but present the recommendation in the clearest manner that requires the least amount of mental effort to comprehend. I love Tracy Allison Altman's suggestion, shown in Figure 9-7 (the rest of that paper is a great read, too) that highlights the link between action and outcome —if you do X, then Y will happen—but also documents the support for the recommendation below. This is a sale: buy this recommended action because of these objective reasons.

Accenture (*http://bit.ly/accenture-analytics*) found that 58% of executives see "outcome from data" as a key analytics challenge. "Establishing the linkage between data collection and analysis on the one hand, and the actions and outcomes predicated by analytics is proving to be a more difficult task for many than data collection or data integration." Moreover, they found that only 39% of execs found that the data they generate is "relevant to the business strategy." This is where each and every member of the analytics org has a role to play. Help embed analytics into the business processes, and help make it easy, clear, and repeatable with relevant data and metrics. Push back where appropriate but with a clear, objective rationale.

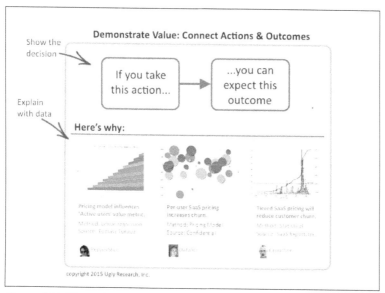

Figure 9-7. Tie actions to outcomes. Set out the action linked to the resulting outcome and below set out the causal evidence. From http:// bit.ly/altman-data-easy. Reproduced with permission.

Collaboration and consensus

I mentioned in Chapter 5 that Nate Silver predicted all US Senate races and also winners in 49 out of 50 states in the 2008 presidential elections. He did so in the face of the pundits who attacked and ridiculed him, claiming that, given their years of experience following politics, they knew better. However, by creating statistical models combining a suite of different polls and opinions (and also using the very latest data that he could get his hands on), the various errors and biases averaged out to produce highly accurate predictions. As Larry Keely of the Doblin Group notes, "No one is as smart as everyone" (cited in Kevin Kelly's *New Rules for the New Economy* [Penguin Books]). In this case, everyone is the electorate reflected in aggregate data.

If a decision is complex or is likely to be unpopular, one approach is to get consensus (social deviance). That will enfranchise stakeholders and make the process more likely to succeed. "What's important is that everyone feels part of the process—it's no good the decision being right if no one supports it," says Robin Tye, Ernst and Young's COO.

In a data-driven world, that means making sure that everyone understands the objective, the data collected, the metrics, and how the primary decision maker is interpreting the evidence. Give others a chance to put forward their interpretations and views, if those differ, and get everyone on board; but also get inputs on other perspectives that that the decision maker may have missed. To help, you can remember this neat mnemonic, DECIDE:

- **D**efine the problem.
- **E**stablish the criteria.
- **C**onsider all the alternatives.
- **I**dentify the best alternative.
- **D**evelop and implement a plan of action.
- **E**valuate and monitor the solution and feedback when necessary.

In other words, make sure that stakeholders are on board with each of these steps.

There is of course a danger here. With too many inputs, you can get group think and a diffusion of responsibility that can slow down the process significantly or increase the chance that you get contradictory perspectives that lead to arguments or frustration. Again, you need to strike a balance, something that is reflected in the data (Figure 9-8).

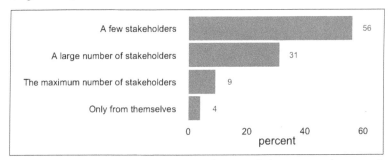

Figure 9-8. Responses to the question, "How collaborative is the typical decision-making process at your organization?" (From "Decisive Action: how businesses make decisions and how they could do it better.") "Decision makers will seek input from..."

Interestingly, the "Decisive Action" report states:

> As for seniority, while C-suite executives and heads of department are most likely to be data-driven decision makers, by their own

reckoning vice presidents and senior vice presidents (or equivalent) are more likely to be collaborative. This may be a symptom of the need for executives of this level to build consensus for their initiatives—something that is alleviated when they reach the C-suite.

Training

Increasing the data literacy of the decision makers is an obvious step to increase ability (mental cycles). The analysts should have done the statistical analysis, so I wouldn't suggest that all managers would need the skills to build sophisticated regression models or understand the mathematical underpinnings of the expectation-maximization algorithm or a support vector machine classifier. Instead, I would suggest focusing more on the principles of sampling and experimental design so that decision makers can better assess whether the data collection or experiment is valid, what types of biases might have crept in, etc. I would also suggest reviewing variance-like metrics, such as margin of error and standard deviation, that reflect repeatability and confidence in the resulting aggregate values.

Warning: this type of training is likely to come with some resistance, so you may need a very senior sponsor, such as CEOs (as I have at Warby Parker), to get the decision makers in a room and give them a refresher course, even if only for an hour.

Consistency

You can make tasks shorter (time) and simpler (mental cycles) by being more consistent in how data is presented. This doesn't mean that every report has to look the same, but a weekly report or dashboard should look the same over time, and the same metrics should be consistent across teams where possible.

For instance, at Procter & Gamble, where they have 50,000 employees accessing dashboards, commonality to align those data consumers is key. In their marketshare heatmaps, green always means above market share, and red means below market share. Don't mix things up unnecessarily. Elsewhere, they have instituted "business sufficiency models" (*http://bit.ly/hbr-pg-data*) that specify what data is needed to address a particular domain. That means, as Thomas Davenport notes, "if you're focused on supply chain issues, for example, the sufficiency models specify the key variables, how they should be displayed visually, and (in some cases) the relationships between the variables and forecasts based on the relationships."

Triggers

Of the three conditions in Fogg's model, the presence of a trigger is possibly the lowest concern of the three, at least in a business decision-making context. I say that because decisions in business are usually in a larger context of goals, KPIs, strategy, and collaborative teamwork in which there is often some real or arbitrary deadline. That is, if someone isn't asking or waiting for the decision, there is clearly something fundamentally wrong in the process or it can't be that important. Of course, someone can postpone a difficult decision, perhaps with the real or fake claim that more data is needed. Make that harder to fall back upon by having a clear, visible project timeline and bake in unambiguous accountability.

One example where there definitely is a need for a trigger is automated processes "run" by statistical, machine-learned models. Such models get stale. The underlying assumptions on which the model was built may no longer hold true; for instance, behavior of the drivers, such as customers or staff, may change. As such, models need regular maintenance to check performance, verify assumptions, and retrain as necessary. However, when algorithms are in charge, humans become more passive and less vigilant, something termed "automation bias." A clear process that sets out a regular schedule and responsibility for model maintenance is needed to combat this.

Conclusion

Decision making is hard. We are beset by a barrage of cognitive, data, and cultural issues and biases. People have preconceptions and egos, and they can get in the way.

Intuition has to be part of a data-driven decision-making process. There is no escaping it. In the conclusion of *Dataclysm*, Christian Rudder acknowledges, "behind every number there's a person making decisions: what to analyze, what to exclude, what frame to set around whatever pictures the number paint. To make a statement, even to make just a simple graph, is to make choices, and in those choices human imperfection inevitably comes through." Related, Scott Berken remarks, "If anyone utters 'the data says,' they are pretending data can have a singular interpretation, which it never does; and this false faith prevents the asking of good questions, such as: is there an equally valid hypothesis based on this data that suggests a different conclusion than yours?"

The key here is to start with the question to be answered—be question and decision focused (*http://bit.ly/altman-data-easy*) rather than data focused. By setting out the objective clearly and unambiguously, you stand a better chance of defining which questions need to be answered and consequently which data should be collected, which experiments should be run, and what metrics you are trying to drive. With that, you stand a better chance of setting out the results aligned with those metrics and objectives, and the decision should be simplified.

What you must do, however, is use the available, relevant data. Don't rely on intuition alone; we are too fallible to do so. Most importantly, don't put up with HiPPOs. If you must make a decision that goes against what the data shows, be honest about when and why, and make sure that it is for the right reasons, such as forcing a longer timescale strategy (such as the Amazon example in Chapter 8).

I covered a number of issues in the decision-making step, including data, culture, and cognition. Which are perceived as the most important or more easily achieved by managers? Better ability to analyze data and more accountability for decision making were the top two answers (Figure 9-9). Both of these are relatively easy to fix. However, all of those factors are achievable. They do require buy-in and support from the whole organization, from data entry clerks to the board. That is only possible with the right underlying open, enquiring culture and correctly incentivized and motivated staff. As one commenter (*http://bit.ly/rosenberg-hippo*) remarked, "As an analyst I can say even further that presenting data that decisively demolishes the HiPPO's viewpoint/agenda can be an invitation to be fired and blackballed at no small percentage of companies." That is unacceptable in a data-driven organization. Culture is thus the subject of the next chapter.

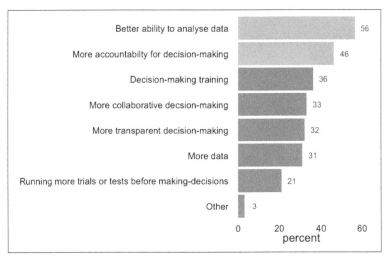

Figure 9-9. Which of the following do you believe would most help your organization improve decision making? (After chart 7 of "Decisive Action: how businesses make decisions and how they could do it better." Economist Intelligence Unit.)

CHAPTER 10

Data-Driven Culture

The biggest problem facing companies who are trying to innovate and transform themselves with data is a culture of "we've always done it this way."

—Gabie Boko[3]

A data culture isn't just about deploying technology alone, it's about changing culture so that every organization, every team and every individual is empowered to do great things because of the data at their fingertips.

—Satya Nadella[4]

If there is one common theme that runs consistently throughout this book, it is the importance of culture. As we imagine data flowing through the analytics value chain, there are a number of different touchpoints; some are human, and some are technological, but they are all shaped by the prevailing culture. Culture influences who has access, what can be shared, and what investments are made into people and tools. Moreover, as I covered in the previous chapter, culture also determines whether the last link in the chain is driven by HiPPOs or by facts.

---

3 Economist Intelligence Unit, "The Virtuous Circle of Data: Engaging employees in data and transforming your business" (*http://bit.ly/eiu-virtuous*) (London: Economist Intelligence Unit, 2015).

4 Nadella, S., "A data culture for everyone," (*http://bit.ly/nadella-data-culture*) The Official Microsoft Blog, April 15, 2014.

In this chapter, I draw out these different aspects more explicitly and in more detail and bring them together in one place to paint a more coherent picture of an idealized data-driven organization. I will first discuss the data-centric foundations: data access, sharing, and broad training to make use of the data. Next, I cover a goals-first culture; that is to say, defining experimental design, metrics, and success criteria up front, and also the ability for results, interpretation, and analysis to be discussed and debated. That is followed by discussion of iteration, feedback, and learning. I round off by discussing an anti-HiPPO culture and top-down data leadership.

In some sense, you can consider these topics, or hallmarks, as a list of key ingredients. Think of all the different cakes and cookies that can be made from flour, eggs, butter, and sugar. The final form depends on the ingredient quality, relative proportions, and the way that they are combined. Likewise for data-driven organizations. Their final forms vary, too. You have to shape the organization to what makes sense for you, given the starting point, the domain, and the size and maturity of your organization. Moreover, you should never expect to be at equilibrium; you will be constantly evolving. Instead, you should invest, experiment, and be patient.

Open, Trusting Culture

> Leadership needs to think of ways to reward those who shared data,
> incentivizing individuals and departments that develop and nurture
> open, accurate and sharable data and analytics.
> —Jennifer Cobb[3]

Data-driven organizations provide broad access to data. That involves providing access to data to staff outside the core analytics org, and also sharing data among business units, teams, and individuals. Let's tackle the latter first.

In Chapter 3, I told the story of Belinda Smith's patio table purchase and how drawing in other data sources provides a richer context about the customer's intent, motivation, and interests. By understanding that context better, the organization can provide superior services and products to meet that customer's needs.

---

3 Cobb, J., "Data Tip #2 - Build a Data-Driven Culture," (*http://bit.ly/cobb-build*) Captricity Blog, October 30, 2013.

For now, let's ignore those external data sources, such as the Census Bureau and the MLS, and consider just some of the possible *internal* touchpoints of a customer at an online retailer:

- Clickstream on company's website
- History of purchases, returns, and exchanges
- Interactions with customer service representatives via email, chat, and phone
- Social media interactions with brand
- Social network data, such as through a refer-a-friend incentive program
- Brand exposure through retargeting

It is not hard to imagine that, typically, these data sources are managed by multiple different teams or business units. For the organization to maximize the potential of the data, the data must be brought together to provide that more complete, richer context. This is where culture comes in.

There has to be a clear signal from the business that the data is not "owned" by those individual teams but that they belong to the organization as a whole. Data leaders (discussed later) need to evangelize the benefits of sharing to the organization as a whole. However, failing that, there has to be the right incentives in place to bust the silos and share the data.

Of course, you have to do all of this without compromising compliance or increasing risk. Those are valid concerns. One-third of respondents in a survey (*http://bit.ly/eiu-fostering*) of 530 executives conducted by the Economist Intelligence Unit said that "their company struggles to achieve a data-driven culture in part because of concerns about the privacy and security issues that arise when data are shared."

Due in part to these practical concerns, but also inertia, the default mode from business owners is likely to be data hoarding. Thus, this is something that the data leaders have be very proactive to prevent. It won't happen passively. That same survey listed "promotion of data-sharing practices" as one of the top strategies (a close second to top-down mandates) that those executives found successful in promoting a data-driven culture (Figure 10-1).

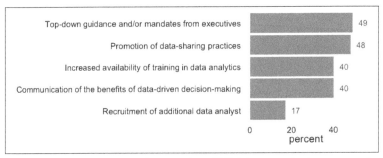

Figure 10-1. Responses to the question, "Which strategies have proved successful in promoting a data-driven culture in your organization?" from a survey of 530 executives sampled by the Economist Intelligence Unit.

By sharing data like this, you also require trust. First, individuals have to trust that the data is reliable and accurate. Second, they need to trust that the data will be used to good effect and not used against them. For instance, in one hospital (*http://bit.ly/hbr-confident*), "one doctor was afraid of his medical data being available to Emergency Room personnel; he didn't want them to see his notes in case he made a mistake." People have to get over this and focus on increasing the overall quality of their data. Third, and this takes up the second theme of this section, is providing broad access to the staff as a whole.

Data-driven organizations are much more open and transparent, and data is democratized, accessible to many individuals within the organization. "Everyone in the organization should have access to as much data as legally possible," said DJ Patil and Hilary Mason (*http://bit.ly/data-driven-report*) (although see Chapter 12). Access can be through static reports and dashboards but also "active access" in terms of business intelligence tools or even the raw data. This too involves a huge element of trust. The organization has to trust that the data will not be abused, leaked to competitors, or used to fuel political battles, but instead will be used in an appropriate manner to further the business as a whole.

Going further, a data-driven organization has greater potential to push decision making further down the org chart and out to the margins. If more employees have access to the data that they need, the necessary skills to analyze and interpret it, and there is sufficient trust, then more decision making can be democratized. For instance, imagine a retail store manager who can use business intelligence tools provided to analyze sales of SKUs in his store; perform seasonal trend decomposition; take into account local conditions, such as weather or construction; skillfully forecast trends; and place replenishment orders to head off stock outs while minimizing back-of-store inventory levels.

Obviously, many decisions, especially any important or strategic ones, are still going to flow up to higher levels of management. However, in most organizations, there are many decisions, especially operational, that could be tackled at the margins, provided that the right data, skills, and trust are in place. It is kind of like our nervous system. Most decisions are routed to the brain for processing, but if you step on a tack, a spinal reflex occurs in which the stimulus goes only as far as the spine before returning back to the muscles to move your leg. "Local" processing and decision making is sufficient to solve the problem.

Broad Data Literacy

If organizations are to take on a data-centered mindset—if there is to be a corporate culture that understands and reveres data—then intimate understanding of data must be embedded in the skills and characteristics of all employees at all levels, especially within the business.

—Accenture[3]

Clearly, analysts need training in experimental design, critical thinking, data presentation, use of business intelligence tools, statistics, etc. However, for a company to be data-driven, this set of skills and evidence- and fact-based perspective should be ingrained at a much broader scale. You need the managers and other decision makers to be data-literate too. Why is this?

- Managers sign the checks to purchase, install, and maintain a new business intelligence tool or predictive modeling service. They have to understand the value that this will bring to the organization.
- Managers sign off on disruption to their teams' workflow and suffer reduced productivity as analysts take classes, train, and

---

3 Accenture Technology Vision 2012. Data Culture. (*http://bit.ly/accenture-data-culture-2012*)

learn new tools. In short, they take a hit during the transition, so they must buy into the longer-term gains.

- Managers make the ultimate strategic and tactical decisions based on the analyses. They have to recognize the flaws and then push back when presented with a sloppy analysis. They should be constantly asking deeper, richer, more probing questions of the data and expecting more from the analysts. They also have to present their findings and conclusions to more senior managers, to the board, or to investors. That is, they have to understand the nuances of the analysis, have confidence in it, and be prepared to defend it.

In summary, managers don't necessarily need to understand the mechanics of how to gather, clean, process, and aggregate the data, but they should have an understanding of good experimental design, basic statistical inference, and the dangers of extrapolation. For instance, I saw an analyst present what I thought was a good and clean analysis to her manager—the decision maker—and then the manager asked me, "So, what's a p-value?" While it is up to the analyst to present the analysis in a meaningful, digestible form tailored to the audience, I believe that in a thriving data-driven environment, there should be some responsibility of the managers to learn some of those basic metrics, terminology, and inference tests, too.

Davenport and coauthors (*Analysts at Work*, p. 15) make this same point:

> As the financial and investment industries (and for that matter, all industries) become more data oriented and analytical, it is incumbent upon senior executives to master some degree of analytical complexity. Otherwise, they're not going to be able to push back when some trader suggests that they take on inordinate and poorly understood risk, putting their institutions and the customers in jeopardy.

And likewise at Strata+Hadoop World (*http://bit.ly/dalessandro-predictive*), Brian d'Alessandro urged:

> As managers and executives in the data business, if you have data scientists or data engineers in your team, you don't necessarily have to learn how to build predictive models, or implement the data hardware yourself, but you should have some statistical literacy because they are going to show up to you one day with a power-point presentation or a report and here is my analysis and frankly you are the last person who gets to call bullshit on any of the analysis that came through.

So what's to be done? A recent report (*http://bit.ly/eiu-virtuous*) found that "data-driven companies are ahead of their more gut-driven peers in offering employee training and implementation support as part of data initiatives (67% vs 53%)." In his 2013 Strata +Hadoop talk (*http://bit.ly/rudin-big-impact*), Ken Rudin describes the approach at Facebook: data camp. He tells of a two-week intensive, immersive camp that not only analysts go through but project managers, designers, finance, customer service workers, and operations, too. They even have a special version for engineers. The camp is structured so that participants face three hours of lectures each morning, part of which focuses on Facebook's data tooling. The afternoons, however, are spent working on a self-selected actual business problem. Working with a mentor for those two weeks, they learn how to explore data, to come up with hypotheses, to ask the right business questions, and to become more business savvy. Rudin says (*http://bit.ly/big-data-bootcamp*):

> If we continue down the path that we're going, and I think that we'll get there, then we'll have a culture where everyone feels that data is something they should be using as part of their jobs. Everybody should be doing analysis.

Not everyone is a Facebook that has the staff, resources, and clout to create such a program. However, every organization can start somewhere, and there are plenty of resources to help. Free, online classes in statistics abound and are offered by Coursera, Udacity, Khan Academy, and the like. There are some excellent books. I happen to like the free and open source *OpenIntro Statistics* (*http://bit.ly/openintro-stat*), but pick a book or set of training materials that match your audience's level and background. The key is to start somewhere, do something, and have buy-in to push staff—ultimately, a broad swathe of staff beyond the analysts—to develop their skills and get comfortable with data, tools, and analysis.

Goals-First Culture

> *Alice: Would you tell me, please, which way I ought to go from here?*
> *The Cheshire Cat: That depends a good deal on where*
> *you want to get to.*
> —Lewis Carroll,
> *Alice in Wonderland*

A focused organization, independent of whether it is data-driven or not, should have a clear direction, a commonly held vision of where the business is heading. The leadership's role is to gather people around that vision, align them, and get them working toward that joint goal. In a data-driven organization, that goal will be more transparent with clearly defined KPIs and associated definitions, clear targets, and a clear current state. That scorecard should be broadly accessible, with each member of the team understanding how their work contributes to nudging those top-level needles.

That set of top-level goals and KPIs will cascade down to business units that then may set their own dependent sub KPIs, which may flow down to lower-level metrics and targets. At some point, you get to individual projects, a coarse unit of "work" that requires setting a goal and success criteria. However, as best practice, it is not just with an A/B test (Chapter 8) that one should define the success metrics and criteria in advance. It pretty much goes with any analytical project. When running a data project, it is always possible to put a post-hoc spin on the data, to pick out something that goes in the right direction, which shows some sort of positive ROI. It is for this reason, in the interests of objectivity, that a data-driven organization should develop a goals-first culture. Define the metrics in advance of the go-live date.[3]

In the case where one is making a next-steps decision based on a number of variables, some of which are likely pros and some of which are likely cons, try to define the relative weights or a ranking for those variables in *advance* of the data collection process. That is, if the approach is to create a weighted decision matrix, define the weights very early on in the process. Thus, suppose that in choosing among three different vendors for a service, you will consider price, volume, and quality. Price and quality are likely negatively correlated in that vendor space. After the fact, it is easy enough to post-rationalize the relative weighting so that any of the three vendors comes out on top. By defining the relative importance of the three variables in advance of data collection, you make a clear case of what is important to the organization and reduce the ability to game the system or cherry pick data points to make a particular outcome win.

---

3 For more on running data projects, see Max Shron's *Thinking with Data* (O'Reilly) and Judah Phillips's *Building a Digital Analytics Organization* (Pearson FT Press).

Inquisitive, Questioning Culture

*"Do you have data to back that up?" should be a question that
no one is afraid to ask (and everyone is prepared to answer).*

—Julie Arsenault[3]

In Chapter 8, I suggested that an experimentation mindset changes
the conversation from opinions to hypotheses and thus that can be
tested objectively. Because they are merely hypotheses, and not an
expression of power or experience, those hypotheses can come
broadly from across the organization. This doesn't mean that everyone gets to test every crazy idea they come up with—there are many
considerations to take into account, including branding, usability,
development costs, and "risk"—but a broader set of stakeholders are
more likely to come up with a broader set of ideas. (Recall from earlier, "No one is as smart as everyone" and "Let the interns speak.")

In addition to giving everyone a voice, a data-driven organization
should encourage an *inquisitive* culture. It should engender an
atmosphere of healthy debate where one can ask for additional
information, challenge assumptions, and discuss recommendations
or additional tests. Have presentations and analyses provide references to the raw data. Frank and open discussion of possible issues
with experimental setup or interpretation and possible improvements can only serve to improve the business, but the key is that the
discussion should be nonconfrontational and neutral—it's about the
data, and not people.

A good model for this are scientists. A key component of classic
Western scientific training is to make young scientists as *objective* as
possible. Part of that culture is an active effort to depersonalize their
work. Scientific journals used to be written in the active voice but
they mostly switched to a passive voice[4] during the 1920s, a feature
that continues today.

While a passive voice can be considered less interesting to read, it
does reinforce the idea that results are far more about the experi-

---

3 Arsenault, J., "How to Create a Data-driven Culture," (*http://bit.ly/arsenault-data-culture*) PagerDuty, October 2, 2014.

4 Example: active voice (focus on doer): "we applied a fertilizer to the plants" versus passive voice (focus on subject): "the plants were treated with a fertilizer."

mental setup and the data per se and less about the people, or the experimenters.

A data-driven organization should encourage that same objective attitude, too. If a website A/B test shows that a larger checkout button does not drive more revenue or a higher conversion rate than the current smaller button, then so be it. It is no one's fault. That is just the way the world is. Instead, celebrate that finding as a new, valuable data point. (You can use that extra screen real estate for something else.)

Michele Nemschoff (*http://bit.ly/nemschoff-data-culture*) goes further:

> Embrace dissent. Challenging the status quo is good, so long as data verifies it. Not all businesses have a C-team that embraces outlandish suggestions. If creating a data-driven environment is a high priority to you, a certain level of dissent should be acceptable. In some cases you should even reward dissent. With the blessing of a C-team member, you need to instruct your employees to search off the beaten path within your data. New ideas—that are data-verified—are tremendous starting points for positive innovations.

Iterative, Learning Culture

Mistakes are the portals of discovery.
—James Joyce

In the previous chapter, I discussed that lack of accountability was cited as a key issue with decision makers. Someone should be keeping score, not only to make the decision makers accountable but for the organization to learn and grow. For instance, when involved in forward-looking activities, such as predictive modeling, it is important to have a feedback loop in which you frequently review the results, dig into individual cases (called error analysis), and understand where you can do better.

I used to be a data scientist at One Kings Lane, a home décor flash sales website. Each morning we opened the doors with about 4,000 products, about 60% of which had never been previously sold on the site. (These items were all limited quantity and would be sold for three days or until we ran out of product, whichever was sooner.) A colleague and I built a set of models to predict how many units of each SKU would be sold by the end of one and three days. We built a dashboard that showed our prediction errors: where our models got it wrong. Each morning, we would come in and spend an hour digging into those errors. What was it about this set of rugs that we predicted so badly? Are people are essentially choosing randomly among a set of very similar items? The daily routine was a lot of fun, in part because we set this modeling activity as a friendly competition between my colleague and I. We traded ideas back and forth, we understood the data better, and our models got significantly better. The key was a constant iteration and feedback, always digging into the edge cases, trying to understand causes, and looking for ways to improve.

The same is true of testing and experimentation, of course. As discussed in Chapters 8 and 9, our intuition is often very poor. More than half of online experiments fail to move the needle in the right direction or indeed at all. However, these are not failures if you evaluate why and learn from them.

Figure 10-2 shows a generic feedback loop. You design and run an experiment, instrument it and measure results, analyze the data, interpret the results, learn, hypothesize, and build a new experiment. Back at the top, around you go again. The "build experiment" step here is essentially a placeholder. It could easily be "build model" or "devise PR campaign." My point is that a data-driven organization should be making the most of *all* data, even the "fails," learning from them and then doing one more thing: *act*, to move the business forward.

This is an aspect that should be deeply rooted in the culture. In a data-driven organization, where everyone is watching the numbers, hypotheses can come from anywhere, and a large proportion of the staff is actively using data, there is a broad engagement and investment. People are able to watch and be watched. When you have a clear set of goals and people are focused on the top-levels KPIs, they will truly care when an experiment fails or a program soars. They will want to understand why and dig deeper and do even better. In a sense, you have to keep up the momentum around this cycle and not stumble when an A/B experiment "fails" but instead view this as a learning that is going to help provide inputs to new, and hopefully better, testable hypotheses next time around.

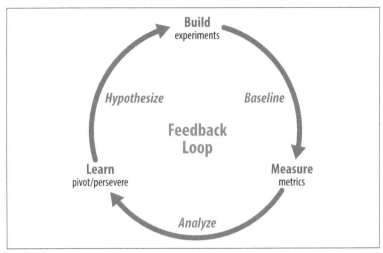

Figure 10-2. A feedback loop: build, measure, learn, and repeat. Redrawn from figure from Andrew Francis Freeman (with permission).

On an organizational scale, too, data-drivenness requires flexibility and iteration: as your organization grows and changes, you may find it necessary to reorganize your data teams and their place in the business structure.

Anti-HiPPO Culture

> *Hippos are among the most dangerous animals in Africa. Conference rooms too.*
> —Jonathan Rosenberg (*http:// bit.ly/rosenberg-hippo*)

As discussed in the previous chapter, HiPPOs are anti-data-driven. They make decisions based on their experience, preconceived notions, and their gut, *without regard to the available data*. This is bad for business, literally. One approach is to force their hand by making all decision makers accountable. If they are making excellent, impactful, gut-based decisions that propel the business forward, then great: that is what counts. However, if they are making poor decisions, they should be forced to change or perhaps more sensibly, be shown the door. HiPPOs will have a highly negative impact on a culture that is striving to be data-driven. Decisions are likely to be suboptimal; and HiPPOs, by the nature of their senior position in the company, hinder an honest, questioning culture. (Recall the quote from the last chapter: "Presenting data that decisively demolishes the HiPPO's viewpoint/agenda can be an invitation to be fired and blackballed at no small percentage of companies.") In other words, they impede an open, collaborative culture where ideas can come from anyone or anywhere, where people will readily admit, "I don't know, but let's test it," and the best, objective, and fact-based insights win out.

I want to be clear that intuition and experience do have a role to play. Sometimes, you just don't have the data available, especially if you are innovating in new, unchartered territory. Sometimes the data is highly informative but someone has to make a final decision, often in the face of some unknowns or uncertainty. I'm talking here specifically about those individuals who refuse to use or consider available data, especially if they have a track record of bad decisions and are unaccountable. Imagine being an analyst working alongside (against?) them. If the data lines up against the leadership, but the leader doesn't budge, it creates a situation of rebellion, which rarely comes out well.

Data Leadership

> *There is no substitute for a corporate leader who*
> *has found religion in data and analytics.*
> —Russell Glass[3]

Data-drivenorganizations require strong, top-down data leadership. They need a leadership that inspires, that promotes a data-driven culture, and actively drives and supports all aspects of the analytics value chain, from data collection through to data-driven decision making and institutional learning. They should be evangelists for data and data-driven practices.

Such leadership allow organizations to, in the words of Davenport and his colleagues, "compete on analytics." In a recent survey, 58% of respondents in outperforming companies agreed that top management leads by example in promoting data compared to 49% in the

---

3 Economist Intelligence Unit, "The Virtuous Circle of Data: Engaging employees in data and transforming your business" (*http://bit.ly/eiu-virtuous*) (London: Economist Intelligence Unit, 2015).

average and subpar performers, or the laggards (Figure 10-3). Conversely, 41% of laggards reported the lack of leadership in their organization prevents greater data adoption compared to only 23% of out-performers.

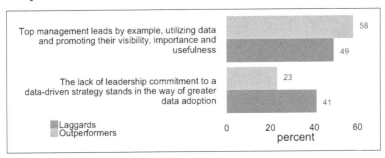

Figure 10-3. Organizations that outperform competitors are more likely to have strong leadership. From Economist Intelligence Unit, "The Virtuous Circle of Data: Engaging employees in data and transforming your business." (http://bit.ly/eiu-virtuous)

A data leader has several constituencies.

First, she has to support the analytics organization per se. That leader must provide them with the data, tools, and training that they need. She should define the organizational structure, modifying it as appropriate as the company evolves, and should also provide a clear career path and incentives for the analysts to be happy, productive, and do great work.

Second, the leader also needs to get buy-in from the rest of organization, especially the business. They need to believe that a data-driven approach is the right way to go. To garner that support, the leader needs to show results, even if they are only small wins at first. With that, the data leader has a better chance of fostering a data-sharing culture, a culture in which the business units are fully sold and part of that organizational-wide effort.

Finally, the leader has to have support from the rest of the senior management team. They hold the purse strings to the necessary IT infrastructure needed, the training budgets, and the key to development of a pro-data/anti-HiPPO culture within *their* teams.

This is clearly a superficial overview of data leadership and requires deeper inspection. Because data leadership is such a pivotal aspect of a data-driven organization, it forms the focus of the next chapter.

CHAPTER 11

The Data-Driven C-Suite

The ideal CDO exists to drive business value.
—Julie Steele[3]

*If the organization wants to be data driven there has to be
an evangelist that makes noise about what it needs.*
—Anon. in Shaw et al. 2014.[4]

So far, we've covered a lot of ground. I adopted a bottom-up perspective, following the data, influence, and impact from the raw data
up through the analytics value chain. I started with the foundation
of a data-driven organization: the data layer (i.e., collecting the right
data and collecting the data right). I also covered the analyst org:
hiring the right people with the right skills, combined in the right
way, who have the potential to do insightful, impactful analysis.
And, I covered the types of statistical and visualization tools and
fact-based storytelling approaches that ultimately can turn raw data
into sales pitches to aid the decision makers. Importantly, I also
highlighted what analysts, and their direct managers, can do to contribute to a data-driven culture and success.

At this point, we turn things around and adopt a top-down perspective. While a data-driven organization and its culture can certainly

---

3 Steele, J. *Understanding the Chief Data Officer*. Sebastopol, CA: O'Reilly, 2015.

4 Shaw, T., J. Ladley, and C. Roe, "Status of the Chief Data Officer: An update on the
CDO role in organizations today," (*http://bit.ly/status-of-cdo*) Dataversity, November 5,
2014.

blossom from below, to reach its full potential, it also needs shaping, sponsorship, and direction from above: data leadership. That is the focus of this chapter.

Someone has to hold the top data position in the company. For a long time, that has been the CTO or CIO. However, they have little time and breadth to regard the data as a strategic asset because they are primarily focused on the basic information *systems* themselves, the infrastructure to "keep the lights on." Fortunately, in the past decade, there has been a shift as more and more organizations view data not just as business "exhaust," cost, or liability, but as an asset per se. In that light, data, information, and analytics take on a greater importance and must be actively managed, cared for, and optimized. To that end, we have started to see a new set of C-level positions: chief data officer (CDO), chief analytics officer (CAO), and chief digital officer (CDO)—if you thought that two CDO positions was confusing, Johnson & Johnson recently hired a chief design officer (*http://bit.ly/wsj-jj-cdo*), so that makes three.

There is a great deal of confusion among these new roles, so I will go through both the chief data officer and chief analytics officer in some detail. (I'll only briefly contrast those against the chief digital officer because that role is less central to creating a data-driven organization.) For each, I'll highlight the role, history, and qualities that make a successful officer. I'll also cover some of the potential impacts to an organization and how you might choose whether your organization needs one, both, or none.

Chief Data Officer

The chief data officer, hereafter CDO, is the oldest of the three roles. The first appointee was Cathryne Clay Doss who took up the role at Capital One, a highly data-driven organization, in January 2002. Since then, the number of CDO appointments has risen rapidly.[3]

---

3 There are around 200 CDOs globally today. Gartner predicts (*http://bit.ly/gartner-cdo-prediction*) that by 2015, 25 percent of large global organizations will have appointed a CDO, and Shaw et al. suggest that numbers of CDOs will double approximately every 15–18 months for the next 5 years.

Currently, CDOs are primarily found in the following sectors:

- Banking and financial services (40% of total)
- Government
- Healthcare

And that itself provides a clue as to at least part of their role.[3] What is the common theme among those areas? Regulation. All of these are highly regulated, or it is the local, state, or federal government itself that sets the rules and regulations. Complying with Sarbanes–Oxley financial reporting or HIPAA compliance in healthcare or anti-money-laundering requirements in banking—all data-centric activities—are complex, closely monitored, and come with stiff penalties. It's a major risk for these organizations.

However, there is more to it than that. These types of organizations have been required to collect and protect data long before 2002. What changed? Likely, they started to realize that the data could be leveraged in new ways, could be an asset and not just a cost and liability, and that could be made actionable in new ways. At a recent Banking Analytics Symposium in New Orleans, only about 15% of participants had a CDO-like role in their organization. Charles Thomas (*http://bit.ly/thomas-cdo*), Wells Fargo's newly minted CDO, speaking at the event said, "You'll start to see more of a trend [in banking] because ultimately, we're sitting on tons of data, and we're not really using it in a relevant and timely fashion."[4]

Thus, the heart of a CDO's role is, or should be, to leverage data strategically. Mario Faria, an early CDO, told me, "The best of breed CDOs are doing more than compliance and governance. They are driving value and using their teams to pursue new ways to leverage data for business needs." With that, let's examine the role in more detail.

---

3 Although the breadth is growing to information services, insurance, and e-commerce (Shaw et al., 2014) and media and manufacturing (via Dave Vellante (*http://bit.ly/abercrombie-insight2014*)).

4 Crosman, P., Chief Data Officers Battle Complexity, Complacency: Wells' Thomas," (*http://bit.ly/im-cdo-battle*) Information Management, October 30, 2014.

CDO Role

IBM defines a CDO as "a business leader who creates and executes data and analytics strategies to drive business value."[3] As such, a CDO's role is an especially broad one, covering a range of areas and responsibilities, both technical and nontechnical in nature. The items discussed here essentially represent an idealized list. No two CDOs have exactly the same role because it is very situational, depending on budget, staff, and where they report (all discussed in the next section).

One potential CDO function is overseeing or leading data engineering and data management. They should define the vision, strategy, processes, and methods by which the organization acquires, stores, and manages its data and its quality. That may mean managing staff such as data engineers and data stewards. As discussed in Chapter 2, this is a foundational piece that, when missing, can lead to garbage in/garbage out and low or misleading impacts.

CDOs frequently oversee the definition of standards and policies. This ranges from policies around data quality and data sharing to service levels for access. They also cover the creation, maintenance, and visibility of data dictionaries across the organization. This is a key component that helps align stakeholders and avoids confusion by ensuring that everyone speaks the same language. This is not to be underestimated. At Warby Parker, my team worked closely with business owners to define a data dictionary, document it, and implement those precise business rules in a central business intelligence tool.[4] This may be the most impactful work that my team has done to date as it has reduced confusion, allows meaningful comparisons of metrics, and contributes to a reliable, central source of truth.

A thriving data-driven organization will have numerous data projects running at any one time, both within teams under the CDO, if any, and in other units. Thus, the CDO's role must be to support those endeavors by providing guidance, higher-level strategy, and coordination. The CDO should also measure and monitor

---

3 IBM Software, "Insights for the New Chief Data Officer," (*http://bit.ly/insights-cdo*) IBM Corp., June 2014. See also "The Role of Chief Data Officer in the 21st Century." (*http://bit.ly/cutter-cdo*)

4 Anderson, C., "Creating a Data-Driven Organization: Two Years On," (*http://bit.ly/anderson-two-years*) April 6, 2015.

the effectiveness of those projects, driving work to maximize analytical ROI and impact.

The CDO may run the analytics org, supervising teams of analysts and/or data scientists. If not, he or she will at least work extremely closely with members and managers of those teams. All of these resources cost money, so the CDO may maintain a budget, spending it on lines items such as data quality programs, hiring good analysts, training, purchasing data to augment existing internal data, and so on.

A key component of the role is identifying and exploiting new business opportunities. That is both an opportunity to generate new sources of revenue and take the business in new directions. Depending on where the CDO sits in the organization, and the budget and resources she has access to, this can mean exploring ideas themselves or providing opportunities for other teams to think and explore data, data visualization, and data products.

What types of opportunities make sense will greatly depend upon the sector and business model. For instance, in government, where CDOs are focused on public accountability and transparency, that can mean identifying and making datasets publicly available—ideally, in a programmatically consumable way[3]—that can provide value to other cities, states, or citizens in general. Success is others using your data and deriving value from it for the common good.

For many, success can mean being innovative with the data that you currently possess. Speaking at Strata+Hadoop World 2014 in New York, Under Secretary of Commerce for Economic Affairs Mark Doms described how the response rate to US census surveys is 88%. To reach the rest, you have to knock on doors, which is very expensive. To maximize their "hit" rate, they augment the census data with that from Social Security to estimate who should be at home and when.

Other organizations, however, are in the business of collating, enriching, and selling data. For those, success centers around finding new data sources, enriching them in novel ways, and educating

---

3 Application Programming Interface (APIs), which is how computers can communicate with each other and share data.

the sales team about new products that may provide value to their clients.

Matthew Graves is CDO of InfoGroup, a data and marketing services organization, which is a growing category of organizations appointing CDOs. Speaking at the CDO Executive Forum in New York, for him, a key component is

> being an evangelist. Working, even in an organization with sales that sells data, data continues to change. Educating them on improvements around the data, new data assets, educating internal sales organization, and our clients. Clients aren't used to leveraging data. That's the whole reason why these companies are trying to create a chief data officer to manage their own data.

Matthew mentioned the one concept that captures the heart of the CDO role: evangelism. To become data-driven, an organization has to leverage data as a strategic asset; and to achieve that, all parts of the organization needs some prodding, and they need some concrete examples of how data is, or could be, enriching and delivering impact. For this reason, a CDO has to have great communication skills with the ability to talk to IT staff in terms they understand and in ways that will stimulate, motivate, and inspire them.

Thus, CDOs should be shaping the culture, influencing others (both laterally in the C-suite and downward in the organization) to change attitudes as to how to view and use data. They should be creating an open, sharing culture, democratizing data by integrating data sources, which includes busting silos.[3] In short, they should be increasing data access and data literacy of the organization as a whole. It is a broad and challenging role.

Secrets of Success

In essence, the CDO is an evangelistic and change-agent role. As Peter Aiken, co-author of *The Case for the Chief Data Officer* (Morgan Kaufmann), told me, "CDOs aren't brought in if things are going swimmingly." If so, what's needed for success? Certainly, a mix of hard and soft skills are critical. For instance, when I asked Mario

---

3 There are of course exceptions. John Minkoff is the CDO of the enforcement bureau of the Federal Communications Commission. Because his team centers around prosecutorial data, he says that no other FCC bureau has access to their data, which makes sense.

Faria what makes a great CDO, he said, "We are able to combine hard skills (data, technology and statistics expertise, vertical knowledge, business acumen) with soft skills (communication, leadership, respect to adversity, willingness to change the status quo)."

Sampling more broadly across data leaders, a survey (*http://bit.ly/aiken-cdo*) conducted by Aiken[3] found that the top three CDO traits were:

- A balance of technical skills, business knowledge, and people skills
- Outstanding relationship building and communication skills
- Politically savvy

This is clearly much more than a technical role.

Where do CDOs report?

So, where do CDOs report? Ideally, they will report to the CEO and be a peer to CTO, CIO, CFO, COO, CISO, etc. Failing that, they should at least report to the business side (COO, CMO, etc.). However, in reality, 80% report to the CTO (Aiken, pers. comm. based on his 2013 survey[4]).

What's wrong with reporting to IT? Aiken (p. 52) argues strongly that "the CDO cannot accomplish data leveraging while subject to the structured deadlines of IT. Further, if they report through someone who is not data-knowledgeable, it will be impossible to improve the data decision-making process." He suggests that most CTOs are not trained or experienced in data management, are slammed, and have a different mindset to managing projects. He told me, "Data operates on a different rhythm than necessarily is going on in software, and it can't be treated like a project. It has to be managed at the programmatic level. And, if you are not managing it at the pro-

---

3 Aiken, P., "The Precarious State of the CDO: Insights into a burgeoning role," Data Blueprint, July 16, 2013.

4 Shaw et al. (2014) state that "CDOs mostly report to the CEO, COO or a key business function. Very few CDOs report to IT and the CDO is often a peer of the CIO." It may be that things have changed significantly in one year. However, Shaw's sample size is significantly smaller. Thus, there may be an element of sample size effects, survivor bias (those sampled are more successful, better supported, and prominent because they report to business), or other bias.

grammatic level, there's got to be a beginning and an end, and data doesn't do that."

In other words, data can support multiple projects simultaneously, and as a foundational piece, will often outlast and transcend those projects. As such, CDOs can better serve the organization through the business side rather than IT.

A mandate to influence

The most shocking revelations from Aiken's survey are that "almost half the CDOs had no budget, over half had no staff, and more than 70% had insufficient organizational support."

With so few resources, a CDO can essentially *only* be an evangelist and a cheerleader. However, that will only get you so far and for so long. Ultimately, you need to show results and, realistically, that will only come from a team and a budget. Recognizing this, Gartner (*http://bit.ly/logan-cio*) suggests[3] "new and aspiring CDOs will face daunting challenges and conflicting priorities as this new and evolving role has little professional structure and lacks established best practices."

To succeed in the role, even if you don't have a team or budget, you have to have a mandate to influence. There are some notable examples where that was not the case. Mark Headd (*http://bit.ly/phila-cdo*), the city of Philadelphia's first CDO, successfully released a number of datasets but hit a roadblock with an API around property tax owed to the city.[4] He encountered heavy resistance from the revenue department's commissioner. Mark said,

> Philadelphia is at a juncture where it is ready to take the next step in its open data evolution. To start sharing data across departments (hell, even across governments) and start identifying new ways of doing things—ways that are more efficient and more effective. I tried very hard to move us past this juncture and onto the next steps. I was not able to do so, and it became clear that I was never going to be able to do so...A self-certifying website is a 20th century answer to the problem of tax deadbeats. An open data API is a 21st

---

3 Logan, D., and M. Raskino, "CIO Advisory: The Chief Data Officer Trend Gains Momentum," (*http://bit.ly/logan-cio*) January 13, 2014.

4 Reyes, J., "Why Philadelphia's first Chief Data Officer quit," (*http://bit.ly/phila-cdo*) Technical.ly Philly, June 19, 2014.

---

century answer to the problem. And that was my single biggest frustration during my time at the city—we were constantly using 20th century answers to problems that required a 21st century solution.

Changing attitude and culture is hard.

Coming to the Bank of America, John Bottega had a stellar record: CDO at both Citi (2006–2009) and the Federal Reserve Bank of New York (2009–2011). He says, "When most firms created a CDO-type position—whether it was a head of market data, a head of reference data, a chief data architect or whatever the actual title—it started as a siloed business focus. Today, it's more of a horizontal responsibility across the enterprise." Having said that, he was given no organization to take on and shape that responsibility and was provided little support. Moreover, he had an especially tough situation. BoA is enormous (more than 200,000 employees), and the different lines of businesses are literally businesses themselves: wealth management, deposits, mortgages, cards, etc. "If you are trying to get people aligned around a corporate goal or objective, it becomes really, really difficult," said Peter Presland-Bryne, SVP, Chief Architect, Consumer Real Estate Division at BoA at that time. "Imagine coming into Bank Of America as chief data officer. It is a corporate level position and you are supposed to drive influence over all these lines of business who are perfectly successful and rewarded in spite of the chief data officer." Bottega's position at BoA was shuttered after just two years.[3]

There are of course a number of counter examples. Some CDOs have the budget, resources, and support that they need to succeed. Charles Thomas from Wells Fargo has, in his words, a "small team" of 600 and a $100 million budget. Kyle Evans, CDO of RP Data, has a staff of 200. Micheline Casey, CDO of the Federal Reserve Board (and CDO for State of Colorado from 2009–2011) had a 2014 operating budget of around $10 million and a team of 25. "If you read the strategy document for the FRB (*http://bit.ly/frb-strategy*),[4] it's the ideal chief data officer job," said Lewis Broome.

---

3 Peter explains that the data team gained traction when BoA focused on business value, specifically deepening relationships with customers. With a "business imperative" coming down from the chairman, Brian Moynihan, the business(es) had good reason and incentive to get on board with data quality, governance, and sharing.

4 Federal Reserve Board. *Strategic Framework 2012–2015* (*http://bit.ly/frb-strategy*), 2013.

"She reports to the COO who reports into the chairman." Moreover, it was the chairman who created the position. So, what is needed then is support from the CEO and the board that data management and leveraging data strategically is a sufficiently high priority to require a top-level C-suite position and, importantly, to back that up with associated budget, support, and protection.

Another strategy for success is to find a partner in crime. For Greg Elin, the first commissioned CDO of the FCC, that was Michael Bryne. "Michael, also the FCC's first Geographic Information Officer—believed like me in the power of RESTful APIs," Greg told me. "I'd like to think there was something special about having these two roles, CDO and GIO, promoting a particular way of thinking about working with data made it easier to bring APIs to such a high profile project [National Broadband Map] in an agency that had never built an API."

The First 90 Days

I asked Mario Faria his strategy for the first 90 days:

> The first 90 days are critical, especially if you are new to the organization you landed. The first month should be used to talk to as many people as you can, from C-level executives to the trainees. You have to understand what it is going on and you have to start building your political bridges.
>
> The second month should be used to start crafting your short, medium, and long term plan. Above all, during this time you should have the mission and vision ready for your organization. With that in place, you are going to have the future view for your team.
>
> The third month, after your plan is ready and approved, is where the true action starts. Here you are going to start to delivering the initial quick wins. You will always need to strike points, make quick and small wins all the time, to show progress to your team, in order to motivate them and to the rest of the organization, to prove it was a wise decision for them to hire you.

Greg Elin:

> Evangelism and looking for distinct opportunities to improve how the FCC collected, used, managed, and distributed data in order to create momentum and change how people thought about data. Important data projects had already started up when I became the chief data officer. The National Broadband Plan had been published and the FCC had launched a broadband perfor-

---

mance test. The Broadband Map was under development. The Chairman wanted a zero-based review of all FCC data sets and we were publishing a list of data sets from three major bureaus for public comment about what to keep, get rid of, and change. So there were many immediate tasks that I was just trying to keep up with and help make a bit smarter in how they worked with data.

My strategy was similar to Mario's. I talked to many people from each of the different teams to get the lay of the land, inventory the different data sources, and get a sense of their relative importance. With each team, I asked them two key questions. With your current data and processes, what do you need help with? That helped identify inefficiencies and automations that we could put in place to deliver those quick wins. I also asked a broader question: what are you not able to do that we can help with? This helped identify new, additional data sources or functionality not in place that formed our more longer-term plans.

Future of the CDO Role

If the CDO role is primarily a data evangelist and change-agent role, what happens when everyone "gets it"? Will it still be needed? Aiken (2013: p. 65) hints that this might be a temporary role when he draws parallels to the chief electrification officer role, a position that came about in the 1880s as organizations switched from steam to the latest hot technology, electricity. Of course, everyone today gets electricity; it's a commodity, so that particular CEO position was largely gone by the 1940s. Could the same become true of data and, in particular, the CDO role?

Greg Elin largely agrees:

> I hope the role of CDO as it is established now as some type of C-suite official responsible for transforming data into an asset for daily use fades over the next couple of decades as using data and analytics becomes an integrated part of the business. Enterprises benefit most when data, and IT in general, is developed integrally with business processes. In other words, CDOs now should be focusing on developing the data capabilities and even self-sufficiency throughout their organization.
>
> Unfortunately, like the many roles created in organizations to address a real need, the role of CDOs will likely remain a fixture past its useful life. The role makes sense now because enterprises

find it easier to have an identified point person to spearhead and manage change.

Richard Stanton (*http://bit.ly/stanton-cdo*), CDO of Penton Media, is more definite: "There's no question the CDO role will become more important. I don't know what that title will be, but the role—the accountability that's currently being played in that role—will be in every organization. I absolutely believe that to be the case."

In a conversation (*http://bit.ly/abercrombie-insight2014*) between Courtnie Abercrombie, Emerging Roles leader at IBM, and Dave Vellante, co-CEO at SiliconANGLE, Courtnie remarked that "I think [CDO] is absolutely here to stay and I think it will cause other positions to morph around it because data is so incredibly important to competitive advantage for companies right now. It really is the new way to be innovative, learn new things about your customer segments…I don't see the role going away at all and it's only going to grow in importance." Dave responded, "I agree, especially inside those regulated businesses…It's going to become the norm." Lewis Broome, however, is not so sure: "I don't think that people have figured out data enough to know whether it needs a role or not." Time will tell.

With that overview of the CDO, let us now contrast that with the chief analytics officer.

Chief Analytics Officer

The chief analytics officer (CAO) overlaps considerably with the CDO position. While the CDO focuses more on the backend (i.e., data management), the CAO focuses significantly more on the strategic use of the data and, as the name suggests, analytics. While the CDO *may* have the analysts report into him or her, the CAO should *always* head up the analytics org and so be closest to the analysts, data scientists, and other data-related roles.

"Data is only strategic if its analyzed, understood, and actionable throughout the enterprise, so the value in all that data can be realized,"[3] said Frank Bien (*http://bit.ly/fc-cao*), CEO at Looker. Importantly, he continued, "the CAO is about creating real business value

---

3 Bien, F., "It's Time To Welcome The Chief Analytics Officer To The C-Suite," (*http://bit.ly/fc-cao*) *Fast Company*, July 28, 2014.

through data analytics and promoting the company's data-driven culture."

This then brings us to the heart of the book. The role is to enhance the data-driven practices and culture, and deliver tangible results to the organization. Bill Franks (*http://bit.ly/cw-cao*), CAO at Teradata, claims:[3]

> As the technology matures, companies are seeing the power of what analytics does. The CAO is a natural extension of that, because the more that analytics is embedded across the organization, the more you need an executive-level position to convey that strategic emphasis.

A CAO should have sufficient vision to see the potential in existing data, understand how it relates, and have sufficient clout to bust silos and bring that data together in the best, most impactful way. The CAO should also monitor the performance of the analytics org, provide training and mentoring, and restructure the organization as necessary. Typically, that would mean greater centralization (*http://bit.ly/forbes-cao/*)[4] into a center of excellence, federated, or hybrid model. That is, a CAO is likely only brought into an organization when there are already pockets of analysts embedded in various parts of the organization, such as within individual business units. As discussed earlier (Chapter 4), that model leads to lack of standards, redundancy of effort, and an unclear career path for the analysts themselves. By centralizing all that analytical activity under the umbrella of a single, visionary leader, you gain economies of scale, standardization, and a better trained, more mentored, and happier analyst team.

As one report (*http://bit.ly/akmeemana-cao*)[5] puts it, "More than just managers, CAOs are the champions for the need to generate value from data... More than senior data scientists, they must work across the executive ranks to make sure that their insights are turned into repeatable action. And, more than IT managers, they must under-

---

3 O'Regan, R., Chief analytics officer: The ultimate big data job?" (*http://bit.ly/oregan-cao*) *Computerworld*, October 3, 2014.

4 Rajaram, D., "Does Your Company Need A Chief Analytics Officer?" (*http://bit.ly/forbes-cao*) *Forbes*, August 8, 2013.

5 Akmeemana, C., E. Stubbs, L. Schutz, and J. Kestle, "Do You Need a Chief Analytics Officer?" Ontario: Huntel Global, 2013.

stand how to steer the company through the turbulent waters of big data and big analytics."

More concretely, the Sandhill Group produced a report titled "Mindset over data set: a big data prescription for setting the market pace (*http://bit.ly/sandhill-cao*),"[3] which listed out the following qualities of a CAO:

Characteristics	Attributes
Analyst	• Possesses superior business and data analysis skills • Formulates and evaluates sound business performance metrics • Brings strong analytics experience that earns the respect of staff and stakeholders
Evangelist	• Helps others understand the value of big data and its many applications • Provides examples that inspire others to embrace the big data mindset
Explorer	• Innate curiosity leads to interesting business questions and innovative, high-impact solutions
Leader	• Staffs and develops a high-performance big data team • Enlists the support and active participation of other organizations • Effectively manages teams directly and on a matrix basis to achieve agreed-upon commitments • Provides a realistic schedule, resource requirements, and cost estimates
Pragmatist	• Operates with a fail-early mentality • Sets appropriate expectations regarding timing and results • Gains consensus across groups with competing interests and priorities • Maintains a sound prioritization of initiatives from across the enterprise
Technologist	• Understands the associated technologies and can be a solid partner to the CIO, CTO, and chief information security officer

As you can see, part of the COA's role is listed as being a *big data evangelist*. In my research, just about every description of CAO's role contained this component. This of course reflects the current

---

3 Netke, S., and M. R. Rangaswami, "Selecting a Chief Analytics Officer — You Are What You Analyze" (*http://bit.ly/sandhill-cao*), SandHill Group, March 3, 2014. I did not have the $1995 spare to read the full report.

hype (*http://bit.ly/gartner-2014-hype*).[3] To me, data doesn't have to be big to be valuable, and what is big today will be small tomorrow. Technologies and terminologies will change, but what the CAO needs to do is get the rest of the C-suite and the rest of the organization to buy into and understand is the power of broad, rich, augmented, and high-quality *contextualized* data—such as Belinda Smith's patio set purchase in Chapter 3. Contextual data is the true foundation for highly impactful and transformative predictive models and recommendation engines or indeed any of those higher levels of analytics (Chapter 1). A CAO's role is to make that happen.

As with a CDO, the CAO will need sufficient support from the highest levels of the organization. Currently, few CAOs sit at the top level of the C-suite. Instead, they typically report to a C-level position on the business side. "The CAO should be viewed neutrally—a Switzerland of the executive suite. The CAO should be under an executive that naturally spans all of the business units that have analytical needs, such as the Chief Strategy Officer, the CFO, and the COO," says Bill Franks (*http://bit.ly/franks-analytics*).[4] "It is often easier to see where a CAO role should *not* report. For example, marketing analytics is quite important to many organizations. However, if the CAO reports to the CMO, then other business units such as product development or customer service might not feel that they get equitable treatment."

The CAO role is newer than the CDO role. According to one report, [5] in November 2013, 477 LinkedIn members listed CDO as their current title compared to only 298 for CAO. (Presumably those are global figures, but they do seem high. In December 2014, I found 347 for "chief data officer" and 248 for "chief analytics officer" for global with "current title only"; in the US, results were 181 and 171, respectively, in line with Gartner's projections.) I found those CAOs most often in healthcare, media, and financial services.

---

3 According to Gartner's 2014 Hype cycle for emerging technologies, big data is close moving out of the peak of inflated expectations to entering the trough of disillusionment.

4 Franks, B., "Do You Know Who Owns Analytics at Your Company?" (*http://bit.ly/hbr-who-owns*) *Harvard Business Review*, September 23, 2014.

5 Akmeemana, C., E. Stubbs, L. Schutz, and J. Kestle. "Do You Need a Chief Analytics Officer?" (*http://bit.ly/akmeemana-cao*) Ontario: Huntel Global, 2013.

As with the CDO, the CAO is fundamentally about change and shifting culture. That is terribly hard to do and often meets resistance. You need buy-in from the business units. Thus, it is not surprising that there are some casualties. In one telecommunications company, the business unit managers were slow to train and use the customer retention and pricing models developed under the new analytics leader. They "didn't see the potential, which, frankly, wasn't part of 'their' strategic priorities," McKinsey consultants said. "In our experience, many companies spend 90 per cent of their investment on building models and only 10 per cent on frontline usage, when, in fact, closer to half of the analytics investment should go to the front lines." A CAO has to invest time, money, and effort in the last mile, getting the frontline business users and their managers to see the value in the models and analytical tools but also train those personnel to realize the value. In other words, this is a weak point in the analytics value chain and must be shored up.

One approach that worked well, at least for one consumer company, is to use the CEO as a forcing function. They insisted that a data leader work with a business unit leader who was not familiar with big data in developing a plan to realize the potential of analytics. "This partnership—combining a data and analytics expert and an experienced frontline change operator—ensured that the analytics goal outlined in the plan were focused on actual, high-impact business decisions. Moreover, after these executives shared their progress with top-team counterparts, their collaborative model became a blueprint for the planning efforts of other business units." In other words, by forcing the analytics leader and the representative of business end users to collaborate so closely and, importantly, making them jointly responsible with success, it created a laser focus on ROI and real actionable impact.

Unlike the current CDO uncertainties, I believe that the CAO role definitely has a rosy future. I'm bullish on it. Even if enterprises "get" data and it becomes a democratized commodity, they will still need a team of analysts and data scientists to ask the right questions, to filter and interpret insights,[3] and to work with decision makers. That team will need leadership from someone such as a CAO.

Chief Digital Officer

The chief digital officer is another new addition to the C-Suite, with the first appointment made by MTV in 2005. Their primary role is to oversee digital strategy. While they are less central to creating a data-driven organization, I mention them here because, first, they are, unsurprisingly, often confused with chief data officers. Second, their role is also a transformative (and transitional?) one, bringing organizations more heavily into the digital age. This has major implications on the data sources available, especially the types, modes, and variety of interactions with users and customers. Those novel data streams, often contextualized with location from mobile devices, provide rich additional context for the analysts and new outlets and sources of interactions with which to place data products such as recommendations, real-time credit approval, and other services.

The chief digital officer is a very rapidly growing role, having doubled every year from 2005–2013 (see Chief Digital Officer Talent Map (*http://bit.ly/cdo-talent-map*)) to more than a thousand today. In fact, there are more chief digital officers than chief data officers and CAOs combined. As the number and uses of mobile devices explodes, and the Internet of Things gains traction, the way that we interact in a digital world is rapidly evolving. The chief digital officer's role is to understand and oversee that change, to identify new services and digital offerings that the organization can provide, and to understand the new ways of engaging with customers. CDOs understand when and how to bring marketing spend from analog to (highly targeted) digital and to make effective use of social media. Importantly, they help to tie all those interactions on those different devices to a seamless omni-channel experience both from the user's perspectives and from an analytics perspective.

"The [chief digital officer] understands and leverages business intelligence data, empowering organizations' user psychologies and consumer profiles in response to brand messaging," said Olivier

---

3 I'm assuming that more of these insights will be autogenerated by machine learning, powered by ever more sophisticated technologies such as next generation deep learning.

Naimi (*http://bit.ly/naimi-cdo*), senior director of the global web platform and analytics for Sony. "Analytics data from digital channels is still an emerging paradigm, so it can be challenging to identify the right metrics. A [chief digital officer] can empower organizations by providing actionable insights by measuring, analyzing, and optimizing business intelligence data from all digital initiatives across multiple channels."

Conclusion

Hopefully, the distinction between these two important roles is now clear. As can be seen, to create a data-driven culture requires active top-down *data leadership*, someone who is focused on the bigger picture of what the organization can and should be achieving with data, information, and analytics. They are the ones that should be focusing on data and analytics strategy, looking out for new opportunities, defining the top-level metrics, and restructuring the organization as necessary to maximize agility, productivity, and impact.

How do you choose whether you need one, both, or neither of these positions? The particular title is not that important—they could be a chief data scientist or head of data—but the key, I think, is that *someone* (*http://bit.ly/franks-analytics*) has this broader, strategic role.[3] First off, very few organizations have both a CDO and CAO. A recent McKinsey report (*http://bit.ly/mckinsey-mobilizing*)[4] does mention at least one unspecified "large financial-services company" that added a CDO "who reports to the CIO but works daily with the chief analytics officer to help knit together data and new analytics tools and to speed frontline change." That, however, is an exception. Generally, to have both would feel a little confusing and redundant.

CDOs historically are more often found in regulated industries, and that is likely continue as other organizations in those areas catch up and adopt a "me too" approach. However, there is mixed opinion as to whether they are a short-term fix or not. The exception is the government sector, which is focused more on transparency and

---

3 Franks, B., "Do You Know Who Owns Analytics at Your Company?" (*http://bit.ly/hbr-who-owns*), *Harvard Business Review*, September 23, 2014.

4 Brown, B., D. Court, and P. Willmott, "Mobilizing your C-suite for big-data analytics," (*http://bit.ly/mckinsey-mobilizing*) McKinsey Quarterly, November 2013.

openness; and in that case, the CDO has a stronger future and a definite edge over the CAO. As mentioned earlier, CAOs tend to be where there is already some analytics around the organization, and their role is to broaden, strengthen, and evangelize that function. If that describes your situation, that could make sense. Generally, if in doubt, I would go for CAO because data is more likely to become a commodity than analytics, and it can be easier to evangelize around value from analytics.

Whoever they are and whatever their title, to succeed at their objective, these data leaders have to collaborate closely with, and have full backing of, other senior executives, the CEO, and the board. They need a budget, a team, and the ability to break through the barriers of individual business units and create an open-sharing culture where data is brought together to provide a richer, more valuable context. This will create an environment where analytics, insights, and data-driven impact can thrive.

Because individual data sources have a long life span and drive many different products, analyses, and projects, the data "should be run as a program, not as a project." This means breaking away from IT and shepherding it primarily under the business. Again, this more naturally aligns with a CAO, but it is better to have a CDO, even one that reports into IT, than to have no strategic data leader.

In the next chapter, I am going to explore one final but increasingly discussed and important aspect of data: privacy (or lack thereof) and ethics. How should a data-driven organization treat personal and sensitive data?

CHAPTER 12

Privacy, Ethics, and Risk

You have zero privacy anyway. Get over it.
—Scott McNealy[3]

An ethical person ought to do more than he's required to do and less than he's allowed to do.
—Michael Josephson

In the previous chapter, I quoted Patil and Mason, who suggest that "Everyone in the organization should have access to as much data as legally possible." While I agree in theory, in practice there are some important caveats when you consider the issue from a privacy, ethics, and risk standpoint. In many cases, who should access which data and, further, what they may *do* with the data, is often more restrictive from a self-imposed ethical and risk perspective than from a legal one. A data-driven culture is one that respects both the power of data and the humanity of the people who are the source of that data.

How should a data-driven organization treat its users' or customers' data from these three perspectives?

I'm assuming here that a data-driven organization has:

- More data

---

3 Sprenger, P., "Sun on Privacy: 'Get Over It'," (*http://bit.ly/wired-privacy*) *Wired*, January 26, 1999.

- A richer context than other organizations
- More points of integration among the nonsiloed data sources
- Greater data access and visibility
- More staff across the organization who are skilled at analytics
- More data scientists who can eke out subtle patterns

Principles of Privacy

In 1998, the Federal Trade Commission published an important document entitled "Privacy Online: a Report to Congress." (*http://bit.ly/ftc-privacy*)[3] Much of the content now seems dated. For instance, then only 14% of all children were online; today, 80% of children under 5 are online weekly (*http://bit.ly/usat-kids-online*). However, one aspect that has stood the test of time are the five fundamental principles of privacy:

Notice/Awareness
"Consumers should be given notice of an entity's information practices before any personal information is collected from them."

Choice/Consent
"Giving consumers options as to how any personal information collected from them may be used."

Access/Participation
"An individual's ability to both to access data about him or her-self—i.e. to view the data in an entity's files—and to contest that data's accuracy and completeness."

Integrity/Security
"Managerial and technical measures to protect against loss and the authorized access, destruction, use, or disclosure of the data."

Enforcement/Redress
A mechanism to enforce the other principles.

---

3 Federal Trade Commission. *Privacy Online: A Report to Congress* (*http://bit.ly/ftc-privacy*), June 1998.

In short, I assume that more data, more access, and more data science translates to more power and more risk.

Data is powerful, but also dangerous. As such, this chapter covers a number of aspects to do with privacy, ethics, and risk, covering some of the dangers and the seemingly nonaligning interests of organizations and their users. I argue that organizations should, as a guiding principle, practice empathy. By acting in an ethical manner —both by setting out policies and also training staff to act in an empathetic manner—and putting users' interests foremost, they will develop and retain their users' trust, protect both their and their users' interests, and so mitigate some of the risk.

Respect Privacy

As the car pulled up to Uber's Long Island Office, Josh Mohrer, Uber's New York general manager, was waiting outside, iPhone in hand. As journalist Johana Bhuiyan stepped out, Josh said, "There you are. I was tracking you." (*http://bit.ly/bi-uber-godview*)[3] He was using an internal tool called the "God View," allegedly widely accessible to Uber's corporate staff, that provides a real-time view of vehicle and customer locations. This wasn't the first time Uber had violated users' privacy. At a Chicago launch party three years before, partygoers watched a live map of where *identifiable* customers, including venture capitalist Peter Sims (*http://bit.ly/sims-uber*), were traveling around New York.[4]

The issue here is that neither of these two customers was informed that their data would be used and shared in this manner, nor did they consent. Yes, Uber may need such access and tools to help improve the service, but neither fall under what the FTC had previously set out: "necessary to complete the contemplated transaction." Both of these examples go beyond that use case.

In these particular cases, no actual harm was done, but it is not hard to imagine scenarios that could be damaging or dangerous: someone

---

3 Kosoff, M., "Uber's Top New York Executive Is Being Investigated After Using Uber's 'God View' Tool To Track A Journalist's Location," (*http://bit.ly/bi-uber-godview*) *Business Insider*, November 19, 2014.

4 Sims, P., "Can We Trust Uber?" (*http://bit.ly/sims-uber*) Silicon Guild, September 26, 2014.

fleeing an abusive partner, a customer being dropped off at an HIV testing clinic, or a celebrity with restraint orders against a stalker. (Danah Boyd (*http://bit.ly/boyd-privacy*) provides additional examples in the context of Facebook's privacy settings.)

A privacy policy, essentially a contract between the user or customer and the business, must set out clearly who is collecting the data, what data will be collected, how it will and will not be used, how it may be shared with or sold to third parties, any consequences of refusing to allow consent, and "the steps taken by the data collector to ensure the confidentiality, integrity and quality of the data."

Uber had clearly violated its privacy policy,[3] but adherence is not the only issue that all companies should consider. Users should be able to comprehend policies. End-user license agreements (EULA) are sometimes very long. While Hamlet is about 30,000 words, Paypal's service agreement (*http://bit.ly/bbc-small-print*) is 50,000 words, or equivalent to the first seven chapters of this book. These documents are written in legalese, but "normal" people are expected to agree to all the terms. An organization can respect its users by trying to write privacy policies that all of us can understand (i.e., are human-readable). (Any insinuation that lawyers are nonhuman is purely coincidental.) A fun example, one that shows both the legalese and the human readable side-by-side can be found at CodePen (*http://bit.ly/codepen-privacy*).

While I may joke about being human readable, this is actually a very important distinction for Creative Commons (*http://creativecommons.org/*), which considers and provides notices in terms of three layers in order to make protections "effective, enforceable, and invisible":

Human

Users should be able to understand what they are agreeing to. Facebook, which has been mired in controversy and complaints over the years concerning sharing settings, has, in fact, made significant strides recently, and its privacy policy (*https://www.facebook.com/policy.php*), while still long, is much more clearly structured and accessible to us nonlawyer users.

---

3 See Uber's Data Privacy Policy (*http://bit.ly/uber-privacy-policy*) and this Slate article (*http://bit.ly/slate-uber-privacy*).

Legal
> Full license in legalese that provides watertight protections.

Machine
> Using technological approaches such as P3P, Creative Commons make its licenses machine readable, and thus indexable and searchable by search engines. (Here is how Lawrence Lessig sees it (*http://bit.ly/lessig-cc*).)

In summary, respect your users by having a policy that they can understand and make an informed decision about, and respect users' privacy by sticking to the principles and terms within the document.

Inadvertent Leakage

The Uber launch party was an example where users' data or context —who was where, at what time—was explicitly shared. However, one of the issues that I envision increasing as numbers of organizations become data-driven, is that as more and more seemingly innocuous snippets of data are collected, and the greater data science firepower they possess, the greater the risk of inadvertent leakage to the wrong parties.

A few years ago, when Edward Snowden's revelations about NSA snooping first came to light and privacy was being hotly debated, I remember trying out a tool called immersion (*https://immer sion.media.mit.edu/*).[3] Immersion analyzes email *metadata* only. Metadata are attributes about an email, such as who it was sent from and to whom at what time, but does not analyze the content of the email itself. You might think that this has limited utility. However, running this on my email account, I was shocked at what it revealed. The tool clearly showed me groups of people who knew each other from different facets of my life, who likely introduced me to others, and the relative strength of those social ties. It essentially showed a very accurate reflection of my social network at that time. All this without accessing the email content. In another example, Latanya Sweeney (*http://bit.ly/sweeney-identify*) demonstrated that you can identify 87% of Americans uniquely from ZIP code, gender, and

---

3 See also Chen, B. X., "Using E-Mail Data to Connect the Dots of Your Life," (*http://bit.ly/bbc-email-data*). *The New York Times*, July 5, 2013.

date of birth.[3] We have increasingly more data and sophisticated tools and skills to paint this broader picture. It is like a Seurat pointillist picture but with data.

These data breadcrumbs across our online and offline world add up, and we data scientists are happy to piece them together. But, we have to do that in a way that is ethical—which is often more restricting than legal—and use that power carefully.

A legitimate legal use case, but one that had unfortunate consequences, comes from Target. In an article (*http://bit.ly/nyt-secrets*)[4] much discussed in the data science world, *New York Times* journalist Charles Duhigg tells the story of how Target marketers approached one of their statisticians, Andrew Pole, and asked whether he would be able to identify customers who were pregnant in their third trimester, before the birth records were made available to them and the competition. They figured that if they could identify these women early enough, they stood a better chance of targeting them with coupons and developing a loyal, over-tired new parent customer base.

Andrew and his colleagues successfully identified the types of purchases that pregnant women tend to make and Target started mailing coupons to them. All of this is legal, but the reason that this story generated so much discussion among analysts is because of the ethics involved and the story of the father of one teen.

Target sends out personalized coupon booklets. Normally, customers appreciate coupons for things that they buy anyway. However, pregnant women reacted differently. They didn't like it. Thus, Target started adding unrelated recommendations, such as a lawnmower coupon next to a diaper coupon, to bury what they knew in the booklets. One Target executive said, "We found out that as long as a pregnant woman thinks she hasn't been spied on, she'll use the coupons. She just assumes that everyone else on her block got the same mailer for diapers and cribs. As long as we don't spook her, it works."

---

3 Sweeney, L., "Simple Demographics Often Identify People Uniquelym" (*http://bit.ly/sweeney-identify*), Carnegie Mellon University, 2000.

4 Duhigg, C., "How Companies Learn Your Secrets," (*http://bit.ly/nyt-secrets*) *The New York Times*, February 16, 2012.

While Target worked hard to disguise what they knew, it didn't get past one concerned father:

> About a year after Pole created his pregnancy-prediction model, a man walked into a Target outside Minneapolis and demanded to see the manager. He was clutching coupons that had been sent to his daughter, and he was angry, according to an employee who participated in the conversation.
>
> "My daughter got this in the mail!" he said. "She's still in high school, and you're sending her coupons for baby clothes and cribs? Are you trying to encourage her to get pregnant?"
>
> The manager didn't have any idea what the man was talking about. He looked at the mailer. Sure enough, it was addressed to the man's daughter and contained advertisements for maternity clothing, nursery furniture and pictures of smiling infants. The manager apologized and then called a few days later to apologize again.
>
> On the phone, though, the father was somewhat abashed. "I had a talk with my daughter," he said. "It turns out there's been some activities in my house I haven't been completely aware of. She's due in August. I owe you an apology."

These product recommendations, manifested in coupons, had leaked the girl's gravid state to a family member. They had leaked not P.I.I. but what Danah Boyd calls P.E.I., personally *embarrassing* information.

Most medical data is covered by protections such as the 1996 Health Insurance Portability and Accountability Act (HIPAA). Here, her state was pieced together by her prior purchases of innocuous products such as unscented lotion. With the right data and tools, analysts have tremendous ability to peek inside people's lives, and so they have to consider the consequences carefully, not just to avoid creeping those people out.

Practice Empathy

I believe that data-driven organizations have to respect their users' rights and sensibilities. While those organizations may wish to push the envelope allowing them to collect more and more data that provides richer fodder for advertising, services, and data products, they will ultimately fare better in the long run if they are trusted by users.

There's a simple test when choosing default privacy settings or developing new data-centric strategies, features, or campaigns:

would you like it if it were your or a close family member's account? How would you feel? If it feels uncomfortable, then don't do it.

At Warby Parker, General Counsel Anjali Kumar has a name for this: the "ick factor." It is a qualitative measure of creepiness, not meant to have any specific legal definition, but instead it is a reminder that we hold ourselves to higher-than-legal standards and must consider the customer's perspective, to exhibit empathy. How would the customer feel about this?

Here is an example (*http://bit.ly/wp-customer-svc*): Anjali was traveling on a train back to New York, and the person sitting in front of her got off but, unfortunately, left his glasses behind. They happened to be Warby Parker glasses. When she returned to the office, the two of us got together and asked: would it be creepy to try and track this person down and return his glasses to him? What's the ick-factor on that? We had a serious discussion and decided that we would be acting in the customer's best interests. Thus, we used our databases to track down the likely customers (remember that we had the frames, gender, rough age range, and knew which stop he got off), narrowed it down, and made the final confirmation using the photo on his LinkedIn page. Anjali then sent that person a new pair of glasses, a copy of "On The Road" by Jack Kerouac, and a note:

> Hi Michael, This might be odd… but you sat across from me on the train ride from NYC to Boston a few weeks ago and left your glasses on the train! As luck would have it, I happen to be the GC of Warby Parker, and there is nothing I like more than a good mystery… I hope these find you in good health! (also, we noticed your lenses were scratched so we made you a fresh pair!) Sincerely, AK[3]

The point is that we took his privacy very seriously. We didn't do it for fun or because we could. Instead, we asked the question among legal and data leadership whether that customer would find it creepy, whether we were doing it for the right reason, and whether that customer would perceive our motivations correctly: to provide great customer service.

---

3 Phelps, S., "Heroic Customer Service by a Senior Executive at Warby Parker." (*http://bit.ly/wp-customer-svc*) *Forbes*, August 1, 2014.class

Pushing the Envelope

Facebook has had an ongoing battle with its users, frequently pushing the boundaries about what is shared and to whom, but a few times has had to retreat when users complained in droves. Mark Zuckerberg has said that privacy controls were "the vector around which Facebook operates" and appears to believe that Facebook is simply tracking changing social norms: "People have really gotten comfortable not only sharing more information and different kinds, but more openly and with more people. That social norm is just something that has evolved over time."

The evolution of their stance, the default privacy settings for different aspects of the site, is striking. Compare the following two figures, which show the defaults from 2005 (upper) with those five years later in 2010 (lower). Both figures from "The Evolution of Privacy on Facebook." (*http://bit.ly/mckeon-fb-privacy*)

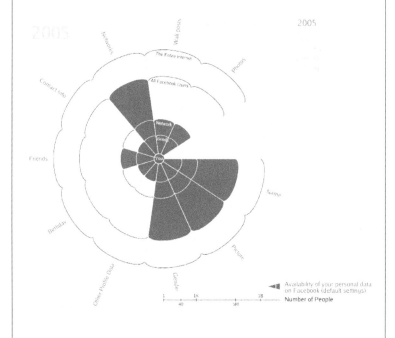

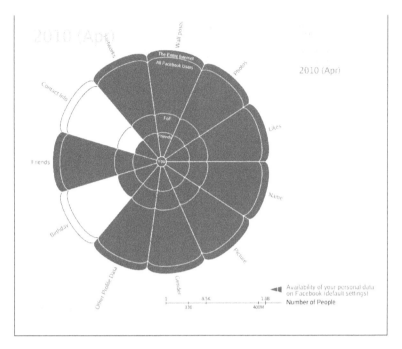

It was a calculated risk, but fortunately the customer did appreciate it and remarked on social media, "I just experienced possibly the very best customer service of all time." (To be clear, we did not advertise what we had done in any way. Our only motivation was to do right by the customer. It was only picked up by the media because the customer, pleased, shared his story though his social network which, ultimately, included a journalist.)

Data-driven organizations have a lot of power. Use it to be the good guys.

Provide Choice

Where possible, provide users intuitive and appropriate controls over how their data is used or shared with others. Simple examples include providing users the ability to control the type and frequency of marketing emails that they might receive, whether to receive push notifications from apps, and whether they wish to receive offers from partner organizations. More controversial, however, is the aspect of sharing data with other parties. This has been a particular issue with various social networks (Facebook being just one example; see box), where changing default settings are ever more encroaching on privacy.

One problem is that even if you do provide controls, many users don't understand the various options available to them. Consequently, the vast majority of people simply accept the defaults. There are at least two things that an organization can do. First, design with empathy. Make the controls simple, intuitive, and clearly documented. Second, put privacy and respect foremost and design with an opt-in versus opt-out mentality. Provide the user choice and control.

Netflix provides an interesting feature in its "account settings" panel. Users can opt-out of A/B test participation (Figure 12-1), something that I have not noticed before with other services.

Figure 12-1. Netflix (http://www.netflix.com) provides customers the opportunity to opt out of A/B tests in the account settings.

You can see the conflict here. Netflix is doing right by its customers, providing choices. However, it is an extremely data-driven organization, a company that A/B tests very heavily. It wants large samples to draw meaningful conclusions from A/B tests as quickly as possible. Opt-outs would reduce sample size, increase test duration, and potentially introduce some bias into samples.

I would hazard a guess, however, that only a tiny fraction of users have actually opted-out. If I am right, this is a win for subscribers (they can opt-out if they have any concerns), and a very low opt-out rate would actually have negligible impact on the testing data and the organization as whole. In this situation, Netflix is, and is perceived to be, good guys without actually giving up much. This should serve as model for other data-driven organizations.

Data Quality

One of the FTC's core principles of privacy concerns is access/
participation. That is, the ability to view the data that the organization has and to be able to contest or correct the information.

I would argue that this is probably the least developed of all its five
principles. Most online services provide users the ability to edit their
profile page and update their current name, address, email, and
other personally identifiable information. Some organizations, especially social networks, allow you to export an archive of your data
(e.g., Twitter and Facebook). What you can't do in most cases is edit
all the historical data, such as prior purchase orders, or review all
the "adjacent" data that the organization may have collected about
you (e.g., from the US Census, MLS, data brokers, social media, and
so on). Frankly, that would be very difficult to provide, would likely
be difficult for the customer to comprehend the disparate set of
database records, might violate agreements with any data that was
purchased from other organizations, and would likely expose some
secret sauce of the organization. Thus, I don't envision much progress being made in this area.

However, data-driven organizations certainly should make it as easy
as possible to review and correct core customer data. It aligns with
the interests of the customers and themselves. With data from different internal sources, for instance from a loan application and
checking account data within the same bank, there are plenty of
opportunities to associate the same customer with different customer IDs or introduce slight variations in address in different entry
points (e.g., "Street" versus "St." or "Apt. 6" versus "#6"). Making it is
as easy as possible to correct and standardize customer's data leads
to higher-quality data for the organization.

If you were to look at my Netflix account, you would get a very
skewed sense of my tastes. You'll see recommendations for highly
diverse shows such as *The Magic School Bus*, *Gilmore Girls*, and
M*A*S*H. Those do not, I should hasten to add, accurately reflect
what I watch. This is because our family shares the account, and so
the shows viewed and the consequent recommendations are really a
melange of four users, not one. While Netflix has the concept of a
profile to help tease out multiple users, this feature is not available
on the device that I use to watch the service.

Create opportunities for customers to provide additional context about their data to influence how the organization views or uses it. Amazon, for instance, provides an "Improve Your Recommendations" (*http://bit.ly/amazon-iyr*) feature, whereby the user can specify that "this was a gift" or "don't use for recommendations." There are many reasons why someone doesn't want an item influencing recommendations and showing similar items in the future, some potentially embarrassing. Whatever the reason, enabling the user to correct, filter, and exclude data, the organization gains a more accurate picture of intent, context, and taste. In the reverse direction, providing the user some context of why a recommendation was made can be reassuring. For instance, my Netflix account currently shows, "Because you watched M*A*S*H" and a recommendation for Magnum P.I., which makes sense. Such explanations can also reveal if there is inaccurate information that the user wishes to exclude or correct. In summary, by adding such features, you can create more of a two-way conversation between the user and the organization, leading to higher-quality data, a more accurate context, and, ultimately, a higher-value service to the users themselves.

Security

I hinted earlier that risk mitigation can often restrict activity more than is legally required. Why is that?

Let's start with a simple example. Many data workers, such as data engineers and database administrators, have access to raw customer records. Those records often have name, address, phone, email, and other PII. That is allowed by law. They have such access because they are tasked with making sure that the information is correctly captured and securely stored, enabling them to fulfill the obligations of the business transactions.

Now imagine an analyst downstream who is running an analysis of the number of sales of different products on different days. There is nothing legally preventing him from having access to those raw records. However, does he really need that level of detail? Should he have access to that data for that analysis? He doesn't need to know that it was Belinda Smith from that particular address with that particular email and phone number who purchased that patio set; he only needs to know that one unit of SKU 123456 was sold on that day.

Most analyses are in aggregate and thus don't need PII.

In his book *Dataclysm*, Christian Rudder, cofounder of dating site OKCupid, presented a number of analyses from the site's data. With the exception of medical data, you can't get more sensitive data than a dating site. Profiles contain photos, gender, age, sexual preferences, interests, and other highly personal information. He states (p. 233) very clearly how data was treated:

> All the analysis was done anonymously and in aggregate, and I handled the raw source material with care. There was no personally identifiable information (PII) in any of my data...Where I had user-by-user records, the userids were encrypted. And in any analysis the scope of the data was limited to only the essential variables, so nothing could be tied back to individuals.

There are a couple of reasons why he would go to this trouble. First, he doesn't want any information to color his analysis, either consciously or unconsciously. As analysts, we want to perform the most objective analysis possible. Additional information can skew our interpretation. For instance, if you saw a user with first name Gertrude (*http://bit.ly/google-gertrude*), do you imagine her to be young or old? Old, right?[3] You can't help making these assumptions and judgements. By not including those additional variables, you reduce the risk of doing so and increase the chance of letting the patterns in the aggregate data shine through untainted.

Second, analysts often make copies of data to perform analyses and models in other tools. Thus, while one may use a business intelligence tool to perform some high-level aggregation, you may need to crunch the data in Python or R to develop sophisticated predictive models. That often means exporting data from the source data store onto files on your laptop. Every copy of the data outside the raw data store increases risk for the organization. Laptops gets stolen. Laptops can get hacked. An analyst working on her computer in an airport or at Starbucks is at risk of "over-the-shoulder attacks," meaning a bad actor looking at the information on her screen. Thus, the less information the analyst has in those files and the more layers of obscurification and protection, the better.

It is for these reasons that many organizations choose to anonymize the information that is exposed in data warehouses and business

---

3 See the results here (*http://bit.ly/google-gertrude*).

intelligence tools for reporting and analysis. Names, addresses, and emails are hidden completely or they are encrypted. For instance, `belinda.smith@example.com` might be encrypted as `f7bf49636a69c6ed45da8dc8d3f445a8a5e6bcc2e08c9a6b2bb6644 6c402f75c` using a SHA-256 hash. (This is a one-way street. You can reproducibly and easily convert from the email to the encrypted string, but it is very difficult, but not impossible, to go the other way and recover the email.) Again, in most cases, the organizations are not legally obliged to do this, but it makes sense to.

The more copies of data, the greater the risk. The more human readable the files, the greater the risk. The more shuffling around and integration of different data sources—which is more likely to be true of a data-driven organization that fosters data-sharing—the greater the risk. One third of executives (*http://bit.ly/eiu-fostering*)[3] say that "their company struggles to achieve a data-driven culture in part because of concerns about the privacy and security issues that arise when data are shared."

We can sum the lessons so far with the following maxims:

- Everyone who needs access to data to perform their function has access.
- Everyone only has access to the data that they need to perform their function.
- Sensitive data, such as customer and prescription data, should be treated with extreme caution: highly restrict access, anonymize, and encrypt.

Enforcement

The FTC said that "it is generally agreed that the core principles of privacy protection can only be effective if there is a mechanism in place to enforce them."

Of course, there are now many protections governing data collection, management, and privacy. Examples include Children's Online Privacy Protection Act (COPPA), which protects children's data and

---

3 Economist Intelligence Unit, "Fostering a Data-Driven Culture." (*http://bit.ly/eiu-fostering*) (London: Economist Intelligence Unit, 2013).

interests; HIPAA, which protects medical information; and PCI compliance, which covers payment data.

Obviously, you have to adhere to those. Those represent an upper bound, legally, of what can be done with the data. However, I would argue this is insufficient. Data-driven organizations must consider these broader issues of ethics and the ick-factor and develop their own internal guidelines and rules. They have to develop a data-centric moral compass. They should consider whether the user expects them to use the data in a particular way and whether those users would be uncomfortable with the organization doing so. Ask and answer, "How would you like it if this was done to you?" That, ultimately, will limit some of the activity that analysts may want to do or be able to do with the data at hand. Like the marketers at Target, there will aways be some group trying to push the envelope—they have their own KPIs to meet after all—so this requires corporate culture, data leadership, and training to set out what is acceptable.

Conclusions

In a data-driven organization, there will always be some healthy tension between different teams, such as analysts who want the chance to build cutting-edge data products and others, such as legal, whose job is to be conservative and minimize risk to the organization. While legal restrictions represent a hard bound, there is a definite, and often large, gray area where activities are both legal but potentially creepy.

An organization must respect its users and draw up guidelines of what is acceptable and unacceptable uses of data. Obviously, you will need to draw a line in the sand for the analysts, the ones that are working mostly closely with the data. At Warby Parker, we set out how each of our different data types (customers, sales, prescriptions, etc.) may or may not be used for different analytical and marketing activities. For instance, our optical prescription process includes date of birth. We believe that it is an acceptable use case for an analyst to better understand our customer base, at the *aggregate* level, by examining the age distribution of our optical and progressives customers but that it is not acceptable for the marketing department to target 25–34-year-olds at the *individual* level based on that source of date of birth information.

At data-driven organizations, however, there will be broader access to data and thus be available to staff whose primary role is not analytical, but who have access to data as part of their role (such as customer service representatives who need access to customer accounts) and who are using data to improve their efficiency impact. Those need very explicit guidelines and training, especially junior staff fresh out of college. For instance, you should spell out that they may not use customer's data, likenesses, posts, etc. in advertisements or Facebook posts without explicit permission from the customer, or that they should not explore data unnecessarily, such as searching databases for famous people, friends, or family. Provide concrete training around this. As the Spiderman comics (*http://bit.ly/uncle-ben*) state, "With great power comes great responsibility."" That responsibility and perspective has to be installed proactively into the organization.

CHAPTER 13
Conclusion

Data is the new oil!
—Clive Humby, Dunnhumby

What does it mean to be data-driven? You will have noticed that the answer doesn't lie in having the latest big data technology or a crack team of unicorn data scientists. They will certainly help, but being data-driven isn't about one particular thing. Instead, as I have argued, it touches upon the whole analytics value chain, indeed thfe whole organization. This is summarized in Figure 13-1.

In Chapters 2 and 3, I covered the bottom layer, the data itself—collecting the right data and collecting the data right. On top of that, you need people with the right skills, tools, and training to make good use of the data.

Certainly this includes the analytics org, but a data-driven organization will be far more inclusive than that and have a much larger user base across the organization.

As I have tried to stress, I believe that everyone in the organization has a role a play. It is a shared responsibility. The core chain runs from analysts, their managers, senior management, data leadership, to the C-Suite and the board. However, in a data-democratized environment where, as Ken Rudin says, "everyone is an analyst," it is the whole staff's responsibility to, among other things, make use of the data, tools, and training available, to embed facts into their processes where possible, to report data quality issues, to generate testable hypotheses, to challenge baseless strategies, opinions, and HiPPOs, and generally to use data to its best effect.

One aim of the book was to appeal directly to analysts and their managers. Their role is often underappreciated. Too often, the focus and discussion concerns top-down change when in fact they can have a pivotal role in enhancing and shaping the culture and organization for the better from the bottom up. This requires being more vocal, visible, and proactive.

Wells Fargo's chief data officer, Charles Thomas, sums it up well: "You'll hear me talk about analysts as action agents—get out of your cubicle, take off the geek hat, put on your business hat and show how those results get moved through the system. You're going to have to take extra steps in making sure you put those insights through the system, operationalize and put them into action." You've got to get out of your comfort zone and promote change and impact.

Figure 13-1. High-level overview of the different components that comprise a data-driven organization. (Modeled after Wayne Eckerson's framework in his book Secrets of Analytical Leaders.)

The analytics organization needs to be organized in the most appropriate manner (Chapter 4). Typically, this will be in some form of federated or hybrid model in which analysts are embedded within the business units but where there is also a centralized unit providing mentorship, support, standards, and a clear career path. Those analysts should be generating quality work, with at least some individuals focusing on forward-looking analysis and higher levels of analytics, such as predictive models and optimization. They should be selling their insights and recommendations to decision makers (the next layer in Figure 13-1) and ideally should be assessed on their actual, ultimate impact to the organization.

Driving the overall analytics program is strong data leadership. While this could come from personnel such as a VP of analytics or chief data scientist, increasingly, at least with Fortune 500 companies, this comes from a chief data officer and/or chief analytics officer (Chapter 11). The actual title is unimportant. What is important is the actual role and whether that person has a mandate, that is, the executive support and a budget to drive an analytics program and culture.

 Appendix B sets out a prototype vision statement for data. A vision statement is an aspirational description of what an organization would like to accomplish in the mid-term or long-term future. In this case, it sets out a future state sets out a future state of being a more data-driven organization in terms of facets such as data skills, literacy, and culture. Think through it and discuss with colleagues. What do you want to achieve?

The final layer, one that permeates everything, is the culture that shapes and is shaped by all of these lower layers. In essence, being data-driven requires these components and best practices in all these layers. For instance, HiPPOs break objective, fact-based decision making. Political wrangling and data silos break a collaborative, open culture.

Many organizations are working hard to become more data-driven. However, any change, but especially cultural change, is extremely hard. One stands the best chance of creating a thriving data-driven culture by baking it in as early as possible, creating it de novo rather than changing it after the fact. This, then, was part of the motivation for writing the book. I hoped to appeal to younger organizations, those that aspired to be more data-driven, and, being small with a lot more hires and growth ahead of them, stood a greater chance of success. In one survey of 368 startups (*http://bit.ly/geckoboard-*

culture)[3], 26% claimed that they are data-driven and "since the very beginning we made sure that data was part of our culture." Another 44%, also claiming to be data-driven, claim that "we have made great improvement and are still working on it." It seems comparable to learning a second language. Many people successfully learn a second language as adults, but it is far easier to do when young.

One thing that I have wondered is whether some online businesses are inherently biased toward being data-driven simply because they are centered around a data product. Imagine an online dating site such as OKCupid, a music recommendation site such as Pandora, or a content recommendation site such as Prismatic. Does being focused around a core algorithm, data science, and data scientists bias toward data-driven practices across the organization? Possibly, but not necessarily. It would be possible to have a core data product that is developed in a testing-focused data-driven manner but in which the organization's customer acquisition or marketing strategies are run by HiPPOs.

What may happen, however, is what is known in population genetics as the founder effect (*http://bit.ly/wiki-founder-effect*) and in the social sciences as path dependence (*http://bit.ly/wiki-path-dependence*). A bias in the founding team, such as a high proportion of engineers and data scientists who believe strongly in instrumentation and A/B testing, can set the early hiring biases, tone, and culture down the road of being data-driven, an environment to which later hires are subject to and influenced by. What is clear, however, is that *every* business can be data-driven. When competing on analytics, there is no restriction on domain.

Throughout the book, I have deliberately underplayed the role of technology. Not because it is unimportant, but I think that, ultimately, culture is a stronger driver. Let me explain. Imagine a data scientist joins an organization and turns up with the latest and greatest toolset (Spark, D3, R, scikit-learn, etc.). If she finds herself in a environment that doesn't have a great data culture, for instance the organization doesn't get A/B testing and it is run by HiPPOs, that data scientist won't be able to make an impact. She will likely leave, frustrated. Now imagine the converse. Imagine the data scien-

---

3 Geckoboard and Econsultancy, "Data Driven Culture: A global survey on the state of data driven culture in startups," (*http://bit.ly/geckoboard-culture*) 2013.

tist turns up to an organization that does have a great data culture, but they don't have all the tools and technology that the data scientist would want. Maybe they have basic relational databases but have never had a need, until now, for a graph database or for a Hadoop cluster. In this environment, that data scientist will be more likely to be able to get the funds and support to create or buy any tools that will make an impact. In short, having the right tools can have a massive impact. However, not having the right culture, or at least drive to create the right culture, is a killer.

Caution: The Rise and Fall of Tesco

Tesco, the UK-based multinational grocery chain, and the UK's largest private sector employer (330,000 jobs), has often been lauded as a paragon of a data-drivenness, an organization whose competitive advantage derived directly from analytics.

In 1995, the company rolled out its loyalty program, Clubcard. This allowed analysts to collect data on customers, target coupons, and reward customers. By being more targeted, coupon redemption rates increased from 3% to 70% (*http://bit.ly/tesco-big-data*).[3] By identifying finer segments, they were able to create new products focusing on high end ("Tesco Finest"), health conscious ("Tesco Healthy Living"), and value conscious ("Tesco Value"). In 1999, they racked up 145,000 different segmented mailings.

It was a huge success. Tesco market share soared to over 30 percent and made it the UK's largest retail brand. Today, it has 16 million active members and detailed data on two-thirds of all baskets. Customers have received more than $1.5 billion in savings from club points. They rolled out products specifically to attract segments such as new parents to become customers, and developed predictive models that factored in weather forecasts to optimize supply chain that saved $150 million in stock. They moved into online shopping, requiring all customers to sign up for Clubcard, and into banking. Today, Tesco has moved far beyond groceries. Michael Schrage (*http://bit.ly/hbr-tesco*) said, "With the exception of, say, an

---

3 Patil, R., "Supermarket Tesco pioneers Big Data," (*http://bit.ly/tesco-big-data*) Dataconomy, February 5, 2014.

Amazon, no global store chain was thought to have demonstrably keener data-driven insight into customer loyalty and behavior."[3]

The analytical powerhouse behind all this was a startup called Dunnhumby, which Tesco later bought a majority stake in. Lord MacLaurin, then CEO, told the husband-and-wife founders, "What scares me about this is that you know more about my customers after three months than I know after 30 years." Dunnhumby is considered "one of the jewels in the Tesco crown."

So how is Tesco doing today? The stock is at an 11-year low. The company lost $2.7 billion failing to expand to the US with Fresh & Easy, and posted a $9.6 billion loss for 2014 fiscal year. The chairman resigned in disgrace after overstating profits by $400 million. It's shedding up to 9,000 jobs and closing 43 stores and its headquarters. "I made a mistake on Tesco. That was a huge mistake by me," said a humbled Warren Buffet. Moreover, Dunnhumby, whose Clubcard program costs $750 million per annum, a price at which is unlikely to show positive ROI, is up for sale for $3 billion.

There is no single reason for the decline. Overstating profits doesn't help. However, competitors have developed their own loyalty programs, most of which are simpler—simplicity appeals to customers! —and instead of abstract "points," they reward users more tangible benefits, such as a newspaper or, importantly for Britons, a cup of tea.[4]

Unfortunately, being data-driven, and even doing it well, doesn't guarantee any success or sustained success. First, most successful strategies can be copied by competitors who can take advantage of free-rider effects. Second, the C-suite are still commanding the ship. If they set the wrong vision and strategy for the organization, even making the best data-driven decisions that support that strategy can still drive the ship into the rocks. The story of Tesco (see box) is one such sad example.

However, I've mentioned a number of studies throughout the book that provide evidence that being data-driven pays off. Organizations

---

3 Schrage, M., "Tesco's Downfall Is a Warning to Data-Driven Retailers," (*http://bit.ly/hbr-tesco*) *Harvard Business Review*, October 28, 2014.

4 Ruddick, G., "Clubcard built the Tesco of today, but it could be time to ditch it," (*http://bit.ly/telegraph-tesco-clubcard*) *The Telegraph*, January 16, 2014.

make decisions better, faster, and can more quickly innovate. Organizations that test more not only know if something worked, but are more likely to know why. Organizations are more inclusive, and everyone can contribute and see how their contributions roll up to company success.

Further Reading

Analytics Organizations

Aiken, P., and M. Gorman, *The Case for the Chief Data Officer* (New York: Morgan Kaufmann, 2013).

Davenport, T. H., and J. G. Harris, *Analytics at Work* (Boston: Harvard Business Press, 2007).

Davenport, T. H., J. G. Harris, and R. Morison, *Competing on Analytics* (Boston: Harvard Business Press, 2010).

Eckerson, W., *Secrets of Analytical Leaders: Insights from Information Insiders* (Denville, NJ: Technics Publications, 2012).

Data Analysis & Data Science

O'Neil, C., and R. Schutt, *Doing Data Science* (Sebastopol, CA: O'Reilly, 2014).

Shron, M., *Thinking With Data* (Sebastopol, CA: O'Reilly, 2014).

Siegel, E.,*Predictive Analytics* (Hoboken: John Wiley & Sons, 2013).

Silver, N., *The Signal and the Noise* (New York: Penguin Press, 2012).

Decision Making

Kahneman, D. 2011. *Thinking, Fast and Slow*. Farrar, Straus & Giroux, New York.

Data Visualization

Few, S., *Now You See It* (Oakland: Analytics Press, 2009).

Few, S., *Show Me the Numbers: Designing Tables and Graphs to Enlighten* (Oakland: Analytics Press, 2012).

Tufte, E. R., *Envisioning Information* (Cheshire, CT: Graphics Press, 1990).

Tufte, E. R., *Visual Explanations* (Cheshire, CT: Graphics Press, 1997).

Tufte, E. R., *The Visual Display of Quantitative Information* (Cheshire, CT: Graphics Press, 2001).

Wong, D. M., *The Wall Street Journal Guide To Information Graphics* (New York: W. W. Norton & Company, 2010).

A/B Testing

Siroker, D., and P. Koomen, *A/B Testing* (Hoboken: John Wiley & Sons, 2013).

On the Unreasonable Effectiveness of Data: Why Is More Data Better?

This appendix is reproduced (with slight modifications and corrections) from a post, of the same name, from the author's blog (*http://bit.ly/anderson-unreasonable*).

In the paper "The unreasonable effectiveness of data,"[3] Halevy, Norvig, and Pererira, all from Google, argue that interesting things happen when corpora get to web scale:

> simple models and a lot of data trump more elaborate models based on less data.

In that paper and the more detailed tech talk (*http://bit.ly/norvig-unreasonable*) given by Norvig, they demonstrate that when corpora get to hundreds of millions or trillions of training sample or words, very simple models with basic independence assumptions can outperform more complex models such as those based on carefully-crafted ontologies with smaller data. However, they provided relatively little explanation as to *why* more data is better. In this appendix, I want to attempt to think through that.

---

3 Halevy, A., P. Norvig, and F. Pereira, "The Unreasonable Effectiveness of Data. *Intelligent Systems, IEEE* 24, no. 2 (2009): 8–12.

I propose that there are several classes of problems and reasons for why more data is better.

Nearest Neighbor Type Problems

The first are *nearest neighbor type problems*. Halevy et al. give an example:

> James Hays and Alexei A. Efros addressed the task of scene completion: removing an unwanted, unsightly automobile or ex-spouse from a photograph and filling in the background with pixels taken from a large corpus of other photos.[3]

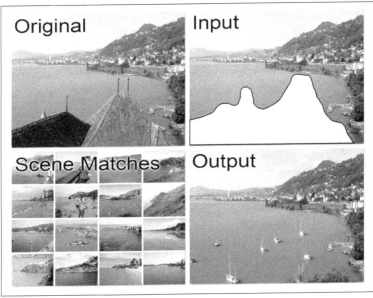

Figure A-1. Hayes and Efros's (2007) figure 1.

Norvig presented the following schematic:

---

3 Hays, J., and A. A. Efros, "Scene Completion Using Millions of Photographs." (*http://bit.ly/hays-scene*) *Proceedings of ACM SIGGRAPH 2007*, San Diego, CA, August, 5–9, 2007, pp. 1–7.

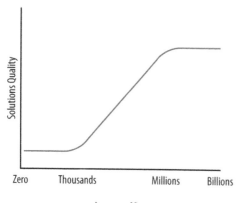

Amount of Data

and described it as a "data threshold" in which results went from really bad to really good.

I'm not convinced that there is any threshold or anything that resembles a phase transition. This seems to me to be a problem of finding the closest match. The more data, the closer the expected match.

Hays and Efros (2007) remark:

> Indeed, our initial experiments with the gist descriptor on a dataset of ten thousand images were very discouraging. However, increasing the image collection to two million yielded a qualitative leap in performance... Independently, Torralba et al. [2007] have observed a similar effect with a dataset of up to 70 million tiny (32x32) images...It takes a large amount of data for our method to succeed. We saw dramatic improvement when moving from ten thousand to two million images.

There is a large difference in those corpus sizes, and a "qualitative leap" is not the same as a threshold (*sensu* phase transition).

More data can dramatically affect the metrics from simple effects. For instance, consider a sample of size n from a standard normal. How does the minimum of that sample vary with n? Let's create samples of different sizes and plot the minimum using the following R code:

```
x<-seq(1,7,0.5)
y<-vector(mode="numeric",length=length(x))
for (i in 1:length(x)){ y[i] <- min(rnorm(10^(x[i]))) }
plot(x,y,xlab="Sample size, n (log10 scale)",
  ylab="Minimum value of sample",type="b")
```

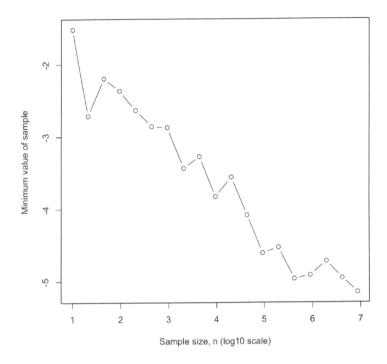

Sample size, n (log10 scale)

The minimum decreases loglinearly. This is a case of extrema from an unbounded tail. Perhaps more relevantly, here, for a minimization problem such as scene matching there is a lower bound: for all intents and purposes, a perfect match. For instance, perhaps someone else stood in the same exact tourist spot and took a picture of the exact same scene but without the obstructing car.

I think this is what is happening in Norvig's schematic. At a certain corpus size, we've found a really good match, and a larger corpus doesn't and cannot improve results.

In summary, for nearest-neighbor-type minimization problems with a non-negative distance function (meaning that the cost function has a lower bound of zero), that distance function will, on average, decrease monotonically with data or sample size.

Relative Frequency Problems

The second class are *counting* or *relative frequency* problems. These were the primary focus of Halevy et al. Norvig's presented a few examples. In segmentation, the task is to split a string such as "cheapdealsandstuff.com" into the most likely sequence of words. These strings are short enough to do a brute force in terms of possible partition, but for each partition, we have to assess the likelihood of that partition. The simplest assumption is to assume independence among words. Thus, if Pr (*w*) is the probability of a word *w* given some corpus we can compute, say:

```
Pr(che,apdeals,andstuff) = Pr(che) × Pr(apdeals) × Pr(andstuff).
...
Pr(cheap,deals,and,stuff) = Pr(cheap) × Pr(deals) × Pr(and) ×
Pr(stuff).
```

One can of course also use n-grams (e.g. for bigrams): Pr("cheap deals") × Pr("and stuff")

A second example that Norvig covered was spell checking. Here we can take a misspelled word and compute the likelihood of the possible variants to suggest the most likely form.

In both cases, we need a corpus that includes both common and uncommon phrases, and we need counts of the occurrences of those phrases to compute relative frequency. The larger and more comprehensive the corpus, the better. I think that there are two statistical effects going on here:

- The larger the corpus, the better the quality of the estimate of the relative frequency. This is the law of large numbers (*http://bit.ly/law-large-nos*).
- The larger the corpus, the more likely it is to include unusual phrases (i.e., the long tail). This is an unbounded effect. The more the Web is indexed, the most new phrases will appear. The problem is exacerbated in that the distribution of words in the English language is a power law. (e.g. Zipf, G. The Psycho-Biology of Language. Houghton Mifflin, Boston, MA, 1935.). This means that the tail is especially long; therefore, especially large samples are needed to capture those rare phrases.

Estimating Univariate Distribution Problems

A third class are *estimating univariate distribution problems*. I recently encountered an interesting example while attending a tech talk[3] from Peter Skomoroch from LinkedIn.[4] He showed a plot of likelihood of a member having particular software-related job titles versus number of months since graduation. What we see from the data is that the distributions of "Sr Software engineer" and "senior software engineer" are almost identical, as one would expect as they are synonyms, as are "CTO" and "chief technology officer." This then presents an interesting way of identifying synonyms and so deduping the data rather than maintaining a huge master list of acronyms and abbreviations. This is only possible because of the scale of data that they have where the distribution they can generate is reliable and presumably close to the true underlying population distribution.

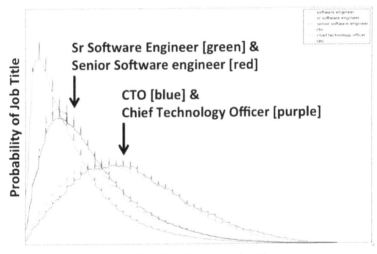

(From Peter Skomoroch, reproduced with permission.)

---

3 Skomoroch, P., "Developing Data Products," (*http://bit.ly/skomoroch-developing*) December 5, 2012.

4 "Analytics Talk: Peter Skomoroch," (*http://bit.ly/skomoroch-analytics*) December 13, 2012.

Multivariate Problems

A fourth class are general *multivariate* or *correlational* problems in which we are trying to estimate the relationship among variables. This could be estimating the relationship $y = f(x)$ or perhaps estimating the joint PDF of many variables. We might use this for word-sense disambiguation (e.g., is the document referring to pike the fish or pike the pointed weapon?) or to build up a dossier of associated features or concepts about an entity (e.g., a company has an associated CEO, head office, tax ID and so on). Here we are interested in the correlations among words or phrases. The problem is that web documents are very high dimensional, and embarking on high-dimensional problems like these we are under the "curse of dimensionality" (*http://bit.ly/curse-dimensionality*) that data become very sparse. Thus, one effect of larger samples is to increase the density of data across state space. Again, with larger samples, we can estimate metrics such as location metrics (mean, median and other metrics of the center of distributions) more accurately. We can also estimate joint PDFs more accurately. The following graph is a simple example derived from this code:

```
par(mfrow=c(1,2))
plot(mvrnorm(100, mu = c(0, 0),
 Sigma = matrix(c(1, .9, .9, 1), 2)),xlab="X",ylab="Y",
 ylim=c(-4,4))
title("n = 100")
plot(mvrnorm(10000, mu = c(0, 0),
 Sigma = matrix(c(1, .9, .9, 1), 2)),xlab="X",ylab="Y",
 ylim=c(-4,4))
title("n = 10000")
```

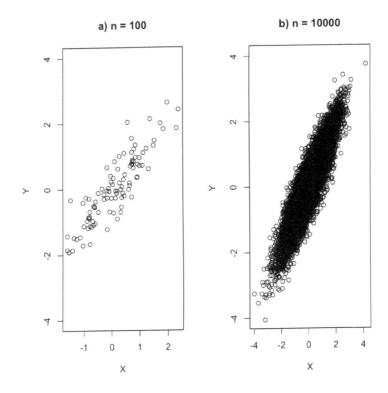

a) n = 100   b) n = 10000

At left is a small sample. It could easily be interpreted as linear. At right, with a larger sample, the true underlying bivariate normal is more obvious. Clearly, this is a trivial example. The point is that for higher dimensions, you will need much larger sample sizes to estimate the joint PDFs well.

This is clearly a cursory answer as to why more data is better. Quality data is still preferred. However, for many organizations, such as Google, Twitter, LinkedIn, and Facebook, where content is user-generated, often free-form text and/or covers many domains (and so deep-cleaning and the use of ontologies is infeasible), then what we see is that having very large datasets can compensate for the noise. It all evens out in the end, and in the case of nearest neighbor problems, the solution will always be better.

Vision Statement

This appendix can serve as a starting point for a vision statement— an aspirational description of what an organization would like to accomplish in the mid-term or long-term future—for a more data-driven version of your organization. The goal should be to highlight where you want to get to, align stakeholders, and stimulate discussion of how to get there. All organizations are different, so tailor it to represent your organization's true vision.

A thriving, data-driven [Company Name] has a/an:

STRONG DATA LEADERSHIP

- Data leaders actively evangelize data as a strategic asset, leveraged to its fullest to impact all parts of the business.
- Strong data leadership understands and supports the needs of the business. It supports the analytics staff by providing them with a clear career path, enables them to perform their best, to be happy and productive, and to maximize their impact.
- Managers expect and rely on data insights to make informed decisions. More generally across organization, data and analytics are deeply embedded into our processes and decisions.

OPEN, TRUSTING CULTURE

- There is a centralized set of coherent data sources without any silos.
- Business units have a sense of data ownership, proactively managing data quality of their sources.

- There is a broad access to data.
  — Everyone who needs access to data to perform their function, has access.
  — Everyone only has access to the data that they need to perform their function. Sensitive data, such as customer and prescription data, should be treated with extreme caution: highly restrict access, anonymize, and encrypt.
  — All staff can easily get a holistic view of the company through highly visible and accessible dashboards, reports, and analysis. Systems are instrumented and alerted as reliable early warning systems.
- Analysts are highly collaborative, proactively reaching out (across departments) to help validate ideas and ensure objectivity.

SELF-SERVICE ANALYTICS CULTURE

- Standard reporting is fully automated. Analysts spend the majority of their time on ad-hoc analysis, data discovery, and forward-looking analytics such as predictive modeling and optimization.
- Business intelligence tools will serve standard data discovery work with a SQL interface supporting all other ad hoc queries.

BROAD DATA LITERACY

- All members of the analytics organization are strong in core analytical, data munging, and statistical skills as appropriate to their role.
- All decision-makers, including senior management, are data literate and have a firm grounding in statistical inference and experimental design.
- There is significant opportunity to share, learn, and develop skills through avenues such as workshops, courses, books, lunch and learns, and mentorship.

OBJECTIVE, GOALS-FIRST CULTURE

- There is a clear, commonly understood vision of where the company is headed driven by a highly visible, often referenced KPI scorecard that motivates and drives strategy, actions, and tactics.

INQUISITIVE, QUESTIONING CULTURE

- There is a respectful environment with healthy discussion and the ability to debate others about their data, assumptions, and analytical interpretation.
- "Do you have data to back that up?" should be a question that no one is afraid to ask and everyone is prepared to answer.

TESTING CULTURE

- Strong testing culture: all reasonable ideas should be tested (both online and offline): gather data, learn, repeat. Objective experimentation is the norm.

Value

Of course, you should then supplement this with reasons *why* staff should buy into this vision:

Finances

Controlling for other factors, data-driven organizations have a 5–6% greater output and productivity than their less data-driven counterparts. They also have higher asset utilization, return on equity, and market value.

Analytics pays back $13.01 for every dollar spent.

Data leadership

Centralized, more supported analysts are happier and less likely to leave.

Self-service

If teams have a better grasp of statistics, experimental design, and have at least one member skilled at SQL, they will be more self-sufficient. That should translate to being more independent, nimble, and scalable.

Testing

Make decisions using both quantitative and qualitative data from real customers. We don't have to guess how customers might react or respond to features.

With ability to roll out tests more easily and to interpret the results properly and consistently at scale, we can innovate more rapidly. We can test dozens or hundreds or ideas per month, optimizing the site.

Activation

Finally, you'll need to set out or agree upon an actual plan, actions as to *how* you are going to realize this vision. What do you need from your colleagues?

Data leadership
Agree upon an analyst competency matrix.

Raise the bar for new and existing analysts. Push existing analysts to further develop their skills.

Open, trusting
Be a proactive partner/business owner in data quality. Develop views, alerts, and other checks to monitor data volume, quality, and issues

Self-service
Learn SQL. All teams will need to be more self sufficient and be able to do more ad hoc queries.

Data literacy
All managers should develop a strong grasp of statistics.

Objective, goals first
Tie all projects back to top-level strategic objectives. Make it clear why we are or are not doing a project, why work is (de)prioritized. Use a concrete numbers such as ROI wherever possible.

So, for each facet of the culture that you wish to achieve, you will need to set out the what, the why, and the how.

Index

A

A/A tests, 161
A/B testing
  A/A tests and, 161
  alternative approaches to, 171-174
  best practices, 160-170
  cultural implications, 174
  data-drivenness and, 9
  examples of, 155-158
  Netflix account settings, 247
  reasons for, 159
  running the experiment, 168-170
  sample size calculators, 164-168
  success metrics, 161
  test plan for, 162-164
Abela, Andrew, 137
Abercrombie, Courtnie, 228
ability (Fogg Behavioral Model)
  actions to outcomes, 196
  aspects of, 195
  collaboration and consensus, 197
  consistency and, 199
  training and, 199
absolute metrics, 116
Accenture, 207
accessible data, 2, 21
accountability, lack of, 186, 195
accurate data, 21, 38
accurate metrics, 114-115
ad hoc reports, 12, 87
aggregated versus raw data, 50
Aiken, Peter, 222
alerting

data-drivenness and, 5
  as level of analytics, 12
  mapping with types of analysis, 87
  operational dashboards and, 149
Altman, Tracy Allison, 196
Amazon, 57, 249
Amelia package (R), 31
analysis (see data analysis)
analysts
  about, 60
  CAOs as, 230
  data quality and, 19
  importance of, viii
  organizing into teams, 76-82
  team skills and roles, 65-68
  tool recommendations, 71-76
  traits and qualities, 69-70
  types of, 59-65
analytical dashboards, 148
analytical paralysis, 185
analytics engineers, 61
analytics framework (Davenport), 8, 13
analytics maturity (levels of analytics)
  about, 11-17
  mapping between types of analysis and, 87
analytics value chain, viii, 10
analyzing data (see data analysis)
anchoring, 189
Anderson, Edgar, 29, 72
Andreassen, Paul, 185
Anscombe's quartet, 95

Anscombe, Francis, 95
arithmetic mean (average), 90, 102
arrangement (data visualization checklist), 139
Arsenault, Julie, 211
aspirational organizations, 15
automation bias, 200
average (arithmetic mean), 90, 102

B

Babbage, Charles, 41
backfire effect, 189
Balanced Scorecard approach (KPIs), 122
bar charts, 134-137
Barr, Stacey, 123
Bayesian statistics, 172-174
Berkun, Scott, 181-183
Bernanke, Ben, 182
Berners-Lee, Tim, 41
Berra, Yogi, 111
Bhuiyan, Johana, 239
bias
    automation, 200
    confirmation, 191
    friend or foe, 192
    information, 185
    recency, 191
    survivorship, 191
biased data, 32, 114, 166
Bien, Frank, 228
big data, 43, 184, 230
Big Thinkers infographic, 145
black swans, 103
Bohr, Niels, 103
Boko, Gabie, 203
Bottega, John, 225
box plots, 96-97
boxplot() function, 29
Boyd, Danah, 240, 243
brain size to body size ratio, 146
Broome, Lewis, 225
Bryne, Michael, 226
Buffet, Warren, 260
business analysts, 61
business sufficiency models, 199

C

C-Suite
    about, 217
    chief analytics officer, 228-233
    chief data officer, 218-228
    chief digital officer, 233
Carroll, Lewis, 209
Casey, Micheline, 225
categorical variables, 88, 92, 97-99
causal analysis, 107-109, 157
Center of Excellence model, 80, 229
central tendency measures, 90
centralized analytical organization, 77-82
chartjunk, 130, 140, 145
charts
    choosing, 134-138
    designing elements of, 138-145
check digit, 27
chief analytics officer (CAO)
    about, 218
    characteristics and attributes, 230-230
    role of, 228-233
chief data officer (CDO)
    about, 218
    first 90 days strategy, 226
    future of role, 227
    mandate to influence, 224-226
    reporting hierarchy, 223
    role of, 220-222
    secrets of success, 222-226
chief design officer (CDO), 218
chief digital officer (CDO), 218, 233
Children's Online Privacy Protection Act (COPPA), 251
click-through rate (CTR), 156
CNN, 128
Coase, Ronald, 83
Cobb, Jennifer, 204
cognitive barriers to decision making, 187-192
coherent data, 21, 39
collaboration in decision making, 197
Colli, Jarred, 175
color (data visualization checklist), 139
complete data, 21, 39

Health Insurance Portability and Accountability Act (HIPAA), 243, 252

HiPPOs (highest paid person's opinion), 175, 177, 186, 201, 214

histograms, 96-97

Hodgkinson, Gerard, 184

Holloway, Todd, viii

Howard, Michael, 57

Humby, Clive, 255

hybrid organizational model, 79, 229

I

IBM, 14, 220

ick factor, 244

immersion tool, 241

imputation, 31

inferential analysis, 100-103

infographics, 145

information

    decision-making issues, 185

    defined, 85

    misinformation and, 189

information bias, 185

inquisitive culture, 211

insertion data entry errors, 25

interquartile range, 90

intuition, decision making based on, 179-181, 186, 192

J

Jain, Piyanka, 77

joinable data, 2

Josephson, Michael, 237

Joyce, James, 212

K

Kahneman, Daniel, 188, 190

Kaushik, Avinash, 119, 151, 177

Keely, Larry, 197

KISS principle, 149

knowledge, defined, 85

Kohavi, Ron, 155, 160, 170

Kosara, Robert, 140

KPIs (key performance indicators)

    about, 89, 111

    common examples, 121-123

    critical elements of, 119, 123

    determining number needed, 123

    executive dashboards and, 148

    goals-first culture and, 210

    target considerations, 124-125

Kumar, Anjali, 244

kurtosis (metric), 91

Kutcher, Ashton, 128

L

Leek, Jeffrey, 86

Lessig, Lawrence, 241

levels of analytics (see analytics maturity (levels of analytics))

Linden, Greg, 155, 175

lines (data visualization checklist), 139

location metrics, 90

lower-hinge (Q1), 90

M

Maeda, John, 5

MAR (missing at random), 33

margin of error, 102

Marr, Bernard, 121

Mason, Hilary, 206, 237

Masry, Samer, 20

maximum (metric), 90

Mayer, Marissa, 10

MCAR (missing, completely at random), 33

McCormick, PJ, 155, 164

McKinsey report, 232, 234

McNealy, Scott, 237

mean

    arithmetic (average), 90, 102

    geometric, 90

    harmonic, 90

measures

    about, 88

    direct versus indirect, 118

mechanistic analysis, 86

median (metric), 90

Mendelevitch, Ofer, 127

metadata

    data provenance and, 36

    immersion tool, 241

metric design
    A/B testing best practices, 161
    about, 4, 111
    accurate metrics, 114-115
    direct measures and, 118
    key performance indicators, 89, 111
    metric defined, 89, 111
    precise metrics, 116
    relative versus absolute metrics, 116
    robust metrics, 117
    simple metrics, 112
    standardized metrics, 113
Micallef, Maria, 124
minimum (metric), 90
Mintz, Daniel, 32
misinformation, 189
missing data, 21, 31-33, 36
MIT, 14, 185
MNAR (missing, not at random), 33
mode (metric), 90
Mohrer, Josh, 239
motivation (Fogg Behavioral Model), 194
multivariate problems, 271
multivariate testing, 171
Murray, Dan, 59
Murray, Scott, 64

N

Nadella, Satya, 203
nearest neighbor type problems, 266-268
Nemschoff, Michele, 212
Netflix test participation, 247
Nguyen, Thomson, 19
NHANES (National Health and Nutrition Examination Survey), 25, 29
NSA, 141, 152, 241
Nyhan, Brendan, 189

O

O'Neil, Cathy, 118
Obama campaign (2008), 159
operational dashboards, 149

optimization
    data-drivenness and, 9
    as level of analytics, 12
    mapping with types of analysis, 87
organizing data, 142-145

P

pairs() function, 30, 95, 99
panel bar charts, 135
Pascal, Blaise, 152
path dependence, 258
Patil, DJ, 42, 120, 206, 237
Peltier, Jon, 135
personal experience, decision making based on, 179-181
personally embarrassing information (PEI), 243
personally identifiable information (PII), 248, 250
Pole, Andrew, 242
power, defined, 165
precise metrics, 116
predictive analysis, 103-107
predictive modeling
    data-drivenness and, 10
    as level of analytics, 12
    mapping with types of analysis, 87
Presland-Bryne, Peter, 225
prioritizing data sources, 44-46
PRISM data collection program, 141, 152
privacy
    data quality and, 248-249
    elements of policies, 240
    inadvertent leakage, 241-243
    practicing empathy, 239, 243-247
    principles of, 238, 248
    providing choice, 246
    respecting, 239-243
    security considerations, 249
Procter & Gamble, 199
prove it culture, 195
provenance, data, 36
proxy (indirect measure), 118
purchasing data, 50-55

strategic (executive) dashboards, 148
summary() function, 29
surprise and delight campaign, 101,
159
survivorship bias, 191
Sweeney, Latanya, 241

T

Target marketing example, 242
Tesco grocery chain, 259
text (data visualization checklist), 138
Thomas, Charles, 219, 225, 256
timely data, 22, 39
transcription data entry errors, 25
transformation provenance, 37
transformed organizations, 15
transparent culture, 195
transposition data entry errors, 25
triggers (Fogg Behavioral Model), 200
truncated data, 35
Tufte, Edward, 140, 145
Tukey, John, 95
Tunkelang, Daniel, 70
Tversky, Amos, 190
Twain, Mark, 189
Twitter example, 128-130
Tye, Robin, 197

U

Uber car service, 239
units, inconsistent, 35
univariate analysis, 89, 96-99
unreasonable effectiveness of data,
265-272

upper-hinge (Q3), 90

V

validating data, 26-28
value (data dimension), 44
variables
    choosing charts, 134-138
    defined, 88
    descriptive analysis and, 92
    exploratory analysis and, 93
variance (metric), 91
variety (data dimension), 43
Vellante, Dave, 228
velocity (data dimension), 44
Vendantam, Shankar, 189
veracity (data dimension), 44
vision statement for data, 257,
    273-276
VLOOKUP function (Excel), 2, 73
volume (data dimension), 43, 52, 184

W

wc (word count) utility, 74
weasel words, 123
Webber, Susan, 118
Welch, Jack, 186
Wills, Josh, 62
Winfrey, Oprah, 128
Woods, Dan, 261

Z

Zuckerberg, Mark, 245

About the Author

Carl Anderson is the director of data science at Warby Parker in New York, overseeing data engineering, data science, supporting the broader analytics organization, and creating a data-driven organization. He has had a broad-ranging career, mostly in scientific computing, covering areas such as healthcare modeling, data compression, robotics, and agent-based modeling. He holds a Ph.D. in mathematical biology from the University of Sheffield, UK.

Colophon

The animal on the cover of *Creating a Data-Driven Organization* is a superb starling (*Lamprotornis superbus*). This vibrant species is common throughout the savannahs of eastern Africa, ranging from Ethiopia to Tanzania.

Superb starlings, once fully grown, are known for their distinct coloring: their heads are black, while their chests, backs, and wings are a brilliant metallic blue-green. A thin white band separates the blue upperparts from bright, rust-colored bellies. Adults measure roughly 7.5 inches long with a 16-inch wingspan.

Superb starlings are very social birds that use long, rambling calls to communicate. They typically live in very large flocks and often care for hatchlings collaboratively. They forage primarily on the ground for insects and berries; however, these plucky creatures won't hesitate to approach humans to beg for food when the opportunity strikes.

Many of the animals on O'Reilly covers are endangered; all of them are important to the world. To learn more about how you can help, go to *animals.oreilly.com*.

The cover image is from *Riverside Natural History*. The cover fonts are URW Typewriter and Guardian Sans. The text font is Adobe Minion Pro; the heading font is Adobe Myriad Condensed; and the code font is Dalton Maag's Ubuntu Mono.

Get even more for your money.

Join the O'Reilly Community, and register the O'Reilly books you own. It's free, and you'll get:

- $4.99 ebook upgrade offer
- 40% upgrade offer on O'Reilly print books
- Membership discounts on books and events
- Free lifetime updates to ebooks and videos
- Multiple ebook formats, DRM FREE
- Participation in the O'Reilly community
- Newsletters
- Account management
- 100% Satisfaction Guarantee

Signing up is easy:

1. Go to: oreilly.com/go/register
2. Create an O'Reilly login.
3. Provide your address.
4. Register your books.

Note: English-language books only

To order books online:
oreilly.com/store

For questions about products or an order:
orders@oreilly.com

To sign up to get topic-specific email announcements and/or news about upcoming books, conferences, special offers, and new technologies:
elists@oreilly.com

For technical questions about book content:
booktech@oreilly.com

To submit new book proposals to our editors:
proposals@oreilly.com

O'Reilly books are available in multiple DRM-free ebook formats. For more information:
oreilly.com/ebooks

CPSIA information can be obtained
at www.ICGtesting.com
Printed in the USA
BVHW091254301118
534437BV00006B/163/P